SCYTHIANS

River Taxartes

an

River Oxus

PERSIS

River Ganges

River
Indus

INDIA

Erythian Sea

NG OCEAN

E GREEKS IN ALEXANDER'S TIME

Lion Cub
The Boyhood of
Alexander

BY

MARILYN BECHELY

George Mann Publications

Published by
George Mann Publications
Easton, Winchester,
Hampshire SO21 1ES
+44(0)1962 779944

A CIP catalogue record for this book
is available from the British Library

ISBN 9781907640018

George Mann Publications

Contents

Prologue

Mother

The god of thunder was shaking the skies above the palace of the kings of Macedon, hurling spears of lightning through the hot summer night. Rain clattered and hissed on the red-tiled roofs, washed away the mud nests of martins under the eaves, and splashed into the courtyard in great warm drops.

A girl leant out from her balcony, as far as her swollen body would allow, and held up her face to the drenching rain. One of the sudden flashes that lit the darkness showed her laughing with a fierce joy.

Behind her in the darkened room, her women huddled like anxious hens, whispering together. "She shouldn't be leaning out like that. Tell her to come in!" This drew a soundless laugh from Phoebe, the oldest of the women. "You tell her!"

"No, but she might listen to you." Phoebe had nursed the princess as a child and came with her from the wild mountainous kingdom of Epiros when she was given in marriage to the young king of Macedon.

"I can't teach her to be afraid! At home she went hunting with the boys, she could ride as well as any of them. As soon as she could walk she would run out into a storm, and those sent to fetch her in would sooner have handled a wild cat's kitten."

"But now she is with child herself – and so near her time –"

"She'll take no hurt. Nor the child. A boy with the heart of a lion – didn't the king dream of it? Here's a royal welcome for him!" Phoebe laughed a little louder.

"What are you whispering?" Olympias turned and came in from the window. Phoebe crossed the room to her side with the long strides of a mountain woman. "I said that Zeus the Thunderer welcomes your son, my lady. Will you come to bed now? Shall we light the lamps?" Olympias caught the woman's face between her wet hands and kissed her. "No, not yet. We'll watch the lightning." She sat in a swan-backed chair by the window while Phoebe dried her hair with a towel and began to plait it in fine braids. In the morning, when it was loosened, it would ripple in tiny waves, like the dark golden sand on the shores of Pella lake. The head of a snake slid between the plaits on her shoulder. It flicked out its tongue and poured itself down her body to coil on her lap, its head resting on the full curve of her womb. Olympias stroked it with the end of a plait.

"Can you feel him there, Menelaos? Can you hear his heart beat? Can you feel him kicking? He is in a hurry." She laughed, and put both her hands beside the snake's head, pressing down on her body and the impatient child stirring within. She had known from the first that she carried a boy, long before the young seer, Aristander, with his bright blue smiling eyes, had given the meaning of the king's dream. "Your wife will bear you a son with the heart and courage of a lion." But she did not think of him as Philip's son – except in so far as that gave him his rank – he was hers, hers and the god's, the gift of the Great Mother.

The downpour had slackened and ceased. Figures moved below the window, carrying torches to relight the cressets on the wall brackets. New flames sprang up, reflecting in the puddles and wet pavements. Olympias gazed at the golden tongues of fire dancing in water and on air, and saw, not the palace courtyard, but the hall of the Great Gods on the island of Samothrace. She had gone there to be initiated into the Mysteries of the old religion – could it have been only a year ago?

Unseeing, she gazed into the fire-bright dark and saw another night in another place. She saw the path in the valley below the Mountain of the Moon on Samothrace, and a procession of tiny lamps, like a dance of fire-flies, moving along it towards the sanctuary of the Great Mother Goddess. She walked in the procession, light-headed after fasting, feeling as though she floated in her fluttering white robes above the rocky path, shielding the flame of her lamp through the wind-filled dark.

A herald's voice cried into the night: "Come, all who are purified and cleansed!" The high doors of the sanctuary stood open, light blazed from torches on either side, and the procession of tiny lamps passed between them.

Inside, the vast hall glowed with firelight. The initiates circled, their shadows stretching and shrinking on the walls with the dance of the flames. The noise possessed Olympias; the clash of cymbals shivered in her bones.

Through the smoky golden light she saw him looking as she passed in the circles of the dance. She saw him through the flying strands of her firelit hair as she turned and beat out the rhythm with her bare feet. He was like one of the gods, big and beautiful, and he moved like a king stallion, stamping out possession of his fields and mares in springtime. When she passed him again, she caught her hair and her veil aside, and lifted her face to the torchlight. She saw him laugh, pleased by her boldness. The power of the Goddess stirred in her. She knew her own beauty.

During the days that followed, throughout the many ceremonies and sacrifices, among the hundreds of unknown faces about her, she was aware of only one – his face, dark and vivid, always there and always watching her.

They were there to learn the secrets and invoke the powers of the oldest of the gods, the Ancient Ones of the earth and the Great Mother who ruled over life and death. The final ceremony celebrated the union between the Earth Mother and the Sky Father, and the birth of their Divine Child.

The herald cried:

"A sacred child is born! Brimo! Brimon!
The strong have given birth to the strong!"

"Ye!" cried the initiates, raising their arms to the sky, and *"Kye!"* reaching down to touch the earth, using the Thracian speech of the old religion .

Then the festival was over. It ended with a great feast. He came looking for her and her guardians. A man, not a god, shorter, coarser, but royal, robed in white with a garland on his dark head and the breath of power about him. Under fiercely swooping brows, his shrewd eyes regarded her with amusement, admiration, and a demanding hunger. She learnt that he was Philip, King of the Macedonians, and that he intended to ask her uncle for her in marriage. She was fifteen. He was twenty five and he had three wives already.

Olympias came back slowly into the darkened room where her women drowsed, waiting her pleasure. She looked towards Phoebe, who sat quietly beside her. The older woman smiled with tenderness. "Where have you been, my lady? Not here. You looked at something far away."

"I returned to the holy island of Samothrace."

"Ah, the Great Mother favours you, child. She has filled your womb with the seed of kings."

Olympias said, "Philip did not marry me for policy, as he did the others. With me, it was for love. He said, "You will be the mother of my sons!"

"And when this boy is born, he will make you his queen."

"So he promised my uncle. He gave the Illyrian wife a royal title, but she has borne him only a girl. The other one is dead. Perhaps the Thessalian will die, too." Olympias spoke the last thought softly, stroking her snake.

Philip's first two wives were princesses who came to him through peace settlements with neighbouring tribes. But the Thessalian girl, whom he had married a few months before his journey to Samothrace, had no royal blood, and was not part of any treaty.

"She danced for him!" said Olympias softly, scornfully, imitating the hissing speech of Thessaly. "She danced for him, like a bought woman, at her father's victory feast, after he helped her people drive out their overlords. I have cursed her. If she has a child, it will die!" She looked straight into Phoebe's eyes. Her own were light and brilliant, a spark reflecting in each one from the torches flaring outside. Behind her in the room a maid dropped a bowl. Olympias turned with a sharp reprimand. She pushed herself up, letting the snake twist round her arm. "Light the lamps. I will go to bed."

The girls hurried to kindle flames in the tall bronze lanterns. From the holes pierced in their sides, yellow light spattered the bed like sunlight through leaves. Olympias lay down, taking Menelaos with her. He slid his flat head under her chin, and she smoothed her hand along the strong undulations of his body, while her eyes glinted wickedly at Phoebe. "Philip is afraid of him – and he a soldier!" They both laughed softly, the laugh of secrets.

Olympias raised herself on an elbow and pointed a finger, glaring and imitating Philip's cry of outrage: "*Ahh!* Get that foul thing out of my bed! How did it come here? Are we *barbarians?*" They laughed a little louder. "But," said Olympias, her voice and hand caressing the snake, "you are not foul, my beautiful one. And you share the secrets of the gods. Let Philip pass a thousand times through the hall of Samothrace and he will never know what is known to you."

Both she and Phoebe knew that the king's anger was caused not only by revulsion for the snake, but by fear of the mysterious power of women and the wild god they worshipped, a fear shared by other men. The sacred snakes, taken to their ceremonies in baskets of ivy, or twined round the wands they carried, were symbols of a knowledge forbidden and dangerous to men. In the unblinking stare of their gold-rimmed eyes, the serpents warned of the age-old mysteries they guarded .

Olympias kissed the snake, her hair falling across it as she lay down again. "Don't the gods themselves appear in the shape of serpents? Sing that hymn to me now." One of the girls brought Phoebe a lyre and she sat by the bed and sang softly, verses from an ancient hymn, which told how the Earth Goddess hid in a cave, protected by her guardian snakes, but the Sky Father took the form of a serpent himself, and entered and gave her the seed of the Divine Child.

The women all slept then, and an unseen presence entered the room. The God of Shadows, the Walker by Night and Bringer of Dreams passed among them.

The crack of the thunderbolt when it fell exploded inside each person's head as though the whole world had blown apart. While they slept, the storm had lumbered round the low hills and now, suddenly, it broke out again overhead with a searing lightning flash and a thunderbolt flung from heaven.

A girl woke screaming and Olympias started up in bed, white-faced. Menelaos darted through the bed clothes and slithered away into deep shadow. Phoebe stumbled to her feet – she had fallen asleep in her chair – and flung herself on one knee on the bed, grasping her lady's hands. Olympias was shaking , not in fear but in exultation.

"I dreamt of fire. The god came to me. His thunderbolt struck my body and fire leapt from my womb. It spread, it went out across the sea, burning on the waves. It went to the ends of the earth, the whole world was on fire. I saw men and women walking in the flames – golden –"

Her eyes, wide and brilliant, stared past Phoebe, beyond the confines of the room. Suddenly a violent tremor shook her and her expression changed, as though she saw or remembered some appalling catastrophe. She cried out, a cry of utter despair that cut like a knife through each of the women huddled at the bed's foot. "It went dark. All the world was dark. The fire died. The god died. *Ohhhh!*" Her voice rose in a mourning wail. "He is dead! It is dark!" And she pulled her hands away from Phoebe and fell back upon the bed, clawing her breast and hair and weeping dreadfully.

Phoebe and several of the women hurriedly made the sign against evil. Phoebe tried to comfort and console. She ordered a warm, soothing drink to be prepared and sent for the Wise Woman to interpret the dream. An hour later she was sending for the mid-wives – the king's son was coming into the world.

Around her mistress's waist she tied the purple scarf given to women initiates on Samothrace. It represented the veil of the sea goddess who nursed the Divine Child and it invoked the protection of the Ancient Gods.

The boy was born at noon the following day. The summer sun was at its height and shining from a clear sky. It was the Month of the Lion.

Father

Waking from his first deep sleep, Philip got up and went to the door of his tent. A shower of falling stars streaked the sky with silver above Mount Pangaion and he grinned and made the sign for good luck. Across the camp red eyes winked from the dying embers on which the men had cooked their meat, and in the distance tall watch fires blazed white smoke and sparks into the dark From the direction of one came the sound of singing, slow and slurred, rising now and then to a raucous shout. Another voice cursed and the song broke up in fuddled laughter. Philip groaned and shook his head.

A boy stepped from the shadows. Light from the torch flaring beside the tent flickered along the blade of his spear and the rim of his shield. He was one of the Royal Pages, boys in training, who guarded the king's sleeping place. "Do you want something, Sir?" Philip laughed, reaching back for his cloak. "Nothing you can do for me, Kleitos."

He walked out beyond the torchlight, paused to relieve himself by a clump of bushes, and turned to look up at the craggy citadel of the town he was going to rename Philippi. A small mining town, the settlers had not waited for Philip to attack, they had invited him in. A good place for a fortress, guarding the gold and silver mines and the road along the coast. Philip narrowed his eyes, visualising the massive walls he would build, dropping from that rocky height and crawling over the lower shelves of the hill.

"Not much of a town yet," he thought, "but by the time it bears my name it will be another fortress between our farms and the cattle raiders. And it secures my claim to the mines – I have them now!"

In the third summer of his reign Philip was campaigning in Thrace, beyond his eastern borders. He counted the advantages his latest conquest had brought. "Regular pay for a standing army – that means trained professional soldiers, and money to hire mercenaries when I need them. Bribes to buy friends and informers – more city gates are opened by silver and gold than by battering rams. I wonder if the shades of the dead know what happens here? If so, my father must be laughing in Hades. He had one silver cup. He used to put it under his pillow at night!"

His father had died when he was twelve. His eldest brother had been murdered by his mother's lover. His second brother, Perdiccas, killed the usurper and became king at eighteen. But six years later he died fighting off an Illyrian invasion in the western highlands and four thousand Macedonians had died with him. Philip was twenty three then and Perdiccas's son a small child.

"So they called me to be king!" Philip kicked a stone. "King of a people like a herd of frightened cattle hunted by wolves. Enemies on every border. But I saved them. I pulled them together, I gave them courage. I bought them time. I retrained the men. And we drove out the Illyrians. A job Parmenion's finished off this summer. What a summer! Fighting beyond our boundaries now, commanding the roads, the river and the mines!"

He laughed, stretching up his arms to the stars. News of his latest victory, the one that pleased him most, had come that day, as he was celebrating the birth of his first son with his Companions. A courier arrived, sweating and triumphant, bursting in upon them without letters or dispatches, simply shouting, "He won, Sir! Balios won the palm! By three lengths!" His racehorse, entered in the Olympic Games, the great five-yearly festival of southern Greece. A fistful of silver for the lucky messenger, more wine to drink to the victory, and Aristander, the young seer, coming forward with a smile in his eyes. "Another triumph, Philip! You don't need me to read these omens. Your boy, born in such a summer of victories, will be invincible!"

Philip and his officers had been lodged in the town, but they came down to share this day of celebration with their men. And what a day it had been! Philip turned back towards his tent. What a day and what a night! He ran a hand through his dark hair, stumbled against a rock and swore cheerfully. "Here, Sir, do you want this?" The Page, Kleitos, was offering him a cup. Kleitos sipped from it first. No king of Macedon drank untasted wine, or slept without a knife under his pillow and a guard at his door. Six of the ten previous kings had been murdered. Philip took the cup and sat on a bench outside the tent.

"Hair of the dog, eh? Who's the officer of the watch?"

"Simmias of Lyncus, Sir. Amyntas's squadron."

"Tell him to make his round of the guard posts now, and pay particular attention to number five." By a jerk of his head, Philip indicated the post from which the last burst of noisy singing had come. It was silent now.

"Yes, Sir!" A different voice answered from the shadows and another boy dashed away to carry out his order. Philip grinned. They were like young dogs, still leaping up for attention and wagging their tails, even after such a day and night as this had been. There were four of them on guard. The other two came forward now and stood with Kleitos, eyeing Philip hopefully. They saw in their awakened king a chance to prolong the excitements of a day they had not wanted to end.

It had begun by giving thanks to the gods. The king had sacrificed sheep and cattle. The thigh bones, wrapped in fat and burnt on the altars were the share of the gods. The rest of the meat was roasted for the men. With wine freely distributed, noise and laughter rose and roared through the camp. The king led a line of torch-bearing dancers, weaving between the fires; then, in full armour they performed the war-dance, leaping the flames. His armed Companions kept close guard about him – his brother had been murdered during a war-dance . Company champions challenged each other to stave fights, boxing bouts and wrestling matches, ringed by their cheering supporters. The king wrestled a winner of three matches and threw him.

As darkness fell, men gathered about the dying fires. They sang rousing cattle raiding ballads and plaintive love songs. One group would begin and others take up the chorus, or start another in competition. Men's steps grew too uncertain to box or dance, their minds too fuddled to furnish the words of another song. The heat of the summer night and the weight of food and drink in their stomachs grew overwhelming. Most of them fell asleep wherever they fell.

The Royal Pages attended the king to sleep in one of the tents. No-one was fit to climb back up to the citadel. Then the four on duty doused their heads in cold water and mounted guard. The night died around them, hot and smoky, stale with the smells of burnt fat, urine and vomit, heavy with the animal sounds of sleeping men, enlivened only by the distant rattle and exchange of sentries at the guard posts, or the clear, cold whinny of a horse from the picket lines.

Being young, and having had their wine well watered, the boys were still elated and restless. So they looked eagerly at their awakened commander. Tousled, unwashed and red-eyed, naked but for the carelessly thrown cloak and sprawling on the bench, Philip was still kingly. Had there been twenty robed and armoured men outside the tent, it would have been Philip who held their gaze by the commanding vitality of his presence. "The most beautiful boy in Greece!" So he had been called in the southern city where he had been taken as a hostage during his brother's wars. Older now, and powerfully built, his broad, dark face was bearded like the portraits of Zeus on his coins. He had a mouth that knew both laughter and ruthlessness, a sudden confiding smile of surprising charm, and a compelling gaze under the flaring brows he inherited from his fierce northern mother.

"What a night!" Philip repeated. He slapped the bench beside him and invited Kleitos onto it. Red with pleasure, the boy took off his helmet and sat beside him, and Philip flung a casual arm about his shoulders. The others crowded closer. There was jealousy between them – the king had favourites.

"A summer of victories!" said the king, tipping back his head and half closing his eyes. Like the boys, now that he was roused from sleep he was willing to hold onto the day of triumph a little longer. "We take the Thracian cities and the mines, Parmenion wipes out another Illyrian invasion, Balios wins the horse race for me at Olympia – and my son has arrived in the world. That's worth a sore head the next morning, don't you think so, lads?" Fervently they agreed. "We licked the Thracians!" said Kleitos. He was a dark, belligerent youth.

"We did, and we'll do more. Since the old king's sons divided Thrace between the three of them, we can pick them off one by one. Neither trusts the other two. We'll master the whole of Thrace eventually, settle it, drain these marshes."

He leaned forward and they crowded up to him – future Companions of the king. "Here's where it all begins, boys, here" – he pointed east and west – "with silver and gold from these mines to fill the treasury, the Thracians running off yelping into the hills, the Illyrians licking their wounds and thinking twice before crossing our borders again, and the Thessalians in the south courting our friendship instead of waiting to pick our bones. Macedon whole and free, no wolves snapping at her belly, though they may still be skulking round her. The year I was born my father was driven out of his palace at Pella by his enemies; when I was your age I spent three years as a hostage in the south; both my father and my brother had to pay tribute to the Illyrians and you know well that Perdiccas was killed fighting them and four thousand Macedonians with him.

But in the future, when you see fires burning in the hills, it won't be Macedonian villages that are going up in smoke, or our cattle being driven away; when you hear a hammer striking the links of a chain, it won't be Macedonians they are putting in bonds for the slave market; when you hear women screaming as the troops take over a city, it won't be our wives who are running from the terror with babies in their arms." He paused, frowning, and then went on. "But we are going to do more than safeguard our frontiers. Give thanks to the gods, boys, that you are young, that you are Macedonians, that you are here. There are great things to be done, and you are going to do them.

They've despised us, the Greeks in the south. They've called us savages, here in the north, although our gods are their gods and our heroes their heroes. Who is our ancestor – we kings of Macedon? Herakles, the greatest of their heroes, the son of Zeus himself. So are we not Greeks too? Now, grudgingly, they allow my horse to run in the Games where only true-born Greeks may compete – so they acknowledge it – and he wins! There's an omen, boys! And they'll acknowledge my son in time. The people of the south are going to look to us – the Macedonians – to win back the glory of Greece.

Their great men are gone, and they've wasted their strength in petty wars, one city against another. We – the people they call savages – will unite them and teach them to be Greek again."

He broke off, his intent gaze passing from one to the other. They stared back, impressed but not understanding. Philip sat back and slapped his thigh, breaking the spell. It was not time yet to voice his ambitions. "We'll hunt tomorrow," he said. "Lion in the hills"

He stood up, the cloak slipping from him, and Kleitos picked it up and pushed it round his shoulders. The sky was lighter in the east. "Wake me when the sun rises," he said, and went into the tent.

He had a soldierly ability to fall asleep instantly for brief periods, but the mood of elation, though quieter, was still on him. He lay stretched out on the hide bed, seeing the sun gleaming on the glossy flanks of his race horse, and the animal's smooth action, wishing he had been there to see him carry off the victor's palm, considering which mares he would put him to next spring. He would strike a new coin of Thracian silver, with the horse on the reverse side, garlanded for the lap of honour, his rider holding up the palm, and on the other the head of Zeus, so like his own portrait. His son, this boy Olympias had borne him – was he like him? He pictured a dark, lusty child, capable of strangling snakes in his cradle, as the infant Herakles had done.

Through a gap in the lacing of the tent, he watched the flames in the cresset burning low, now that night was passing. When he turned over and closed his eyes, a small golden flame still danced inside each eyelid. The God of Shadows and Whisperer of Waking Dreams passed the sentries unseen and entered the tent. The king lay half asleep and remembered... Torchlight on Samothrace. Ships riding at anchor, casting shapely shadows across the bright path of the sinking moon. Torches spilling light into the dark ripples along the shore; torches smoking against the stars as the initiates climbed the path to the holy places of the Old Gods.

He believed now, whether it was true or not, that he had known when he first saw her that she would be the mother of his sons. Fearless, fighting sons. "Sons take after their mothers!" so the old women said. He had seen her weaving through the dance, the torches turning her hair to fire under the thin smoke of her veil, enormous grey eyes shining, a glowing flush on her white skin, young and ardent, proud and unafraid. He had desired her, the Great Mother roused men to such thoughts. She had seen him, too. He found her looking boldly, meeting his eyes, not turning away. She lifted her veil and he laughed at her daring.

He had been two days on the island, taking part in one of the great festivals to which rulers from many countries were invited. He had come seeking the power and protection promised by these ancient, timeless gods, lest he, all too soon, follow the path his brothers had taken into the Underworld. He saw the new initiates arrive and watched her in the dance. And through all the ordeals and ceremonies of the following days, he sought her out and watched her. Many women cried out or fainted from emotion, but not she. She was always in the forefront, fearless and intent. At the final purification, when the blood of the slaughtered bull splashed onto her, she did cry out – but in exultation, not revulsion.

He knew then that he would have her. But when he discovered that she was a princess of Epiros, he thought that perhaps the gods had had a hand in it. Epiros was a country on his western borders which also regarded the Illyrians as enemies. An alliance with the royal family would be to his advantage, but he had to promise that he would make her his queen. Olympias could be no minor wife.

So she had borne his first son. Neither of them had doubted that she would, even before his dream. He had dreamt that he sealed her body with the mark of a lion. Two of his seers had warned him that it meant she would be unfaithful, but Aristander, the young Lycian, had said: "No man seals an empty vessel. Your wife will bear you a son and he will have the heart and courage of a lion." And in Lion Month the boy had come, to fulfil whatever destiny fate and his father had prepared for him.

Olympias would bear him other sons. He would sire a pride of lions. His Thessalian girl's child had died at birth – the midwife was blamed – but she, too, was young and still aroused desire in him. Like his stallion, he could cover many mares. His sons would command his squadrons and rule his provinces – a new race of Grecian heroes. He and his brothers had united against common enemies, for the moment he forgot that his half brothers had become dangerous rivals.

He stretched out fully on the creaking bed. He felt his own genius, his own strength, he knew the power of his own mind, the force of his will, the fire in his heart, the vigour of his body. But, mindful of the vengeance of the gods, who strike down a proud man over-confident in his happiness, he turned on his finger the ring of magnetic iron given to him on Samothrace, and invoked the protection of the Old Ones. And then he slept.

There was a clatter in the doorway, Kleitos saluting. "Sir, the sun is up!" Between sleeping and waking, as he heard the rattle of metal before the boy spoke, his hand slid under the pillow and grasped the hilt of his dagger. Vividly then there sprang to his mind the memory of another time when his hand, warm from sleep, closed on the cold bronze. Olympias screaming: "Don't kill him! Don't touch him! He belongs to the god!" With a shudder he recalled the all-knowing, cold eye of the snake regarding him as it slid slowly from his bed, ill-wishing him, it seemed.

Child

The sun flared over the brown plain, summer dry. Philip pushed up his helmet to wipe the sweat that was running into his eyes. Above the red mark left by the rim, his forehead was paler than the sunburnt face below. He squinted through the dust and glare at the walls of Methone.

Methone was a Macedonian city on the coast, a day's ride from the capital at Pella. In the reign of Philip's brother it had been captured by Athens, the most powerful city-state of southern Greece, and used to harass merchant ships going in and out of Pella harbour. Now Philip was taking it back.

The strong winds that prevented the Athenian fleet from sailing north in summer bent the dry grasses and scurried dust and grit into the faces of the men loading the catapults. These machines, lined up like great wooden dragonflies, hurled stones and iron bolts into the city and bombarded the weakest part of the wall. The screech, rattle and thud of their straining ropes and sliding shafts had been going on monotonously since dawn. Now Philip saw a crack widen as a trickle of crumbling masonry broke from the ramparts.

He stepped out from under the roof of planks, covered in wet seaweed, that protected the engineers from enemy missiles, pointing towards the weakened spot. Another volley of iron bolts, some of them inscribed *'from Philip'* hurtled towards it. The king shouted for the rams to be brought up.

The arrow came out of the sun. A marksman on the wall had seen his chance. He drew his bow as the king stepped out and loosed the arrow when he looked up. The edge of the helmet Philip had pushed up his forehead deflected the blow and broke its force, otherwise he would have been killed outright, but the heavy Cretan arrow head broke his brow bone, shattered his right cheek, and cut into his eye.

His Companions ran, seizing him as he fell, and clustered round him as they carried him under the housing, concealing the extent of his injury from the men. The bombardment of the city went on, the soldiers for the most part unaware that their Commander lay stricken with a mortal wound.

The child woke in the dark, already listening, aware of unusual noises before his eyes opened and he came out of sleep. The lamps were flickering in his mother's room. The bed of Lanike, his nurse, was empty. He slid from his cot, wide awake now, running naked in the direction of the men's voices. One of them he recognised, Kleitos, his nurse's younger brother.

Except for the king and the guards on the doors, men did not come to the apartments of the women and children, but Kleitos was an exception. He was useful to the queen, bringing her news outside the official messages. After his audience with her, he would come to find his sister, pick up two-year-old Alexander, toss him up onto his shoulders, gallop with him round the room, and tumble him down onto the lion skin on the floor. There they would tussle until the child was breathless with laughter. Then Kleitos would pull the lion skin over his own head and shoulders and crawl towards him, growling. Father had killed the lion with his spear. Alexander pretended to kill the Kleitos-lion with a stick, though when he rolled over and lay still, the child always crept forward to touch him in sudden fear, only to scream with delight as Kleitos came to life again and leapt up roaring. He loved Kleitos, and if he was here he would find him.

Torches were alight on the stairs. He found his way down, scrambling determinedly from step to step, a small, pale frog with a long black shadow. The Pages who should have been guarding the doors to his mother's reception rooms were crowded half inside, listening. He squeezed between them, knee-high, scarcely noticed.

Inside, there were other young men besides Kleitos, hot, dust-spattered, red-eyed, as though they had ridden hard, and a big, red-headed man he had sometimes seen with his father. His mother and her women had their cloaks and shoes on, and his mother wore a belt with a knife in a leather guard hanging from it. He paused, taking in the strangeness of it all, looking from between the sturdy legs of one of the messengers, while the red-haired general was speaking.

"Madam, I won't deny that the wound is serious. But the king has the best of doctors and the doctor's letter, as you can see, gives his opinion that the wound is not fatal. Nothing has been said to spread alarm."

"Philip is strong," said Olympias, pacing the room.

"He is, but we must prepare for any outcome. Philip trusts me to look after your safety and that of the child. His half brothers are in Methone, but we know they'll get no troops from Athens to support them at this time of year."

"You are advising me to go."

"No, I have sufficient troops to protect you here, at least for the present. But no-one knows a traitor until he shows himself. If you wish to go secretly to Aigai and then on to Epiros, I can provide a strong guard of your own people. You could leave tonight. If you wait for further news you may wait too long."

Olympias watched him, measured him with her eyes, wary as a lynx. She did not like him. Could she trust him? When the king died any rival might try to seize the throne and murder the king's family. Who knew the rival until he declared himself?

Feeling the whispering danger hidden in the room, the child suddenly darted forward and tugged at the edge of Kleitos's tunic. "What happens, Kleitos? What happens?"

"Hey!" Kleitos looked down. "Nothing. Be quiet."

"What *happens?*" He kicked and beat Kleitos with his fists, in a rage at not knowing. Kleitos grabbed him and he screamed in anger.

"Alexander, come here." His mother took him. "Be quiet now." Her voice stilled him. She held him hard. They stared together at the men confronting them. She said to the general: "No, I won't run away. We will stay here. Philip would expect it. He will recover. You will defend us here if necessary."

The waiting women moved from their frightened huddle and murmured in relief. They would feel safer in the fortified palace than riding mountain tracks in the dark.

Antipater nodded, and gave his orders to the young men – double guards on all the doors and no mention of the king's injury outside these apartments. No word was to get about that Philip lay at the point of death. The safety of Macedon, as well as that of Olympias and Alexander, lay in his survival. Left without king and commander the country would be savaged again by civil war and foreign invasion. Philip's shield and spear were their only safeguard.

Macedonian kings led their men into battle. Philip marched at the head of his spearmen. His brother had been killed fighting at the head of his troops. Death was a daily possibility, yet Philip had never seriously expected it. He had assumed that the gods knew how much he had to do and were willing him to do it. Now, for the first time, he thought he might die, and during the second night, when the effects of the drugged wine and herbs wore off, the pain was so great that he almost wished he might.

The gods of Samothrace promised a good life after death to those who learned their secrets. The words of the priestess of the Underworld, seated on her throne flanked by blazing torches, came back to him.

"You have seen what I passed through,
and yet I rose again, and so will you.
Here is the initiates' secret –
that death is a passage and no more."

Beyond the Gates of Death he might walk with warriors and heroes in the Fields of Light. It seemed to him, in the darkest time of that night, that the Gates were opening for him.

But in the wolf-light of early morning, when his doctor came with cheering words and ministrations, he was ready to try to swallow some food. He recalled the urgent needs of his people, the plight of his wives and children, and the great work, the great dream, he had not even begun to fulfil, and he joined his doctor in the fight to save his life.

He was fortunate in having one of the finest surgeons in Greece, a man also called Philip, who was determined, not only to save his life, but also to salvage what he could of the king's looks. With infinite care and patience he operated on the splintered bones and torn flesh, balancing the king's present suffering against his future dignity and his own reputation. How far he had succeeded could not yet be known, but it was certain that Philip would never again be called beautiful.

This did not yet disturb him. He was thankful merely to be alive. Methone had been taken; he briefed his commanders from his bed, giving up pain-killing drugs in case they clouded his mind. When he lay wakeful, his thoughts turned to his next campaign in Thrace, and the trouble brewing in the south of Greece that might give him opportunities there. Yet he saw, when the doctor removed his bandages, the faces of his young Pages flinch, and he dwelt briefly on the thought that in future people might turn away their eyes when they were talking to him. He was used to admiration. He did not ask for a mirror. He waited for what he would see in people's faces.

Alexander was riding his horse to go to his father, like the noisy, sweaty young men who galloped to and from the palace several times a day, and whose coming and going sent people running with shouted orders or whispered messages.

His horse was a picture on the floor made from tiny brown, black and white stones from the river. When he patted the sides of the horse and shouted: "Go! Go fast!" he felt the little bumps smooth and warm under his hand. The horse was half a man. It had the body and legs of a horse, the head, chest and arms of a man. The horse-man held a bow and arrow, and beside him in the picture ran two boys carrying a hare and a spotted fawn that he had shot.

Alexander pretended to ride and watched his mother. Ever since the night he had gone downstairs in the dark the sense of danger that came with the excited boys and the red-haired man had not gone away. Everybody moved and spoke as though they thought of something else, as though they listened and watched for what was not seen or heard. He picked up the sense of fear as a small animal might, and watchfulness became a part of him, too.

But this morning was different. Anxiety seemed to have blown away, as the wind blew away the cloud shadows and splashed sunlight across the picture on the floor. And his mother moved like a bird, with the joyful swiftness of the swallows diving under the eaves.

She was wearing a saffron robe, catching the colour of the sun. Phoebe had coiled her hair like a crown, and she wore a diadem of gold flowers with tiny bees hovering above them. From her ears hung little winged figures of Eros, the god of love. Philip had sent her the diadem and ear-rings after the birth of Alexander, when he took the Thracian cities where the finest gold craftsmen worked.

Lanike came for Alexander now, and he ran away from her. His mother swooped and caught him, spinning round with him while he shrieked delight. "Come now, I will dress you. I will dress you myself." Lanike brought a white tunic with a gold key border of the queen's own weaving. Olympias put it on him and teased a comb through his tangled bright hair, while she sang to him and let him ride on her knee. He loved the glitter of her ornaments and her perfumed skin, and let her lift him afterwards to look at one of the pictures painted on the wall. He liked the bright splashes of red on it.

It showed some of the horses that were half men fighting with bows and arrows against warriors armed with spears. It was at a wedding feast – wine, fruit and blood spilled to the floor, women were screaming and running, trying to escape, and the hooves of the horse-men reared up, dark and dangerous.

Alexander was interested only in the horses. He pointed to one lying on the ground. "Horse tired," he said. "No," said his mother, "the horse is hurt. They are fighting. Look, this man is hurt. An arrow has hurt his arm." She pointed to the wound and the trickle of blood coming from it.

"Not cry," he suggested.

"No, not cry. He is a soldier. Alexander, listen." He always listened to this special voice, the one she used to tell him stories, or when she wanted something from him. "Father has been fighting. He has been hurt. An arrow went into his eye." She put her hand over her right eye.

"Not cry?" he repeated. "No, Father doesn't cry. He is coming home today. He will have a bandage over the sore eye." She drew a corner of her veil over her face to show him. He laughed and pulled it away as though it was a game.

"No, we're not playing. Listen. *You* mustn't cry. Kiss Father. Like this." She kissed him. "Nothing will hurt you. Father is still the same. It's only a bandage over his eye." He regarded her with his wide, searching gaze. Impossible to know how much he understood, how much he would remember, but it was important today that he should please the king, that his behaviour should be noticed and approved.

He was not now Philip's only son. Philinna, the king's Thessalian wife, whose first child had been born dead, had given birth to a boy he had not yet seen. Phoebe had brought the news to Olympias during the night.

"She has birthed, my lady. It is a boy. He is healthy."

The Wise Woman was brought to the queen by lamplight. A tiny person, so old that her age was forgotten, her shoulders bent, she moved like a pecking bird or a questing mouse. Her clothes hung round her like dark seaweed, but she had bracelets of gold on her withered arms and little golden birds dangled from her ears. They murmured together, Olympias, Phoebe and the Wise Woman. Then Phoebe was given a small leather bag, and the queen hung another gold jewel to glimmer in the ropy folds of the old woman's neck.

That was in the last watches of the night, as the sun was lightening the eastern sky. Now it was riding high at mid-day, and the king was entering the courtyard of his palace, to the applause of his household.

If the journey home had been a trial to the wounded king, Philip would not show it. He came out of the shadow of the porch with almost a swagger, acknowledging the cheers and greetings of the secretaries and Companions waiting for him in the sunlit court. He was accompanied by his doctor, his Pages, and an older man with two fine hunting dogs in leash. He and the king were both in civilian dress. Philip wore a long cloak and a purple kausia – the round cap of Macedon – with the royal diadem, a strip of gold-embroidered purple cloth, tied round it. Heavy bandages swathed the right side of his head; his face below the bandages was darkly bruised.

He paused as the blast of sunlight hit him, looking up, his good eye half closed as he took possession once more of the splendid palace he might never have seen again. Built fifty years before by King Archelaus, it was talked about even in the great cities of the south. The walls had been painted by the finest artists and the floors covered with mosaic pictures in tiny brown, black and white stones. Scholars came from all over Greece to see them – here – in the savage north! Water splashed into a pool in the courtyard; rows of pillars supported the delicate balconies of the upper storeys, and magnificent stone lions, with sleepy, smiling faces, not at all fierce, sat above their black shadows guarding the flight of steps to the royal apartments. These were old friends from Philip's childhood. He smiled at them, and put a hand to his face as the movement hurt his wound.

The sun caught two figures coming down the flight of steps, Olympias hand-in-hand with Alexander. She had no women with her. They came out of the darkness into the shimmer of light – white and gold, the sun glinting on her ornaments. Startled, the men fell silent.

Philip, caught between disapproval and amusement at her boldness in coming to greet him publicly, and unbidden, in front of the men, decided to be gracious rather than carping and stepped forward, a painful smile again twitching his lips. She made a graceful welcoming gesture. "May the king live! Welcome home, Philip." His hand brushed her shoulder as she uttered a carefully worded, formal greeting, expressing thanks to the gods for his recovery. Then she lifted Alexander towards him. "Your son greets you, too."

He drew his hand back. It embarrassed him to be confronted by this child in public. Everyone had heard of the prophecy – "a boy born with the heart of a lion – invincible." He remembered the night when he had celebrated his birth in that summer of blazing victories. He had imagined a lusty, dark infant, capable of strangling snakes in his cradle as Herakles had done, and so, he thought, had everyone else. But Olympias had given him a child who inherited all of her beauty and none of his own sturdiness. Alexander was small, fair-skinned, with large, clear grey eyes and dark gold hair – the only resemblance he had to a lion. With his fine bones he could have been mistaken for a girl. And now Philip had another son.

He had been told that Philinna was safely delivered of her second child. She was a tall, well-made girl, and her people were a warrior race, great horsemen, too. He was told that the boy was big and healthy. He would be the one to fight at his side. As for Olympias's child – how had he fathered such a one? He imagined the jokes, the hidden smiles. So he drew back and saw Olympias stiffen, her eyes threaten. Everyone felt the sudden hot stillness. A dog growled and Lysimachus bent to settle it. The child followed the movement and pointed. "Dog!" he shouted joyfully. "Dog!"

"Ha!" Philip exclaimed, pleased. "You like dogs, do you?" He grabbed him, swung him up, then down towards the hound. Alexander fondled the rough head and let the dog lick his hand. Philip tossed him up again, the dog gave a sharp bark, and Lysimachus, laughing, recited some lines from a poem of the Trojan War:

"Then, taking up his dear son, he tossed him about in his arms,
And kissed him, and prayed to Zeus and the other Immortals,
'Grant that this boy may be as great in strength as I am,
and rule strongly in Ilion.'"

"But that prince squalled when he saw his father put on his helmet," said Philip. "I hope my son would behave better."

Alexander regarded him thoughtfully. He put up his hand to touch his curly beard, stroking it like the rough head of the dog, and then seized hold of the dangling ends of the royal diadem, which glittered and attracted him. This brought cheerful sounds of approval from the king's friends, who saw in it a happy omen, and Lysimachus exclaimed: "A crown prince indeed, Philip! He claims his inheritance." Philip's large callused hand closed over the boy's small one. "So," he said, "you want to be king, do you?" Olympias feared a pouting lip and a scream of anger, but Alexander's gaze was taken suddenly by the blood-stained bandage. "Father hurt," he said gravely, and reached up and kissed him gently on the cheek. Philip kissed him, too, and handed him back to his mother. "He'll do," he said.

Olympias glowed. Alexander could not have done better if he had been old enough to teach. At ease together, they went through to the inner court, where a statue of Herakles, draped in a golden lion skin, stood above an altar. There they gave offerings of wine and incense in thanksgiving for Philip's homecoming. Alexander was given a handful of shining granules to throw onto the fire and watch them rise in sweet white smoke. The following day there would be sacrifices in the temples and public squares, offered in gratitude for the victory and the king's life. Olympias had dedicated several hundred white rams and oxen to be offered for her in different parts of the city. But now the king's doctor was claiming him. Enough had been done, and more than enough, in one day by a man recovering from so serious an injury. As soon as he had rested and taken food, his surgeon wanted to examine the wound.

In the summer dusk at the end of the day Alexander was playing a last game in his mother's room. Kleitos had brought him a small wooden horse, red-brown, the colour of Balios, his father's famous race horse. Olympias lay propped on one elbow on the lion skin on the floor, her loose hair falling over her shoulders, while Alexander crawled round the furniture racing Balios against imaginary horses. They heard a guard salute in the corridor and a moment later Philip entered. He had bathed and changed into a white robe, and a clean square of cloth had been folded and tied over the injured side of his face.

Olympias stood up, but before she could speak he reached out and took hold of her arm. "Look!" he said in a hard voice. "Don't look away. Look!" Deliberately he raised his other hand, untwisted the loose knot, and drew the cloth away.

The whole side of his face was bruised, purple and yellow, and his forehead was still swollen. Through the brow and across the deformed cheek ran a dark red wound. At the ends, where it had begun to heal, the flesh was puckered; in the centre it was still wet and oozing. The swollen eyelids were closed across the dark pit of the eye socket, gummed together by yellow matter. Having exposed his disfigurement, Philip stepped back and stood watching her. But he was testing himself more than her. He had considered how he would react when he saw the shade of horror cross her face, her mouth tighten or tremble, her eyes look away. He did not think that she would weep, but it was possible. He had to confront her, and know, and deal with whatever came of it. But Olympias also knew the meaning of courage, and she met his challenge. Her expression did not change. Her eyes smiled at him as though he came to her unspoiled and she could look at him with pleasure. "Honourable scars, Philip," she said. "A mark of your valour. To me you are finer than before."

The soldier in him thought, "A mark of valour! Crass stupidity, to lift my helmet in range of the wall!" And he was not deceived. She did not speak from love, she was acting the part of a great queen. But she was doing so with grace and saving his pride and she had not flinched from him.

He wanted her as he had wanted her on Samothrace. He caught her and pulled her to him, and kissed her on the mouth and then on the neck as she turned her head into his shoulder.

Alexander, kneeling on the floor with Balios in his hands, watched without understanding until he saw the king take his mother into his arms. Philip's face appeared above her shoulder, turned towards the last of the light. The undamaged side was hidden against his wife's hair; it was the dreadful, discoloured, blind mask that confronted the child they had both forgotten. The horror of the thing that was no longer his father, that had taken hold of his mother and was devouring her, screamed through him, as though ice had a voice and his body was frozen in a blue-white glittering terror that came out of his mouth in a piercing shriek.

His parents sprang apart. Philip regarded the screaming child with helpless shock. His small body was rigid, his pale eyes wide and staring. Olympias ran and gathered him up, stroking and crooning. He clung to her, not for comfort but to keep her from this monstrous man. His scream became a long, indrawn gasp for breath and over her shoulder he cried out at him: "Go way! Go way! *Go way!*" Lanike came running. The king blundered from the room. For this he had not been prepared.

In the night Alexander woke from a bad dream and was hot and feverish. Lanike gave him a cooling drink and his mother took him into her own bed. Philip also lay wakeful, disturbed by thoughts as painful as his wound. And in her house beyond the rose gardens, Philinna rocked her son, a big, healthy baby whose lusty cries meant no more than that he was hungry and demanded another feed. He was to be called Philip after his father – Philip Arridaios.

Lion Cub

Philip II

Alexander

Chapter 1

The Army

As mid-day approached the holy city of Dion drowsed into a sleepy silence. Heat spread like honey through the dusty courtyards and flowers wilted in the rose gardens. Leaf shadows lay black and still on the ground, and on warm stones small lizards, baked brown and motionless in the kiln of summer, lifted their little pointed faces to the sun.

South of the city, beyond the farmlands, rose the long blue ramparts of Mount Olympos. For several days summer storms had gathered round its summit, now soft white vapours rose from the deep gorges in the mountain side, to drift upward and cloud the peaks. There, where earth and sky merged into one, Zeus, father of gods and men, had his earthly throne. Dion was his city, where the Macedonians had kept his feast days time out of mind. King Philip celebrated his victories at Dion.

A solitary horseman rode at a limping trot above his shadow along the wide road that came from the south, his hoof beats tapping on the noon day silence. He passed the gate into the fortified city and along the straight road to the palace, where dogs stretched out in the shade raised their heads to watch him go by and then flopped down again. At the palace steps he dismounted, answered the challenge of the sentries and disappeared into one of the buildings like a bee returning to the hive. Presently, the hive began to stir. Two officers marched briskly across a courtyard, clerks hurried to and fro, somewhere a trumpet sounded and shouts of command were heard. A detachment of soldiers formed up in the forecourt.

A pack of boys came running through the striped shadows of a colonnade, the dust smoking from their flying feet. A smaller boy about four years old stopped abruptly, feet astride, to watch them. His legs were brown with dust, his face dirty, and his tunic of good woollen cloth had a torn piece hanging from the side. There were wisps of straw caught in the tangles of his bright hair, and he carried a brown and white puppy against his chest, which was trying to struggle up onto his shoulder and bite his ear.

"Ptolemy!" His voice was imperative and clear-pitched, and startled the puppy into giving a shrill bark. *"Ptolemy!"* Louder, on a higher note, it cut through the babble of boys' voices. "Where are you going?"

A tall, big-boned, gangling boy swung exuberantly round a pillar on his out-flung arm and yelled: "To meet the king! The army's home!" The others whooped and trotted to a stop, waiting for him. They were all aged between twelve and fifteen, big, loud-voiced confident boys, sons of the king's Companions.

The small boy darted forward. The sun caught him, glowing. "Take me! I'll come!" Ptolemy laughed, not unkindly. "You can't, Alexander. We're going to ride out of the city and meet them on the road. They're an hour's ride from Dion and no-one expected them until tomorrow."

"Father likes to surprise people."

"Yes, well, perhaps you can go with the official reception. Your mother could ask the general. You'd like that – to go with the soldiers. But we want to be the first to cheer them and then ride back with the Royal Squadron –" Several of the boys punched their fists into the air and shouted, *"Philippos! Philippos!"* scaring a flock of doves into the air with a startled clap of wings.

"I can come! I want to be first. Father wants me to cheer him." He stood looking up at them, his wide grey eyes brilliant with desire, and Ptolemy thought, not for the first time, how hard it was to disappoint him, simply because he never expected it. The other boys, sweating and tousled, stood with thumbs hooked over their cord belts, or leaning against the pillars, and grinned down at him. Kassander, the red-haired son of the general Antipater, pointed at the puppy.

"Where did you get that?"

"In the stables. Kritsi had a litter."

"It's a mongrel."

Alexander wasn't sure what this meant, but he knew it was disparaging. He said fiercely, "He was the bravest. The others wriggled down in the straw, but he came out and tried to bark at me." He turned back to Ptolemy. "I can come."

"No, you can't," Ptolemy repeated.

"On Piebald!" said Kassander and rolled his eyes. This was the sedate pony on which Alexander had learnt to ride. He was fond of Piebald and this mockery of his friend offended him. He frowned up at Ptolemy, pushing out his lower lip. "You can take me up in front of you."

"Alexander, they wouldn't let you out of the city with us alone, and there'll be no-one to ride guard. All the men will be needed on duty."

"I'll sit behind you and hide under your cloak."

"If I let you," said Ptolemy, "and you got out without being seen, the guards would be in trouble. It's Alexis and Lysander on the gate today. Do you want them to be punished?"

In the act of shaking his head Alexander saw a friend approaching. Lysimachas strolled in the shade, reading, undisturbed by the activity around him. A guest-friend of Philip's from Arcania, he stayed in Macedon to enjoy the hunting and the books in the fine library collected by King Archelaus. Alexander had been drawn to him by his skill in training his clever dogs, and his readiness to tell wonderful tales of the gods and heroes. He ran up to him. "Lysimachus, Lysimachus, come with us!"

Several boys groaned and rolled their eyes at one another. A wild gallop, lusty cheering at the pitch of their lungs, recognition by the king and a return to the city sharing the triumph of their heroes, the Royal Squadron of the Companion Cavalry, all this threatened to diminish to a nursery outing, a sedate ride in the company of an infant and a middle-aged scholar. Following Kassander's lead, most of them slid away, to meet again at the stables. Ptolemy, and one or two others who felt an obligation, stayed. Alexander tugged at the scholar's long tunic. "Lysimachus, come with us to meet the soldiers."

"Alexander, where are your manners?"

He let go of the robe. "Pardon. But please, Lysimachus, will you come? Ptolemy is going but he won't take me on my own."

"Indeed not. Have we your mother's permission?"

"She won't mind. She has people with her from Epiros. Lanike says I'm not to interrupt. You know she lets me go anywhere with you. We're going to cheer the soldiers because they won the fight and beat the temple robbers. Father Zeus will be pleased if we cheer them. So will my father."

Somehow it had become Alexander's undertaking, as any enterprise in which he was involved seemed to do. A sudden glint in Lysimachus' eyes signalled the onset of a story or a game. "Ah! The prince Achilles goes to welcome his royal father, the favourite of the gods! Well then, Achilles, mount your centaur. Chiron will carry you – at least as far as the stable yard. You can leave that puppy there until we return."

He crouched as he spoke. Alexander, alight with joy, tucked the pup inside his tunic, scrambled onto the man's back and was hoisted to his shoulders. "Why am I Achilles? Who is Chiron? What kind of horse is a centaur?"

"Achilles is a prince. Chiron is his teacher. He is half man and half horse. That's a centaur."

"I know! I know! There's a picture of him on the floor in Mother's room. I didn't know his name. Which of the boys is Achilles?"

"Oh, the tallest, I expect," said Lysimachus. "The centaurs are a wild tribe, drunken and savage. They live in the mountains of Thessaly. But Chiron is wise and good."

"What does he teach Achilles?"

"Stories and songs. The knowledge of medicine and how to heal wounds. Hunting skills and the use of weapons."

"Teach them to me. Is Achilles brave?"

"The bravest prince who ever lived."

"Then I will be him. I shall fight with a sword. Can a centaur go fast?"

"As the wind. Hey up, hey up!" Lysimachus ran off with a galloping stride, bouncing the laughing Alexander. The puppy, having closed its eyes to sleep, squeaked in protest. Ptolemy, grinning ruefully, and the boys, flushed with embarrassment at finding themselves in the company of a nursery child and a man who played like one, followed with their tails down.

Once they were mounted and out of town they felt better. Lysimachus had recruited an escort of two grooms and a young cavalry man recently promoted from the Royal Pages. He had been wounded during his first campaign in Thrace and had to remain with the home garrison when the king went to fight in Thessaly. Alexander had found him petting his horse in the stables, and afterwards sought him out as often as he could escape from the womenfolk to listen to army talk and tales of battle. He thought of Kebes as a friend. To the boys he was what they hoped to be themselves in a few year's time. They respected the long purple scar across his thigh, competed to ride beside him, and laughed loudly at his jokes.

Ptolemy rode beside Lysimachus with Alexander in front of him, in cheerful acceptance of the changes to his plan. He had a sense of humour which enabled him to take life as it came, and to make the best of it. Besides, he liked Alexander. Kinship between them and the little boy's affection often put him in the role of an elder brother, which he enjoyed. It gave him a sense of his own manhood, and he had sometimes the odd feeling that the king's son needed his protection. Also, he was half aware already of a quality in Alexander that burnished everything that happened in his company to a special brightness.

He was shouting now for Lysimachus to ride faster. They were out of town and trotting along the Sacred Way, past the shrines of the gods. The eyes of the painted statues stared far away beyond the heights of Mount Olympos. Before them on their altars lay the blackened embers of that morning's sacrifices. The riders acknowledged the gods as they passed, and then the road led in a wide curve past the theatre and the stadium – where games and chariot races and drama contests were held in the month of Dios to honour the god – and out towards the foothills of the mountain, skirting its long ramparts until, at the edge of the sea, it joined the main highway to the south. Most roads in Macedon resembled rocky, winding, dried-up river beds in summer and were made impassable by snow and floods in winter, but this was King Archelaus's well-made military road that ran from north to south the length of the kingdom, along which an army could march swiftly with its heavy baggage train, winter or summer.

"Lysimachus! *Now* go faster!" With a grin, Lysimachus pressed his horse from a canter to a hand gallop and the others followed. They were riding through farm lands, where men were burning the stubble of the barley harvest, and goat-herds piped to their flocks, browsing in the shade of orchards. Macedon was a fertile land. They passed country people coming into town with laden carts and donkeys, driving small flocks of sheep and goats, and herding oxen with their fierce dogs. They were coming to the markets that would provide for the victory feasts and sacrifices, and for the summer festival of Olympian Zeus. They shouted cheerful greetings in the rough Macedonian dialect and Alexander shouted back. His parents spoke attic Greek with him, but the soldiers and servants taught him Macedonian.

The sun chariot began its long descent down the western slopes of the sky. Its fierce white light became golden, although it still burned on their shoulders. From the mountain a purple stain began to spread across the sky, towards the glittering sea on their left. A low rumbling echoed through the dark cloud, the voice of the god, a reminder of his majesty and eternal presence.

Alexander raised wide eyes to Lysimachus. "The god is speaking. Is it to welcome Father?"

Lysimachus said: "What your father has done can only be pleasing to Zeus."

When they came to a stream with a little water left in a stony pool they washed their feet, hands and faces and watered their horses. From flowering sprays of wild clematis and myrtle they made crowns for themselves and sprays to tie on their horses' head stalls. They rode on quietly, garlanded and gilded by the westering sun, like centaurs and princes riding out of the old legends, while Father Zeus spoke to them continuously from his purple cloud.

From beyond the hills another sound came. It was at first like the distant whispering of an innumerable company, so that Alexander imagined a gathering of thousands of the big green grasshoppers that rasped away the summer in upland meadows. Against the lowering dark sky a lighter cloud of yellow dust began to rise. Alexander felt his throat tighten and a shiver ran down the nape of his neck. What was coming was sinister and beautiful.

The sound became the beat of marching feet, the trampling of horses, the rattle of weapons and harness, and the shrilling of pipes. Their own horses trembled, feeling the vibrations through the ground. The dust cloud advanced and darkened and spread wider across the sky. The light glittered on spear points like sunfire on the crest of breaking waves, and from beyond the last fold of the hills a dark tide of men flowed towards them.

Lysimachus led his charges to the top of a hillock by the side of the road. From there they watched the dark flood become head-tossing horses dancing like waves of breaking surf before the steady surge of marching foot soldiers. Between the beaten earth and the thundering of the god in the sky, their noise filled the air – the hammering of hooves and the rasping saw of thousands of marching feet keeping time to the strident rhythm of the pipes. The blue caps of the infantry, under the cold gleam of the iron spearheads, made another sea, grim and menacing, in contrast to the blue water that lay sun-laughing beyond the sandy marshes east of the road.

The cavalry were walking their horses. As they approached, Alexander's gaze ate them up – tall men, sunburnt and scarred, clad in their squadron colours, marching with clanking swords at their sides, through the dust that whitened their boots and drifted up under their horses' bellies. He could smell the hot dust and the horses, choking out the scent of the warm, crushed herbs of the hillside. The smoky cloud hung like a panoply above the march, unrolling back to the far horizon, and the tide of men stretched into the distance and beyond vision. Back there, out of sight, rumbled the heavy wagons carrying the baggage, the supplies, the portable parts of the siege engines, the sick and wounded, and the earthenware vessels holding the burnt bones of the dead.

These Alexander did not know about yet. He did not hear what the boys were shouting beside him, he was unaware of Ptolemy's horse dancing under him, though his legs gripped its sides and his body balanced without thought. He saw, heard and smelt only one thing – that great animal, the army of Macedon, on the march.

As the troops began to pass by the hill, his lips moved soundlessly, and he beat one clenched fist on another in time to the pipes. First came the cavalry of the vanguard and a file of pioneers, their task was to see that the road was clear; then the servants of the god, leading two white goats; the altar on carrying poles; the fire bearers, and, following these, the king's seers. Aristander was chief among them now. He rode handsomely on a white horse, a large white cloak spread around him, and a wreath of laurel on his head. He was like a god himself, his face had the look that was on the statues of the immortals, remote, far-seeing, unmoved.

After these tokens of the god's presence came the escort to the king, first a herald and a trumpeter, then a file of the Royal Shield Bearers and a unit of the Bodyguard.

The king rode in the midst of his Bodyguard, a man returning home with a great prize won. He sat straight and easy on his war horse, his head thrown back a little, the hint of a smile on his lips, one hand guiding the reins and the other resting on his hip. His purple cloak swept down from his shoulders and spread over the haunches of his horse, the cuirass of his parade armour was banded with gold and embossed with golden lions' heads. On his head he wore a gilt diadem and a crown of laurel leaves. His broad square face was darkened by the summer sun and winter winds of his mountain campaigns, and marked by the suffering he had endured. His blind eye had healed well. Philip, his doctor, had gained a reputation for his successful treatment of the king's injury. A deep, puckered groove ran through his brow onto his right cheek, which was flatter than the other one, and his eyelids were half closed across the socket, but his scars were not repulsive, nor even too disfiguring. He might not be called beautiful again, but men would not turn their eyes away from his injury. Philip had learned to make use of it. A foreign envoy seeking favours or a soldier making excuses could be confronted, either by the stare of one fierce blue eye in which all Philip's formidable personality seemed concentrated, or by the other, blindly closed on hidden thoughts, and they seemed to find either disconcerting.

A group of Royal Pages followed the king, carrying his helmet, shield and spears and leading his spare horses. Parmenion, his friend and second-in-command, accompanied him, riding at his side, and behind them Parmenion's tall eldest son, Philotas. Kassander and his friends had achieved their purpose and were keeping pace with the front rank of the Royal Squadron, as jubilant as hunting dogs, trotting home beside their masters with waving tails.

Ptolemy's little group began to cheer: "Philippos! Philippos! Philippos!" Kebes beat his sword on his shield and Alexander slapped his hands against his knees in rhythm with the chant. The clang of the shield and the high-pitched boys' voices cut through the general noise and Philip heard them. Grinning, he turned his head to the right, his blind side, and acknowledged the applause with a salute. There had been many such small groups along the way, shepherds and farmers and villagers gathering to greet the returning army and its commander. Philip would not have given a second look if it had not been for the banging on the shield. Slewing his body round further, he recognised Kebes, and shouted in the voice that carried across drill-ground and battle-field: "Kebes! Is the wound healed? Come down and join us."

"Yes, sir. Thank you. Sir, your son is here."

Kebes' voice did not carry so well; the king nodded and would have ridden by, but Philotas urged his horse forward and spoke to his father. After one startled glance to confirm his words, Parmenion passed his message to the king. Philip looked again, reined in his horse and gave a command. Parmenion raised his hand. The king's trumpet sounded, making the horses flick their ears, then another took up the call and another. Hooves clattered to a halt, marching feet stamped and were still. All along the darkened, spear-glittering way, companies halted one by one and their flutes shrilled into silence, as successive trumpet calls shimmered into the distance, like a flat stone skimming across the lake at Pella. The king sat still in the midst of his guard, looking up at his son.

Alexander's stomach clenched on ice. The great animal had been halted for him, its bronze claws raised and motionless, its latent power breathing through its sudden quiet. Its mouth-piece was the king; from him would come the red roar of anger.

He knew his father very little. He was a nursery child still, living in the women's apartments with his mother, his nurse and his baby sister. The king was seldom at home in his palaces. All the year round, in winter snows and through seed-time and harvest Philip fought his campaigns

– to the dismay of his enemies. Between campaigns he was busy with administration – dispensing justice, road building, land draining, settling new towns; with politics – organising his network of agents and spies throughout the Greek world; with military matters – training and developing his army. Everything was done by the king. When he had leisure he spent the rest of his prodigious energy in hunting and feasting and in pursuit of the victories of love. He seldom came to the queen's rooms now. Alexander saw his father in fleeting glimpses, striding through a courtyard with his Companions, whistling to his dogs as he rode out of the stable yard accompanied by his young Pages, or as a distant figure on the drill field, his trumpeter sounding orders while the chevrons of horsemen wheeled to left or right, or the files of infantry formed lines and squares. He knew Philip chiefly from the talk of others. He heard the Pages boast of his courage and whisper sly jokes about him which he didn't understand. He heard his mother speak of him now in a stinging, scornful tone; Lysimachus use his name with affection and respect, and Kleitos with vigorous devotion. But however they spoke of him he sensed the man's power. He was Father, Commander, Priest and King – only a little less than a god, and more real than a god to a small boy.

If Alexander had been on his own pony he would have ridden forward. It was his way to go to meet the challenge of anything that frightened him. As Ptolemy did not move, inactivity in the face of danger made his skin creep and his face whiten. Lysimachus, smiling, rode a few paces down the slope and called: "May the king live! Greeting, Philip. The boy has come out to welcome you." A murmur of laughing approval ran through the nearest rank of Companions. "Come down!" shouted the king. Ptolemy took his horse to the edge of the road, the colour came back into Alexander's face, and he looked across hopefully at his father.

The king looked and liked what he saw – a self-possessed child with a good seat on the horse, straight back and legs, and a bright, direct gaze. He gave him a salute, which Alexander copied with care. "May the king live! Welcome home, Father." His glance flickered to the laurel garland on the king's head and he gave a brief nod of satisfaction. "You beat the temple robbers."

"Ah!" The king's bearded chin thrust forward. "They said Philip of Macedon turned tail and ran away. They should have known him better. We showed them that like the Ram he only pulled back to run at them and butt them harder!"

On a wave of the Companion's laughter, still full of his victory and its consequences, Philip prodded his horse forward a few paces. "Come, try a war horse, boy!" He leant over and grabbed Alexander and swung him up, his strong arms holding him high above his head, laughing up into his face. The boy laughed back, glowing with delight, and from behind Philip Kleitos shouted: "Basilikos! The little king!" It took the soldiers' fancy – the pretty, laughing child with a torn tunic and a garland of wilting flowers on his tangled, sun-bright head, and they took up the cry in Greek and Macedonian, and some of them banged on their shields, as they did when choosing and acclaiming a new king.

"Not yet! Not yet!" roared Philip good humouredly. "Plenty of time. Let the Ram butt a few more backsides before you shout for the Lion. Now, ride with me, boy." He lowered the child, and Alexander scrambled astride the horse in front of his father, feeling the big animal's muscles quiver and the stiff fur of the panther skin shabraque under his bare legs. "Parmenion," said Philip, "the city is sending out delegations and princes to do us honour. It's time we put on our finery. Order the men to dress for parade and the cavalry to mount." Grinning, Parmenion did so. Messengers galloped back and forth and servants came running. Officers issued crisp commands. The Foot Companions took off their caps and put on the bright blue helmets they had been carrying at their shoulders, officers took their dress shields out of covers. Like birds in springtime displaying feathered crests and glowing breasts, or snakes emerging in new-polished scales, the army took on a new pride. The cavalry mounted their horses and the Bodyguard grew taller and more splendid under their high-crested helmets, those of the officers spined in gold with waving tails of red or white horsehair. Black boars with white sickle tusks strode across their round bronze shields.

The Royal Pages brought the king his helmet. It had a high, curved crown, like a cock's comb, it was silvered and gilded, and had a great swinging tail of scarlet horsehair and two tall white plumes. They shook out his cloak and uncovered his ceremonial shield, the device showed his ancestor Herakles strangling a lion. It was carried before him by one of the Bodyguard. Suddenly inspired, Kleitos took off his own white and purple cloak, folded it in half, and pinned it round Alexander's shoulders, and then straightened the wreath on his head. "Pity we haven't a helmet to fit him," said the king. "All ready? Trumpeter, forward!"

Again, Parmenion raised his hand. Trumpets blared: "Royal Squadron – at a walk – forward! Shield Bearers – forward – march!" Once more the calls shimmered into the distance, repeated with their prefixes for each company. The great animal stirred, rattled its claws, and began to move, one segment after another, scaly and shining.

And now Alexander was part of it. He sat straighter than ever, all his senses at full stretch, incorporating its nature into his blood and bones. On either side were the broad backs of the pacing, tail-swishing, head-tossing horses; one snorted warm air across his legs and he heard its harness rattle. Around him the men tossed their jokes to and fro like a ball game; he saw white teeth laugh in a black beard, eyes smile at him across the top of a dented shield, black hairs on the back of a strong hand, the stitching where a leather cuirass had been patched, and a savage, half-healed scar along a brown arm. The smell of dust, horses, leather and sweat filled his nose and tickled the back of his throat. Behind him was his father's powerful frame. If he leant back a little, he could feel the hard cuirass, the iron plating under the leather, and the knobbly little lion's heads pressing into his shoulder blades. Down his neck blew a gust of hot breath when the king's laughter roared or when he shouted a command.

On either side of him, his father's big, scarred hands guided the reins, capably, doing hardly anything at all, yet the big horse moved gently, obediently. Alexander himself grasped a lock of the horse's black mane in one hand and rested the other on his father's knee, feeling the thick ridge of a cockled scar along his thigh.

Parmenion nodded at the king. "He shapes well, Philip."

Philip glanced down at the lion-gold head, crowned by the drooping garland put on for his victory, and for the first time felt deep affection for his son and pride in his presence. He had timed his arrival to coincide with the summer festival of Zeus, now he remembered that it was the child's birth month also. Maybe the gods had not mocked him after all. The boy was confident enough and had a hard, strong little body. Philip recalled that Lysimachus had spoken well of him and said that he showed no fear of dogs or horses. He must get to know the child. Philip Arridaios, his second son, was a toddler now, certainly big and well-made, but he had a vacant look and there were rumours that he suffered fits, rumours that he had been cursed from birth. Well, Philip paid no heed to rumours – there were always whisperings among women – but he would take care to protect his new wife, already pregnant with his child. Between his campaigns in Thessaly, Philip had married again – not, this time, a girl who happened to dance at a feast and catch his eye, but one deliberately chosen from a noble Thessalian family to seal his victory – beautiful Nikesipolis. His thoughts shifted to dwell pleasantly on his recent triumphs and the great prize he had won.

'Thessaly – too powerful on our southern border – always a threat to Macedon. The wealthiest state in Greece. With the finest horsemen, too. When the Companions learn to wheel and change their line of attack as swiftly as their squadrons did on the Crocus Field, we'll have something to be proud of. Cavalry three thousand strong and feared all over Greece. Well, they're mine now. And the grasslands where the horses are bred and pastured. And fairly won – by words rather than the sword.

I took trouble. Their lords know me well enough, now. They trust me. A man like themselves who talks horses, comes to them for his battle chargers and his racing stud, hunts and drinks with them, is generous with his gifts, marries two of their women, makes them his kin. And if a man is descended from Herakles it means something to them!

When the Phokians attacked them and they came to me for help, I was ready. But that first victory was too easy. Made me too cock-sure. Only a small force of Phokians and their general not too clever. Daresay he feared me, too. Philip of Macedon has made a name for himself. But he can still be a fool.

They threw their whole army against me then and their commander led them himself. He was no fool. And I'd never been careless before. Poor reconnaissance – no excuse for that. Let him trap me in that circle of hills where he had all his catapults set up. Cut us to pieces! The men wouldn't fight again. The first time they've turned against me. It was worse than after Perdiccas's death when they daren't go back to face the Illyrians. I reminded them of that. How we took our revenge the year after. I talked myself hoarse – fine stirring speeches – and they came round, but I wasn't sure of them. I had to find a better general than me to give them heart. And who better than a god?'

Philip had found a leader for his army in Apollo, the Far-Shooter, Apollo, the god of light. The city states of southern Greece had been at war for four years and the Phokians had run out of money. They robbed the treasuries of the temple of Apollo and melted down the gold to pay their troops. Philip returned to the attack after his defeat as though he and his men were the avengers of the god. When his troops were drawn up for battle on the Crocus Plain they wore wreaths of laurel, the tree sacred to Apollo, and sang Apollo's hymn. Whether or not the Phokians believed that the deadly arrows of the Far-Shooter flew above the Macedonian spears, or saw his terrible bright shadow between them and the sun, their nerve broke before the thrusting onslaught of the phalanx, the slashing charge of the cavalry. The Macedonians and Thessalians were heartened, and Philip made no mistakes this time. Retreating soldiers are at the mercy of their enemy. Six thousand Phokians and their commander were killed and three thousand were taken prisoner.

What followed was almost unbelievable – but it had happened. The proud lords of Thessaly had chosen Philip, a foreign king, to be their head of state. They had elected him their ruler for life. This was the great prize he had won!

So he had good cause to ride at ease, to smile when he heard the voice of the god overhead, knowing that it could only be the voice of approval; to beam upon the harvest of the summer farms that would not burn again while he had life and strength; to acknowledge the cheers of his shepherds and goatherds, his villagers and citizens, knowing that he had earned them; to laugh with the comrades-in-arms who had shared his defeat and his triumph, and to perceive unexpected promise in the four-year-old son who had hitherto been a disappointment to him.

As they approached the city, the regent and his escort and other officials came out to welcome him. At the entrance to the Sacred Way, the king took the ritual cup of wine and poured a libation to the gods. Then only the king, with his Companions, Pages and Bodyguard, and units from the Royal Squadron and Shield Bearers, went on past the theatre and the shrines into the city. The rest of the army split up into detachments and rode or marched to their encampments in the foothills of the darkening mountain or on the wide sea plain before it. From the city gates to a long way past the stadium people lined the route, with soldiers from the home garrison saluting as the king went by.

Alexander sat before his father in a kind of dream, taking this in, too. It was the first time he had been the focus of a cheering throng. The voices came up to him in waves of sound, it seemed they rode on the noise like a ship cresting shining billows. Flower petals and barley grains showered over them, caught in their hair, the folds of their clothes and the horses' manes and were trodden into a mosaic of bruised colours under trampling hooves and marching feet. Trumpets sounded from the gate towers, braying hoarsely into the sky, which glowed now like a polished shield, and where the voice of the god was now silent, as though he had given his acclamation and would not join in with a mortal throng.

Among the cries of "Philippos!" were some for "Alexandros!" the people being delighted to see the child there. One of the Bodyguard tossed his new title to the crowd – "Basilikos, the little king!" – and they took it up, laughing. It was the first time he had heard his name in the mouth of the people. They were cheering him as well as his father. He felt his father's arm swing up to acknowledge the cheers; he raised his own hand, and the cheers and the laughter grew louder.

"Alexandros basilikos!"

"Philippos! Philippos!"

"Hold him up, Philip, let's have a look at him!" roared an old soldier, an ex-Shield Bearer in the front of the crowd. Philip took hold of Alexander's waist. "Stand up, my son. Stand on my legs." He stood, flushed and glowing, as the people cheered themselves hoarse. When they passed between the gate towers, his father's powerful arms hoisted him off his feet and held him high, while the guard saluted, and he returned the salute for himself and for the king. Then Philip's battle-field voice bellowed cheerfully behind him: "Alexandros basilikos! The little king!"

Chapter 2

The King's Son

"I rode on Father's war horse," said Alexander. Hellanike was bathing him. His mother had been pacing the room, his little sister half asleep against her shoulder. He had watched her, waiting for her anger to cool. Now, as she sat down, he thought it was time. He had told her nothing yet, wanting to keep his shining afternoon all his own and unspoilt. If she was angry her tongue would rip it to shreds as her hands had torn the silk scarf. But she did not answer, although he knew she heard.

Before he had returned to the women's rooms Lysimachus had taken him to the top of a watch tower. He had seen the soldiers' fires, red and gold, winking across the plain, as though the great beast they had travelled with had a thousand eyes and was bidding him goodnight.

"When your father came to the throne," said Lysimachus, "those men were dressed in sheepskins, fighting each other in war bands with whatever weapons came to hand. Now they are all Macedonians."

His voice lifted slightly, and began the spell-making speech of the bards:
"So, with hearts made high, they rested after battle,
as the watch-fires burned numerous about them,
as in the sky the stars are seen in all their glory.
A thousand fires were burning there on the plain
and beside each one sat fifty men in the flare of the blazing light."
Alexander was tired, but he pricked like a dog scenting quarry.
"What's that? A story?"
"A great story. A long poem about a war."
"About Achilles?"
"Yes, Achilles was fighting there. I'll tell you more, but now it's time to return to your mother and to bed."

He took a last reluctant backward glance. Out there was the world of men. They would be singing as he heard them sometimes late at night, in Hall or in the barracks, and joking and laughing, cooking their suppers and drinking. It was a different world from his mother's scented lamp-lit rooms where the women fussed over him, and chattered and whispered, or wept at a spiteful word, where danger did not leap up with a flashing sword but slid through the shadows, noiseless as a snake.

He returned to them reluctantly, tired but full of the importance of being out so late with the men. He met visitors on the stairs outside his mother's reception rooms, among them a very pretty girl in a gleaming red robe who smiled and leant down to greet him. "Are you Alexander? I thought so. You are very like your mother. May I give you a kiss?" She spoke in the soft dialect of Thessaly. Hellanike came swiftly and drew him away into his mother's room. Olympias was pacing to and fro, twisting a silk veil in her hands. The Wise Woman hopped and fluttered beside her like a bird with a broken wing. "So – she is with child, this new wife of Philip's – but it is a girl child she carries. My lady, have I ever lied to you? She will bear him a daughter."

The queen swung round upon her. "Daughter or son, what does it matter? This marriage is an affront to me and mine. Could he not be satisfied with paid women? Must he take a new wife before all the world? And who is she, this new wife? A princess from an ancient house, bringing a strong alliance? No, the daughter of some petty lord in Thessaly. My marriage settlement brought him the province of Orestis. What was her dowry? A string of race horses? And this is the woman he chooses now to be the mother of his sons! This is the worth of the promises he made on Samothrace. Yes, in the House of the Great Mother. He would love forever. Love! He knows only lust. He can hardly have met this chit before he got her with child. He has shamed me before the world. Does he think he can mock the gods, too?"

The piece of silk in her hands ripped apart with a shocking sound. Alexander cried: "What is it? Mother, what has he done?" Her stormy eyes swept over him. "You, too!" she said savagely. "He would throw you aside, too." Phoebe cried suddenly, fiercely, "He was bewitched! She cast a spell on him!"

"You talk like a fool!" said Olympias. "Philip is easily bewitched. Any pretty face can cast a spell on him. The only magic this girl used is in herself. You have eyes, you saw her. She is beautiful, charming – clever. What other spells did she need to enchant Philip? He was willing enough to be caught."

She turned upon the Wise Woman. "So, she will bear him a daughter. She is sixteen. How many sons may she bear him in the future? Look into the palms of her hands and tell me that. And am I past child-bearing at twenty? Look! Look! What do you see?" She thrust her right hand, palm upward, under the old woman's chin. The crone had looked there many times. She did not look again. She closed her eyes and shook her head slowly from side to side. The queen seized a handful of loose clothing at her neck and flung her to the ground.

Then she caught hold of Alexander and knelt, holding him away from her with hard hands, her storm-grey eyes staring into his. "That woman who kissed you. That is your father's new wife, his brood mare bought in Thessaly. Her name is Nikesipolis. You are not to go near her, do you understand? As it is with the others, so with this one. Do not go to their houses, take nothing from them – ever – not a cake, nor a fruit, nor a cooling drink – not on the hottest day, however thirsty you may be. Never take anything from them, nor from any man or woman who serves them. Do you hear me and understand?" He nodded angrily, frowning, twitching his shoulder under her biting hand. She had told him such things before.

"Then remember." She straightened up. "If Nikesipolis comes here at my command you may speak to her, but remember, Alexander, they are enemies, these royal wives. Never trust them or their servants. If you see that I am kind to them, know that it is so that I can keep watch on them. I have given Nikesipolis my cousin Doris to serve among her women. You may trust her. Pay heed to anything she tells you."

She turned back to the Wise Woman, who, crouching by the basket where the house snakes lay, was whispering to them and clattering a little string of silver charms to and fro, so that one of the snakes, the largest, had raised its polished head and was moving it from side to side, following the glittering sound. The queen pulled a ring from her finger, held it out for a moment, and dropped it into the lap of the Wise Woman. She gathered up the snake and stood, holding its looped body high, supporting its head so that she could gaze into its eyes.

Alexander, watching her stand with the snake like a warrior with his bow, armoured in her mystery, knew that whatever threat came from his father's other wives, his mother was the strongest and most dangerous.

Yet she had been hurt as well as angry. He had seen the track of tears on her cheek. He wanted to give her something and all he had was the wonder of his day. So when Lanike had finished bathing him and had taken the baby to her cradle, when he had his mother to himself, he said again, as though he had more to tell, "I rode on Father's war horse." This time she looked at him. "Tell me," she said. He leant against her knee. "The people shouted for me," he said, wondering what she would say. "They called me the little king. Father said it, too." He felt her suddenly become more aware, although she did not speak. Searching for something else to impress her, he came out with – "The god in the sky was shouting, too. Lysimachus said it was for Father."

The queen laughed; the soft laugh she had that made things seem uncertain, the way when he lay in bed shifting light from the lamps made the shadows of familiar pieces of furniture into horses and monsters. It gave him the same shiver of pleasurable anxiety. She said, "There was a thunderstorm the night you were born. A thunderbolt fell close to the palace. It made a fearful noise."

"Why? Was Father Zeus angry?"

"No, I think he acclaimed you."

"Like the men bang their shields and shout for the king?"

"Yes, like the men shout for the king. It woke me. I dreamed of fire. I've never told you this, have I? You must remember it." She took his hand. "I dreamt of a great fire that came from me and spread out over all the world. A terrible, beautiful fire with golden flames streaming into billowing clouds, red as the sky at morning or evening. It flamed across the sea and burned on the mountains, through cities and forests and deserts to the end of the world." She stopped, drawing back from the sharp, black pain of the dream's end, which could still pierce her with sorrow, even in memory.

A little frown had gathered between Alexander's brows. Already he knew the importance of omens. "What did it mean, Mother?"

"Perhaps the god had a special message for me. You remember how Zeus once loved a princess and gave her a son, who was born when his mother was struck by the god's lightning?"

He cried out in distress – "But she was burned! She was burned all to ashes!" His mother sat safely beside him, but his sense of time and place was confused, so that he felt danger threatened her now.

"Hush!" She stroked his hand. "She burned because she questioned the truth of the god. She did not believe that it was Zeus who came to her in the shape of a man. She demanded to see him in his glory. He appeared to her radiant and terrible, with lightning flashing about him. A mortal could not withstand it. She was destroyed, but Zeus saved their son from the ashes. He is the god Dionysos whom we worship. A god born of fire and a mortal mother."

"Yes, I know." He had been to their ceremonies, carried there by Phoebe before he could walk. He grappled with thoughts beyond his understanding. He knew she was telling him something splendid about himself – something splendid and frightening. There were secrets hidden in her eyes, and she spoke in her soft, special voice, but he could not find the meaning her words concealed. He returned to what he understood.

"Did it hurt you, the fire? Was I burned?"

"No, no! I told you, mine was only a dream. You were safely born. You were beautiful." She kissed him and said, touching his hair, "You see, if the god came to give me a son, I would ask no questions. I would not be like that poor, doubting princess."

"Am I a god's son?" In surprise he thought he had grasped the secret her eyes had promised him. It seemed only a little more magical than being a king's son in a world where the centaurs were as real to him as cavalry men and the snakes that shared his own and his mother's bed drank milk from silver dishes as though they, too, were princes. But the queen laughed, tapping his hand with her finger. "Oh, we are talking of dreams – stories and dreams. But the sons of the gods are braver and more beautiful than other men, and so are you to me. What will you be when you grow up – another Jason to go in search of gold and kill a dragon? Another Perseus –"

He broke in – "Lysimachus told me that Prince Achilles was the bravest. Was he a god's son?"

"Ah, no, but his mother was a goddess. Do you know that we are descended from him, you and I?"

"What does descended mean?"

"Long ago his son took a princess, captured in war. She came to Epiros, my country, with her child, and from them came our royal family." She counted on her fingers. "I don't know how long ago it was, but you are, perhaps, his great-great-great-great-great-great-grandson." He copied her, marking off the 'greats' on his fingers. She went on: "The king is of the family of Herakles, but you and I share the blood of Achilles." Unconsciously, he absorbed the knowledge that she put his father on one side and ranged herself and her son against him. He asked, "Mother, when will I be king?"

"When Philip dies."

"When he's killed fighting?"

"Perhaps. But first you must grow to be a man."

"I'm four now."

"Yes, this is your birth month, the month of the Lion. Tomorrow, after the thanksgiving for the victory, the king and I will make offerings for you at the altar of Zeus."

"Can I do it myself?"

"No, not yet. But you may wear your new red sandals, and I have had a crown made for you, like the king's."

"Give it to me now!"

"No, it is not a toy. Sleep now." She kissed him goodnight. "Keep it as a surprise for the morning."

They were quarrelling! He heard them as he came down the stairs to his mother's reception room. Lanike had dressed him early and given him permission to go to the queen because he was impatient to have his crown. Raised voices came from behind the heavy door below, which stood partly open; he heard their anger, his father's loud and iron-hard, his mother's like a stinging whiplash. He stopped, his stomach tightening into a cold knot. They were quarrelling about the new wife.

He heard his mother's voice, hot with fury: "And do you want to breed more stupid sons, that you must take another Thessalian mare?" And his father's, sharp with temper held in check. "Keep your tongue, you witch. What had you to do with that? I've heard talk. The boy was well enough at first, I'm told, and learning to speak. What curse did you lay on him? By god, if it could be proved –" She laughed. "Where do you learn these things, Philip? In the barrack room, on the back stairs, in the bed-chamber? Palace gossip. Is this what the pretty boy who shares your couch at supper whispers in your ear?" There came the crash of a piece of furniture falling and then the queen screamed. Alexander leapt the last five steps to the floor and sped into the room. Kleitos and a guard had been standing outside the door with one of the queen's women, but they were frozen in their places, and he was past them, had pushed the heavy door and slid through the crack as swiftly as a lizard vanishes between stones, before Kleitos' hand, out-stretched to grab the back of his tunic, closed on empty air.

His father had hold of his mother's wrist in a powerful grip and her fingers were spread wide. Her nails had clawed streaks of scarlet down his cheek, but Alexander could not see this, his father had his back to him. What he saw was the man's hand uplifted to strike and his mother's face, her eyes pale and wild. She was blazing with cold fire, like a snared leopard, and excited by the danger of provoking Philip, but to her child she looked like a flower about to be broken in the grasp of a bear-like man. She bent her head suddenly – she and her son shared the same quickness of movement – and bit the arm that held her. With a shout of surprise and rage, the king struck his blow.

There was a chair behind him. Alexander, still running, leapt upon it, and from there sprang onto the king's back, clinging like the kitten of a feral cat, holding on with his knees and one arm, beating the other clenched fist on the back of his father's head. The queen's cry became a gasp of derisive laughter, as the king let go of her to grab at his cloak, which was half-throttling him, dragged tight by the boy's weight. His golden oak-leaf crown was knocked sideways as his hands, reaching up, found Alexander's arms and grasped them hard. He stooped and swung him off his back.

Philip glared at the ferocious child, who was kicking at him viciously with the red sandals. "Leave her alone! Leave her alone! Don't touch her. I'll kill you!" Even the lips of the small face were white with anger, the large grey eyes flashed with a light as dangerous as the sun on a naked sword. "I'll kill you!" He meant it. The sword was in the child's voice also.

The king did not see a likeness between the outraged queen and her son. He saw only the fury of Alexander. And suddenly he laughed. A great roaring laugh that emboldened Kleitos and the guard, with Hellanike and the serving woman peering over their shoulders, to push the door wider and take a step inside.

"By the dog!" roared the king. "A warrior!" He caught sight of his guard. "Did you see him, Kleitos? Or was he too quick for you? Here, take him." He slung the child, now crimson with shame and close to tears, towards the man, who had to be quick to catch him.

"Put me down!" Alexander twisted and fought, biting and kicking, as Kleitos held on to him, laughing. "You've bred a lion cub here right enough, Philip. What shall I do with him?"

"Take him out," said Philip, barring the passage of the queen. "Keep him with the Bodyguard. Slap his behind if he gives you any trouble. I'll take him to the sanctuary with me. He deserves it." He pointed to a small gold wreath on a table. "Take that. Close the door."

Hellanike darted forward, like a dog stealing a bone, and took the wreath. They left, shutting the door swiftly on the smouldering truce about to close the royal battle within.

"Put me down! Put me down!"

"Call a truce," said Kleitos. "Sit here beside your huntsman." There was a statue in the courtyard of a young man astride a horse, his hounds leaping round him. Kleitos managed to unfasten the pin and toss his cloak over the horse's shoulders while keeping a grip on the child. A group of the Bodyguard were laughing at them. Seeing this, Alexander became rigid and silent. Kleitos lifted him onto the horse. He watched for a chance to slide off again and escape.

"Look!" said Lanike. "Here's your crown." She held the gleaming circlet before him, thin oak leaves of gilded silver, as perfect as those on a living tree. He turned his head, refusing to look at it. Lanike coaxed him: "Grown people quarrel sometimes, just as children do. Don't think too much of it. Come now, don't sulk. Is this how a big boy four years old behaves?"

Kleitos said, "Your father wants a fighting son. He won't beat you. He dreamt you would be a lion cub before you were born. Isn't that so, Lanike?"

Alexander felt his unwilling interest quicken. His mother had had a special dream about him, too. But he wouldn't look at the man. "Go away," he said. "We don't want you. I'll stay with Lanike."

Kleitos put his foot on the back of a stone hunting dog and leant forward, between him and the sun. He had been promoted from the Royal Pages into the Bodyguard and wore their uniform, a purple tunic and a cuirass bearing a lion's head. He had grown a thick black beard and his black brows grew low over his eyes, meeting above his nose. He wagged a big finger before the boy's face.

"I was with your father in Thrace, the summer you were born. We were in Philippi; the Thracians ran off and we just walked in. Before that we'd taken other cities. Philip was celebrating the news that he had a son when two more messages came. Parmenion had smashed an Illyrian invasion, and his horse had won the palm at Olympia. Well, Aristander read those omens without any trouble. ' Three victories to herald the birth of a boy! He'll be a soldier nobody can beat – invincible – another warrior like Achilles.' That was it. Well, we drank to that, you may guess. And the king drank the most. What a day and a night that was!" He laughed, slapping his knee. "Even the prisoners wanted to join in. The king gave ten of them leave. They mimed a cattle raid. It was so good that some of us thought those who fell down were really dead. Afterwards your father led them in a war dance. Then he set them free. I tell you, boy, you'll have something to do, whatever your birth omens, to equal your father, whether fighting, dancing or drinking!" He drooped a wink at Lanike. "And much else besides." His small dark eyes smiled, half mocking, half affectionate.

50

Alexander was caught between reluctant pleasure at his part in the story, and the resentment any child feels against a cocksure adult who knows things about him that happened when he was too young to be aware of them. Also, he sensed something taunting in those last remarks, and his pride had not yet recovered from their handling of him, Kleitos and the king. He lifted his chin, like his father. "Don't touch me again," he said, preparing to slide down from the horse. Kleitos recognised the move towards a truce, and Lanike held out his crown once more. "Will you put it on, Alexander?" He did so.

Kleitos relaxed. In a gruff whisper he said aside to Lanike, "His mother's temper, but she's a wild cat, uses teeth and claws." The pin that had fastened the cloak lay loosely stuck in the folds. Alexander snatched it and jabbed it into Kleitos' shoulder just below the band of the cuirass. Kleitos shouted, spun round and aimed a cuff at him, which he ducked, sliding from the horse. Lanike scolded. The Bodyguard laughed.

Kleitos caught him. A trickle of blood was running down his arm. They stared at one another in hurt and surprise. Alexander discovered that you could love and hate someone in the same breath. "I'm sorry," he said, and meant it. "I've had worse wounds," said Kleitos. "If you're sorry, give me a kiss." Alexander kissed him. He smelt of onions.

A stir, the sound of voices, the king's laugh, made them all turn their heads. He was coming briskly down the steps into the courtyard, accompanied by his Pages and the Commander of the Bodyguard, followed by the queen and the royal women, glowing like spring flowers in saffron, white and blue. Nikesipolis gave Alexander a little wave. His wondering gaze went from one to the other, the genial king, the queen, calm and dignified, the people around them, smiling and talking. Lysimachus was there. The tightness inside Alexander loosened a little at the sight of him.

The king paused beside them. Alexander frowned at his sword belt. If he had thought of it before leaping on his father's back he might have pulled the big sword from the scabbard and killed him. Philip's voice overhead was brisk and friendly. "Alexander, go with Kleitos and Lysimachus. They will show you what is done and explain things to you." To the men he said, "Not too close, but let the people see him. If I want him with me, I'll signal." And to the Commander of the Bodyguard, "Detach a troop to guard them." He marched off.

The queen sank gracefully to one knee before her son and carefully adjusted the gilded crown, smoothing back a lock of hair. "That is beautiful, darling. You look like a king. Behave like one. I shall be watching you. So will Father Zeus. Remember you are very special to him." Her eyes looked deeply into his, saying more. She lifted the hands of her champion, one after the other and kissed the backs of them. His father had shamed her and struck her; there was a bruise on her cheek. When he was a man no-one would ever make her cry; he would kill all her enemies and bring her the finest jewels in all the world. She would throw away Philip's gold. He would kill his father if he hurt her again. You could curse people to make them die. He had heard his mother do it. He lifted his face to return her kiss. "Go with Lysimachus, darling. He will tell you what to do."

Lysimachus stooped towards him, and this time Alexander did not object to being carried, but reached up to him. The man felt strong and steadfast. Alexander put his arms round his neck and clung to him. Having no children of his own, Lysimachus was deeply touched, and returned his embrace. "Well now, are we ready?" Their escort marched beside them. Alexander looked up from Lysimachus' shoulder, his face bright. "Shall we ride? Can I ride on my own? Will my horse have a panther skin?"

"You did well," said the king. They were returning from the shrines along the Sacred Way. Alexander had watched from a distance while the first offerings were made, but when the time came to give his birthday bull, he was called up, to walk with his father round the altar fire and scatter the barley meal.

"Hail Zeus, chief among gods and the greatest, Lord of All,
be gracious to me, all-seeing father ..."

His bull stood waiting patiently. Its horns were gilded and it wore garlands of flowers round its deeply folded, silky neck. Alexander watched its vacant, melancholy eye; he was close enough to see the thick fringe of white eyelashes. A fly crawled across the bull's cheek, making its skin twitch. Alexander stepped up to it and brushed the fly away, sliding his hand down a glossy fold of its neck. Lysimachus drew him back.

The king cut a curl of stiff white hair from the head of the bull and gave it to his son. Then he put a hand on its forehead and stroked down. The bull lowered its head and gave a mild, throaty bellow. The onlookers murmured satisfaction. It was a good omen, the animal consented to its death. The king took up the sacrificial knife, as the servants of the god grasped the horns...

The blood of the bull soaked into the ground, an offering to the Great Goddess, the Earth Mother. Its thigh bones, wrapped in fat, burned on the altar, and the smoke rose up to heaven to please Zeus, the Sky Father. Meat from the carcass was carried off to be cut up and roasted for the people – men and gods rejoiced together.

The child had felt his throat swell in pity when the white bull sank in ruined beauty to the ground and gasped away its spirit; a blue film crept over its round dark eye, sealing it in mysterious emptiness. But Lysimachus, stooping over him, told him it was going to live with the gods. Offerings were made for the queen, and then Alexander was released from the ceremonies to go with Kleitos, Lysimachus and their guard to enjoy the festivities.

Buskers and peddlers had followed the crowds to the shrines. They watched a fire eater and a sword swallower and Lysimachus bought him stuffed dates from a stall. Curiously, he stared at other children and they stared back at the boy wearing a crown of golden leaves, with his military escort. He offered a greeting in Macedonian to three sun-dark brothers in homespun farm clothes and shared with them his handful of sticky dates. Then a hot and breathless Royal Page found them and summoned them to take their places in the procession returning to the palace. Alexander was sticky and happy, his gilded crown, forgotten, lodged lopsidedly on his tumbled hair. The king grinned down at him.

"You did well. I was proud of you. Very well indeed, for a first time." To Antipater, riding close behind him, he said, "I can remember the first time I saw an ox have its throat cut."

"Not an ox," said Alexander, "but I've seen a goat before."

"You have? Where? When was that?"

"My mother killed a goat for Dionysos. In the sacred grove at Pella. In the dark before the sun was up. I held a cup for the blood and she let me pour wine for the god. I did it very well. Then we danced and the god was pleased."

The king's fierce brows had drawn together. "That's women's business. I won't have you mixed up in that. Does she take you there often?" The child's face stiffened. His mother was being attacked again. "Answer me! Does she take you there often?"

He wouldn't answer, however angry it made the king. Philip glanced at him and changed his tone. "I'm not angry. Listen to me. Dionysos is a great god. He is present when a tree sends out its leaves, when a foal is born, when the grapes ripen and wine is pressed. He is a giver of life and joy, but he is dangerous, too. You'll see men tipsy and happy; you'll see them drunk and half mad, not knowing what they do. When the women serve the god he sends such madness upon them, but it comes from himself, not from wine. And it is not for men to see."

Philip had chosen his words carefully. The god Dionysos was honoured in Macedon. The palace at Pella was full of his images. As a beautiful young man he rode naked on a panther across a stone floor picture. Draped in a panther skin he led a procession of pipers and dancing women along a carved stone frieze. On the side of a golden bowl he reclined with a wreath of ivy in his flowing hair, raising a wine cup to his lips. On a painted plate he travelled in a ship whose mast had sprouted vine branches laden with grapes. To his worshippers he offered abundant life, but upon those who neglected or scorned his worship his vengeance fell savagely. The Greek poet Euripedes, who spent his last years in Macedon in the time of King Archelaus, had written a terrible play about him. A young king forbade his worship. Dionysos sent the royal women mad. Hunting like hounds upon the mountain, they seized the king and tore him, thinking it was a lion cub they killed. His own mother lifted her son's head on her spear, not knowing what she did.

The child, while his father talked, had kept to his own thoughts. A few months earlier, on the second day of the winter festival, he had been brought to a shrine of Dionysos with other small children, and given a little wine cup. His was of silver, theirs of painted earthen ware. Then his mother had led a procession which brought the image of the god back to his sacred grove after the winter. She rode in a car draped with garlands of ivy, dressed like a bride, and beside her the mask of the god's head was fixed on a pine bough draped in a cloak, so it looked as though she rode beside the stiff figure of a bearded man. And the people waved pine branches and threw flowers and chanted: *"Brimo! Brimon!"*

The crowd along the way were cheering now. "Philippos! Philippos!" Philip acknowledged the cheers, and, remembering his son's age, asked, "Is this too hard for you?"

"No."

"Listen then. Every day the king must sacrifice for his people. If you become king you will do the same. Every day at dawn you will make the offering to Father Zeus, and you will make the proper offering to each of the gods on their feast days. At the feast of Dionysos you will sacrifice to him. If you do not, both you and your people will suffer for it. But there are secret rites and ceremonies of Dionysos which are only for women. Men must have nothing to do with them. Do you understand?"

He paused again to acknowledge the shouts of the people, and added, cunningly, "Your mother has done nothing wrong. Do not mistake me. When you are an infant it makes no matter. At your age, the god will welcome you for your mother's sake, and take no more notice of you than of a lamb or kid that strays into his sanctuary. But when you are grown, when you are a big boy and leave the women's' rooms to live with the men, the god will be angry if you pry into his secrets."

"I am four!"

"Yes indeed. When you are seven you will be nearly a man."

Later, the king said to Antipater when they were alone: "I must have her watched. What does she think she is doing – teaching him women's magic? I've seen him with those snakes of hers wrapped round him, talking to them as though they were his brothers. It won't do, I suppose, to take him from her before time, but it's three years yet, and he's forward for his age. I'll get Lysimachus to keep an eye on him. He seems taken with the boy and he won't annoy the queen. He can have him out riding, teach him to hunt small game. And, by god, when I do get him away from his mother I'll find him a tutor to strip him of her fancies and make a soldier of him!"

"Have you anyone in mind?" asked Antipater.

"Not yet, but I'm thinking."

"The boy's deeply attached to his mother."

"Of course, at his age. But he has the proper stuff in him. You saw how he stood up on that horse yesterday and took the roaring of the crowd – enjoyed it, by god. He'll take the war cry the same way in time, mark me. He's my son as well as hers. His eyebrows slope like my father's, did you notice that?"

"He has your chin," said Antipater. "And the look of you when he pushes it out."

Philip laughed. "Stubborn, you mean. That'll do him no harm. Now, what do we make of these reports from Thrace? What's Kersobleptes been up to? Philippi's not in danger, but we can't let him get away with trouncing the garrison in the field. I'd better go myself."

Chapter 3

The Grandchild of Achilles

"Lanike! Lanike! Their horses sit down for them!" cried Alexander. "Their horses sit down!"

He had been playing with the Persian boys, and, disbelieving the tale that their fathers' horses were trained to lower their haunches to enable their riders to mount easily, had been taken to the stables of the guest house to see for himself. The horses were splendid, taller than those bred in Macedon, or even in Thessaly. When caparisoned they wore bridles spangled with silver ornaments and tall red plumes nodded on their headstalls. But the wonder was that they would lower their haunches for their riders to mount!

"Even Chiron never saw such a thing!" Alexander exclaimed.

"And who is Chiron?"

"Oh – it's what I call Lysimachus. We play a game. I'm Achilles and he's Chiron and we go hunting together. Like the picture on the floor there."

"Tch!" Hellanike raised her brows and shrugged. She had a poor opinion of Lysimachus, who had won a special place in Alexander's affections – a grown man playing at children's games!

"Can I bring Araxis and Obares here to play with my soldiers?"

"Ask your mother's permission. I daresay you may."

"I wish I had brothers. A sister isn't much use to me. Araxis and Obares have nine brothers and lots of sisters. Why are there only two of us?" He was six now, and his sister Cleopatra three.

"Because that's how it is."

"Arridaios can't play either." Alexander sighed heavily.

"Be kind to Arridaios," said Lanike sharply. "He can't help the way he is."

"I know. I let him have some of my soldiers, but he spoils my battles. Araxis and Obares are twins. I like them. We climbed the plane tree by the south gate. I climbed the highest. I went right up. Why are Persians wicked?"

"There's good and bad, I daresay. But the Great King is wicked. And they're all barbarians."

"What are barbarians?"

"Foreign people. They talk like savages – ba – ba – ba – so we call them barbarians."

Alexander was puzzled. He knew that the Great King was wicked. Lanike had sometimes tried to scare him into being good with threats of his cruelties. The Persian king was an ogre who stalked through the dark when the nursery lamp had gone out, together with the one-eyed Cyclops, the three-headed dog of the Underworld, and other monsters. He knew that Persians were enemies. Long ago, in the time of Alexander the First of Macedon, King Xerxes had brought a huge army across the sea to conquer Greece. He had buried children alive, Lanike said, and had the sea whipped when it sank his ships. But these Persians, who had come to stay at his father's court, had gracious manners, they were beautiful in person and in their dress and they fascinated Alexander. "I don't think our Persians are barbarians," he said. "They can speak Greek." Perhaps they were different from other Persians.

They had rebelled against their Great King and been defeated, that's why they were here. Philip had welcomed the rebels and their families and given them houses suited to their rank. The children's great-grandfather, Artabazus, had ruled his own lands in Persia like a king. He was still a prince in exile, the head of a large family – his eldest sons were grandfathers, too. To Alexander he was like the mysterious wizard king in whose far-off land Greek heroes had once slain a dragon to win a fleece of gold.

Artabazus was in his seventies, tall and vigorous, with a penetrating eagle stare. He wore clothes in glowing colours, long tunics with sleeves and wide sashes, loose trousers gathered into soft, high boots. Alexander had never seen trousers before, or people who covered themselves in clothing from neck to ankle and wondered if they had the same bodies underneath. The Persian spoke Greek with a foreign accent that intrigued the Macedonian boy. They delighted in each other. Artabazus would take Alexander on his knee to tell him stories and they shared surprise in the novelty of each other's customs and beliefs.

"Artabazus told me about his country," said Alexander. "It's just across the sea. Do you know Achilles fought there? He fought people called Trojans. They had a rich city there. Do you know that the general Father lived with in Thebes went to help Artabazus fight the Great King? Artabazus said he marched through Macedon, but I wouldn't remember it because it was when I was small. He won two battles for them. Do you know that the Great King fights from a chariot? How can he manoeuvre fast enough on the battlefield? When he rides out to war they drive an empty chariot in front of him. It's covered in gold and it's for the sun god to ride in, but no-one can see him, of course, so it looks empty. I should think it gets in the way. Do you know —"

"Do *you* know," said Lanike, exasperated by this talkative Persian, "do you know that the first king of Macedon carried away the sun in his cloak?"

Alexander stopped in mid-thought with his mouth open, tilted his head to one side, and ate her up with his eyes. "How? Why? When did it happen?"

"Sit down then, and be still, and I'll tell you. Long ago, three princes came from the south. They were grandsons of Herakles."

"Herakles killed a lion," said Alexander, "with just his bare hands."

"Yes he did. So they say."

"Father kills lions but he uses a spear. Herakles was brave but Chiron says that Achilles was the bravest man who ever lived. Is it true?"

"How do I know who was the bravest man who ever lived? Do you want to hear this story?"

"Please, yes."

"Then listen. These three brothers came into the north. They went to the house of the king and asked for work. In those days the king and queen lived like the hill people do today. The king told the oldest brother to look after the horses, the next one to herd the oxen, and the youngest one to mind the sheep and goats. The queen did the cooking, just like any farmer's wife —"

A bubbling laugh came from Alexander. He pictured his mother in her jewels and veils, and Doris in the kitchen court, red-faced in front of the hot ovens, heaving out the trays of bread with her brawny arms.

"You may laugh," said Lanike, "but she did. Every day she baked loaves of bread, and the loaf she baked for the youngest prince swelled up to twice the size of all the others. After it had happened several times the queen told her husband and he called the boys and told them they must leave his country."

"Why? They hadn't done anything wrong."

"He thought it was strange. That it meant trouble."

"Go on."

"Well, the eldest brother said he must give them their wages before they left. The sun was shining through the smoke hole in the roof. It made a bright round patch on the floor, like a big gold piece. The king pointed to it and said, "That's all the wages you deserve and that's what you'll get." The two older boys were angry but the youngest said, "We'll take what you give, O king." He took out his knife and scratched a line round the sunlight on the floor. Then he bent down and gathered it up three times and put it inside his cloak."

Alexander considered the sunlight splashing onto Chiron's picture on the nursery floor. "He couldn't have," he said after a moment. "Not really. He must have pretended. Sorry, what happened next?"

"The boys rode away and the king called his Companions and asked them what they thought it meant. They told him it was a bad omen, that the boy would come back and take his kingdom, first one piece, then another, then all of it."

"Did he?"

"Wait! Wait! This made the king angry, as you may guess. He sent his Companions galloping after the boys to kill them."

"But he couldn't do that! Not before they'd given him cause. They were his guest-friends. They'd eaten bread and salt at his table."

"So, maybe. But what would you have done?"

"I wouldn't have sent them away in the first place. If the youngest one was brave I'd have made him my friend and let him help me in my wars, like Father and Parmenion. Father says that in Athens they choose ten generals every year, but he has only ever found one, and that's Parmenion. What was this boys name?"

"Perdiccas. But he wasn't killed. He crossed a river with his brothers and the river rose in flood behind them, so the horsemen couldn't get across."

"The gods were with him, then. I expect he took the kingdom."

"Yes, he did, in three battles, as it was foretold. He built our city of Aigai, his first city. The gods told him where it should be. He sent a messenger to the temple of Apollo to ask the priestess, and the answer came:

'Zeus has given you rule over a rich land. Go then in haste
to the pastures where flocks graze, and where you see
snow-white goats with shining horns lying fast asleep,
sacrifice to the gods, and build your city on the level ground,
and live there in happiness, you and your children.'
That's why our city is called Aigai, the goat pasture."

"Are you a goddess, Mother?"

"And why the soldiers have a white goat to lead them on parade."

"I expect so."

"But Pella is the biggest city now. The king lives here."

"Aigai is where our kings are buried. Perdiccas said when he was dying that his sons should bury him there, and that if ever the bones of a king of Macedon were not entombed at Aigai, then the kingdom would pass away from his family and into the hands of another."

It was later the same day. Alexander was playing with his soldiers on the floor of his mother's room. They were of painted clay. Cimon the potter had made them. He had equipped those on foot with long spikes of wood in imitation of the great spears, or sarissas, which Philip's army carried into battle. There were not many foot soldiers in the toy army, and even fewer cavalry men – just ten of them on stiff little horses and a commander in a white cloak. Alexander had made the enemy himself, squeezing the man-shapes out of clay from the spoil bins in Cimon's workshop, and putting them to dry in the hot sun. The enemy broke easily, not having been fired in a kiln.

He disposed his forces; the infantry phalanx in the centre, three files deep; the cavalry, five on each side of the phalanx, the right and left wings of his army. The white-cloaked commander led on the right. Facing them, the enemy in a long double line. Alexander paused to consider whether they were Illyrians or Thracians – or Persians. He decided upon Thracians, his father's campaigns being in the north just then. He was muttering to himself in Macedonian, imitating the brisk voices of the officers, and the grouses and jokes of the men. There was one soldier with a broken nose who had plenty to say, but as he was a fighter with a reputation for bravery, a double-pay man, who was keeping up the morale of his section, the commander pretended not to hear him. Indeed, he called him by name as he addressed his troops before the battle, encouraging them to show the same dash and courage.

Alexander whistled trumpet calls: 'Prepare to advance!' 'Infantry forward!' 'Cavalry charge!' Kneeling, he pushed forward his infantry, then swept his right wing into the enemy line, keeping the white cloaked commander in the lead. As the cavalry charged he pitched into a sudden, piercing battle-cry in full voice:

"ALALALALAI! ALEXANDROS!" It startled his mother, who stood weaving at her loom on the far side of the room. She dropped her shuttle, which trundled over and over across the floor, unwinding a thread of scarlet wool across his battle ground. As she came to pick it up, she gave him a laughing look:

"And with that Achilles raised the war-cry,
and drove his powerful horses forward.
The glitter of bronze rippled like laughter across the plain,
And the earth resounded to the feet of marching men......"

Alexander sat back on his heels and pushed a lock of hair away from his eyes. The words had a splendid sound, but his cavalry had just broken through the enemy line. Now his spearman should advance in a solid front. He was divided between the need to win his battle and his wish to hear more about Achilles. His cavalry were in the midst of the enemy and unsupported. "Tell me later, Mother," he said, "after the battle."

After the battle there would be a victory feast. The commander and his companions would recline on couches, garlanded, drinking red wine. The hall would be ablaze with torches and resound with laughter and song. Young soldiers would link arms and stamp out a war dance, heads tossing like horses, until the commander-king himself leapt up to lead the swaying lines. Then the bard would take up his lyre and recite stories of old battles, great heroes, and the famous dead. "Tell me later, Mother, about Achilles..."

Alexander's battle was won. The defeated foe were scattered, fled, or their broken bodies heaped on a funeral pyre. The victorious troops rested, feasted, their wounded lay wrapped in clean linen. Their commander, the god who had dispensed their fortunes, sat by his mother's knee and bit thoughtfully into a grape from a cluster he held on his lap. "What were you saying just now?"

"Some lines from the poet Homer. About the Trojan War."

"Artabazus told me! Achilles fought the Trojans. Did he win?"

"He killed their champion, the dearest son of their king."

"Was he a spearman or a cavalry commander?"

"It wasn't like that then. Men followed their chieftains to war. Lords and princes drove in chariots to the battle field and then dismounted to fight."

"Achilles was the best. Chiron told me."

"He was big and beautiful and brave.

'Swift-footed Achilles, stormer of cities,
breaker of the battle line!'"

The boy's face quickened. He put down his grapes and turned to his mother, his mouth a little open as if the story could be tasted, his eyes searching hers to catch any hidden meanings. "Tell me about him."

"His mother was a sea goddess," she said, "a daughter of Ocean, Thetis of the silver feet. Thetis was beautiful and many gods loved her, even Zeus himself, but there was a prophecy that her son would be greater than his father, so no-one would marry her. Zeus gave her to a mortal man, King Peleus of the Myrmidons. At first, Thetis refused him. She was a goddess, what was a king to her? When he tried to claim her, she changed in his arms into a lioness, then into a scorpion, then a serpent." Alexander's gaze rested on his mother's snakes, coiled in a jewelled tangle on the sun-warmed floor. They were asleep, but he knew how quickly they could move, pouring themselves away like water. "But Peleus held her fast, whatever shape she took, and so he won a goddess for his wife. Hellanike must cut your hair."

Alexander caught her hand as she lifted it to put back a lock that flopped heavily into his eyes. "If you were a goddess," he said, "I'd catch you and marry you." His mother laughed at him. Her eyes were like his, although he did not know it, the colour of grey light on shining water. There was a little cleft in the centre of her full lower lip, again like his own. She wore a thin green veil over her head, the edge of it shivered against her cheek when she laughed. Tiny waves rippled across her hair, like the soft ridges left in the sand by the shores of Pella lake. He knew what the smooth little bumps would feel like and put up a hand to stroke them. She took hold of his fingers. "Your hands are dirty. Do you want to hear more about Achilles?" He nodded.

"Thetis loved him very much. She wanted him to live for ever, like a god. Do you know what she did?"

Alexander shook his head. "She took him while he was still a baby to the River Styx, that black river that flows past the Underworld, between the land of the living and the land of the dead. The water is like snow-water when it comes down from the mountains, icy cold. She held him three times under the water."

A chill crept along Alexander's spine. "Right under? Didn't he drown?"

"No, the water flowed all over him and made his body immortal. But each time she held him by the same foot, so there was a part of him that the water did not touch, and there, in his ankle, he could be wounded to death."

"So he didn't live for ever?"

"No."

The lightest of shadows crossed his face. He picked at a scab on his knee. "What happened to him? How did he die?"

"The gods gave him a choice when he became a man. He could live long and die of old age and be forgotten, or he could go to war and die young but win a name that would always be remembered."

Alexander looked up. "But that's like living for ever."

"Yes, it is."

There was a silent pause. For a moment he was afraid to ask, so what happened? Achilles must have made the right choice, and yet in stories of the heroes such things were never certain. People made mistakes and suffered for them, and then the story hurt. He said, "But we're talking about him. So he must have chosen fame."

"Yes, he did. The High King Agammemnon led all the Greeks to fight the Trojans because a Trojan prince had stolen his brother's wife. Achilles was very young when the war began. He still had long hair and no beard. So his mother sent him away to one of the islands, and when the Greek messengers came to fetch him he was with the king's daughters dressed as a girl, and they couldn't find him."

"Did he want to be dressed as a girl, then?" exclaimed Alexander in astonished scorn.

"Would you?"

"No, of course not. I'd want to go to war."

"Well, so did he, but his mother and father forbade it because they feared his death fate. But now! One of the messengers was very cunning. He went away and blacked his eyebrows and put on the red cap and striped cloak of a Phoenician merchant. He came back with a box full of pretty things for the princesses to buy – combs of ivory and necklaces and jars of perfume. Only one of the girls didn't take anything, or even look. Then the merchant drew out from under a length of cloth a handsome old sword, well-polished and bright. At the same time a trumpeter sounded the alarm, and this girl sprang forward and seized the sword and whirled it round her head."

Alexander let out a shout of laughter and slapped his knee, a habit he had acquired from Kleitos of which he was rather proud. "So then he went to war?"

"Yes, he led his father's men."

"Why didn't his father go?"

"He was too old."

"Was Achilles a better fighter than his father?"

"Oh yes. The king had done brave things in his younger days, but his son surpassed them. And the poets sing of his deeds and tell the tale of them over and over again, so his fame lives on, as he was promised."

Alexander said gravely: "It was a gift to him from the gods. That's what it was, Mother, wasn't it?"

"Everything comes from the gods," she said. "This was their gift to him and his mother. They gave him his strength and his beauty and his courage. And in the end his everlasting fame. But remember that he was allowed to choose. He could have refused the gift."

Alexander remembered the story of a man who had lived to be so old that he had withered away, only his voice could be heard, feebly chattering like the rasp of a grass hopper on a summer's day.

"How did Achilles die?"

"He fought and killed the Trojan prince who had slain his best friend, although his mother had warned him that if he did his own death would soon follow. And so it was. He led an assault on the main gate of the city and an archer stood on the gate tower and shot him through the ankle. He bled to death."

"An archer wounded Father. Archers are not brave. They fight from a distance. I shall fight with a sword." He looked at her as though trying to capture some thought. "Was Achilles really the best?"

"Indeed he was. *Divine Achilles, like a god.*"

"Then he gave something too," said Alexander. His brows drew together as he searched for words to express his thought. "The best life. When he died, it wasn't as if he was giving away nothing. Do you see, Mother?"

"Yes I do." She kissed him.

"Shall I be famous like him?"

"Who knows? But we are of his blood."

"You told me. His son was my great-great-great-great-great grandfather. He captured a princess and they had a baby."

"A Trojan princess. He carried her off as his prize when the city was destroyed."

"A *Trojan* princess?"

"The widow of their champion, whom Achilles slew."

"But then we have Trojan blood in us, too. Like Artabazos and Araxis and Obares."

"They were brave people," said his mother. "You can be proud of that, too."

"Artabazus will be *very* pleased," said Alexander, "when I tell him that

I'm a bit of a Trojan." He stood for a moment leaning against her, lost in thought. Then, reaching up one arm to encircle her neck and pull down her head, he whispered into her ear: "Mother, are you a goddess?"

She laughed and shook her head. "No, but perhaps I will be the mother of a second Achilles. That would be enough for me." He glowed at her, not certain that he had understood, but aware of love and admiration and returning both with passion.

Chapter 4

The Great King

Alexander was running through the outer court on his way to make more clay soldiers when he came upon the two elder Persians, Artabazos and Menapis, strolling in the shade of a colonnade outside the room in which the king gave audience to visitors. They were dressed for a court occasion in silks which held the light like cups of wine. Their beards were plaited and their hair arranged in curls like rows of snail shells below the high round hats that looked so strange in Macedon. They smelt delicately of perfume.

Alexander stopped to admire their splendour. "It must take a long time to do your hair like that. Mine's always tangly. Lanike says it's a waste of time to curl it. Why are you in these clothes?"

He was concerned to discover that they were waiting for an audience with the king. "My father's in the Court of Justice. It may take a long time. Somebody's sister was dishonoured and a man was killed. Now there's a blood feud between the highlanders in the footguards. And then there are envoys from Thessaly for him to see. Ptolemy's on duty, he's going to take me riding afterwards and he said I might have a long wait. Would you like something to eat and drink? Shall I tell the steward to bring cakes and wine?"

No, they assured him, they had been given refreshment and needed nothing. "Then I'll stay and talk with you. It's very boring to wait with nothing to do." Artabazos made a graceful gesture. "That would delight us both."

"Well, I should like it, too. Our men don't plait their beards. Do you do that before a battle?"

"I have always done so," said Artabazos. Alexander nodded. "It makes you feel proud and brave." The woven strands of hair, black streaked with white, framed his face like the cheek straps of an elaborate helmet.

"A flowing beard," said Menapis dryly, "offers the enemy a handhold."

"Father's is cut short," said Alexander, "but he doesn't like wasting time with the barber. The barber talks too much. I won't grow a beard. Is the Great King brave?"

"All our men are brave. Ours is a hard country, it breeds brave men just as yours does. And the bravest of the brave are the Ten Thousand Immortals who guard the king."

Alexander was silent. His father's Royal Bodyguard numbered seven. After considering he said: "Only the gods are immortal. Soldiers are not gods."

"They are called Immortals," said Menapis, "because as soon as one dies he is replaced by another so they always number ten thousand. It seems to me that you have lost some troops." He pointed to the broken soldiers in Alexander's hands. "Did you win your battle?"

"Oh yes, our casualties were light. The Thracians were cut down in retreat. I led the cavalry charge. Father always leads the spearmen on the right. Where does the Great King fight?"

"He takes the centre."

"In his chariot. My mother told me that in the time of Achilles all the leaders rode in chariots to battle but they jumped down to fight. Does the Great King do that?"

"No, he fights from the chariot with javelins and arrows."

"I should like to try riding in a chariot, but in battle I shall fight from horseback. A horse thinks with you. How many squadrons has the Great King? Who leads them?"

"The armies of the Great King are too many to count, Alexander. He rules not one country but many, joined together in one great empire. It stretches from the other side of this sea across plains and deserts and mountains as far as the land of the elephants – from all these lands he can summon men to fight for him."

The new word, elephants, caught his ear, but he held it at the back of his mind while questions streamed from him – how does he summon them? how long does it take them to come? how does he find food for them all? "Lanike told me that when the Great King crossed the sea and marched through Macedon his armies drank the rivers dry." The Persians' answers were too vague to satisfy him. He regarded them thoughtfully for a moment, and then brought out the new word, carefully copying the Persian accent. "Please tell me, what are e-l-e-phants?"

Artabazos' brows – black with a white frosting – rose dramatically. He flourished an expressive hand. "Creatures so big that they could not pass through that archway. Grey or brown, with baggy, wrinkled skins like old cracked leather, and a long, curved tusk growing from each side of their jaws." Artabazos placed a finger at either side of his mouth, then swept his hands forward in a long upward curve. "Their ears hang down as large as carpets and they flap them to and fro." He waved his hands at each side of his head. "And their noses grow into a long trunk" – his arm suggested sinuous length – "a tube of muscle like a thick snake, with two finger tips at the end. With his trunk an elephant can pick up a straw from the ground or uproot a tree!" He paused, and once more raised his brows, as though to ask, "Now, what do you say to that?"

Alexander gave him a cool smile for courtesy. He had heard tales of three-headed monsters and fire-breathing dragons and a flying horse, and he loved such stories, but he intended to hold an adult conversation, not to be amused as a child. "It's not true, is it? It's like the flying horse and the snake-headed monster, they're true in stories but not in real life."

"Not true!" exclaimed Menapis. "Would a Persian lie to you? From boyhood our fathers teach us three things – to ride, to shoot and to tell the truth. In the east, princes train war elephants. I have met men who have seen them. These elephants can lift men in their trunks and dash them to the ground, or trample them underfoot, beating them into the earth like squashed flies. The princes ride in towers on their backs and discharge their spears and arrows from that height. Horses who have never seen elephants are terrified of them."

"How do men tame elephants so that they can ride them?"

"There are men in the east who are skilled in such work. They call the elephants their children and whisper into their huge ears. They sit on their necks and guide them by the pressure of their feet. Their knowledge is passed down from father to son."

The boy nodded. This he could believe. "It is their mystery, then. A god must help them. I should like to know how they do it. It cannot be at all like breaking horses. I shall find out one day. How far away is the land of the elephants?"

The Persians exchanged a look, wondering how to convey to him the vast distances of their empire, not one land but many, twenty or more ancient kingdoms, each ruled by its own satrap, but owing allegiance to the Great King. They drew breath and began.

They told him first of the heartlands, high under the sun, where the mountains gave back the light of the sky, purple at dawn, golden at noon-day, flame at sunset. They told him of the lowlands, the black fertile plain between the two great rivers, Tigris and Euphrates, where wheat ripened twice a year; and the marshes, where men lived in reed houses on floating islands. They told him of the grass lands, where golden-maned horses ran like the wind's own children; and of vast deserts of sand or salt or stone, where shining lakes and false, floating cities appeared to deceive the traveller. And they told him of a curtain of mountains hanging in the sky, peak above snow-clad peak – beyond which lay the kingdom of the elephants.

As he listened a longing seized him so intense that it felt like the pain of a great hunger, a longing to see all these lands, to gallop the grassy plains, cross the burning deserts, boat among the islands of the marsh, and climb the high passes of the mountains to discover the worlds beyond. "King Archelaus built roads. My father is making a new road into the western mountains. Our army can march all the way to Illyria now with its baggage train. Are there roads everywhere across Persia? Are there roads across the desert? How do you build roads on sand?"

They told him of the camels that crossed the trackless deserts in long-striding teams, swaying like ships above their gliding shadows, steering by the sun and the stars; of the caravan routes that led through mountain passes, following the way of nomad shepherds; and of the Royal Road that connected the great cities of western Persia – Susa, Persepolis, Babylon. He asked how many day's march it was from one city to the next, and they told him how the King's Messengers galloped the Royal Road in relays, with fresh horses waiting at each staging post, through summer heat and winter snow, *faster than anything else which is mortal.'*

He was leaning against Artabazos' knee now, the elder having seated himself on a stone lion. His grey eyes, so full of light, gazed into a magical distance seeing, as the old man described them, the fabulous cities: – Babylon, encircled by towering black walls in which there were a hundred gates of bronze; Persepolis, city of palaces, where the king's horsemen could ride ten abreast up the stone staircase into an audience room that held ten thousand: – Ecbatana – Susa – their names sang and they shimmered before him like the false cities of the desert, opening their gates for him, showering his way with flowers.

He wakened slowly from the daydream, brushing a fly from his face. Artabazus smiled at him affectionately. "Now we have shown you Persia. You have seen it all."

"And what," he asked suddenly, "is beyond the kingdom of the elephants?"

"The encircling ocean," said Menapis, "the end of the known world."

Alexander frowned in thought. "And the Great King rules all the lands you told me of?"

"All, from the Hellespont to Hindi."

"But not to the end of the world?"

"No. Not to the end of the world."

"How does he become Great King? Do the soldiers acclaim him?"

"No. One of the old king's sons succeeds him, usually the eldest, sometimes another if he is stronger. The Magi, wise men who serve God, look for signs in the stars to confirm his right. Then he eats a cake of figs and drinks a cup of sour milk. He puts on the royal robes and worships before the Holy Fire. Then he is King of Kings and his person is sacred."

"But if the men haven't chosen him, why do they fight for him?"

"They believe that the Wise God has chosen him and so they are loyal to him. It is a matter of honour. It is also in their interest. Without a great king to unite them under his rule, the lands of the empire would become separate warring nations again, and return to poverty. A wise man has said that ten years of famine follow every year of warfare."

Alexander wished to ask why, then, had these two satraps rebelled, but he knew that it was discourteous to embarrass a guest. Artabazos met the wondering gaze of his expressive eyes, and gave a slight shake of the head. "I know your thought, Alexander. But there are some men in positions of power who abuse it. We defended ourselves against a king who would have robbed and dishonoured us."

"Lanike says the Great King is wicked."

"Let me tell you of one who was not. Kyros was our first Great King. He should be a pattern for all kings to follow. Then men would serve them gladly."

Alexander leant, warm and loving, within the old man's encircling arm. "What did he do?"

"I'll tell you. In the beginning there were two nations in our land. The Medes who were rich and powerful, and the Persians who were poor farmers – shepherd folk."

"Like our hill people."

"Yes, like your hill people. The king of the Medes let his daughter marry a Persian chieftain and she had a son called Kyros. The king had a dream – he dreamt that a vine grew from his daughter and spread over all the kingdom."

"It seems," said Alexander, "that people always have dreams when a son is born. My father and my mother had one for me. What did the king's dream mean?"

"The Magi told the king that it meant his daughter's son would one day take the kingdom away from him."

"That's just like Lanike's story about my people!" cried Alexander. "But then it was a loaf of bread and a boy pretending to catch the sun."

"Is it so? Tell me your story afterwards. Let me finish the story of Kyros. The king sent for a general who was called Harpagos. He told him to take the baby and kill it. Harpagos took the baby and gave it to a slave who kept flocks. He told him to leave it out on the hills to die of cold, or for wild beasts to devour."

"I expect a god came and saved him," said Alexander confidently.

"No. It was the herdsman's wife. That same day she gave birth to a boy who was born dead. She told her husband to wrap the dead baby in the royal grave clothes and leave it out on the hills, and they kept the living child to grow up and be a comfort to their old age. They thought no-one would ever know. Harpagos sent soldiers to bury the dead child, and the slave woman raised the prince as her son, the son of a shepherd."

"Did he know who he was ?"

"Not until he was ten. Then he was playing with some other boys. They chose him to be their king. Kyros gave them their duties – one to be a guard, another to be a messenger, and so on. One boy refused to obey and Kyros struck him with a whip. He was a lord's son and he complained to his father, who told the king.

The king sent for Kyros and his foster father. 'How dare you,' he said, 'the son of a slave, strike the son of a nobleman, one of my Companions?'

Kyros answered boldly. 'The boys chose me to be their king. But he would not obey my orders, so I punished him.' He did not speak like a slave, and he had his grandfather's looks, so the king guessed the truth. He threatened to torture the shepherd unless he confessed everything. So the whole story came out."

"But he didn't kill Kyros?"

"No, he saw that he was brave and handsome and he wanted to keep him, because he had no sons. And the Magi told him that the prophecy had been fulfilled because Kyros had played at being king. So he sent for Harpagos and told him that the prince was alive and that he was glad of it. He asked him to send his own son to play with the prince, and to come that evening to a sacrifice of thanksgiving and a banquet."

Alexander was watching the old man's face. It was too soon to rejoice. He had more to tell. He told it in a whisper. "At the banquet Harpagos was served with a special dish and after he had eaten the king told him he had eaten the flesh of his own son – that was his punishment for disobeying the king's command."

The dark, unfathomable eyes of the Persian looked into Alexander's, wide and pale with shock as he felt the father's agony. The child twisted as though to pull away from his encircling arm, but Artabazos said softly, in a voice that promised consolation, "Hear the rest of the story."

"Harpagos killed the king."

"No, he waited. Kyros was sent to live with his real mother and father. He grew up brave and generous and everyone who knew him loved him. When he was a young man of fighting age and trained in warfare he received one day the present of a hare."

"A hare?"

"A dead hare, for the table. The huntsman who brought it whispered to him to skin it himself. Under the skin he found a letter. It was from Harpagos. It said, ' The lords of the Medes will not endure the cruelties and tyrannies of this king any longer. Raise an army among the Persians and come, we will join you. Overthrow him and you shall have his kingdom.'"

Alexander straightened up, bright and expectant once more.

"Yes, you've guessed. They won a great battle and Kyros became ruler of both Medes and Persians. That was the beginning of the empire."

"And he killed the king."

"The king was his grandfather remember, and he was old. No, he didn't kill him. Kyros was not a vengeful man. He let the king live in retirement in peace and dignity. And he did not treat the Medes as a conquered people. Medes and Persians became one under his rule. He went on to conquer other cities and provinces, for he was a great warrior and commander. He spent his life in the saddle. But he allowed all those who came under his rule to keep their own customs and religions. He valued each tribe and nation for its own excellence, its talents and ideas, and let each manage its own affairs. That's why he was loved and obeyed."

"And he conquered all the lands you told me about? But not to the end of the world?"

"He thought he had. On his tombstone the words are carved: 'I am Kyros, King of the World, Great King.'"

"King of the World!" He said it wondering, softly, it sounded magical.

"I have seen his tomb," said Menapis, also softly, "a plain chamber of rock. It stands on the Plain of the Water Bird. The stone still gives back the light of the sky as it did in the mountains where it was hewed."

In the silence that followed, Alexander regarded them thoughtfully, feeling their melancholy. "Do you want very much to go home? My father will help you when his wars are done. The Macedonians will win back your lands." To his distress he saw moisture glisten in the crease below Artabazos' eye. "Do you miss Persia so very much? I'm truly sorry." Artabazos stooped to kiss him. "Your mother's roses have the perfume of Persia," he said. "So they bloomed in my paradise at home."

Alexander sprang away, tugging at his hand. "Come then! Come and smell them. My mother will be pleased. And I can show you the shrine of Herakles and the stone dog that's just like Bia!"

"Dear child, it would not be seemly for us to enter the inner court, so near your women's apartments. We can see and enjoy the roses from here."

"I'll bring you some!" He was gone before they could protest, returning with his hands full of thorny blossoms. He began to divide them into two, separating them carefully. The Wise Woman came drifting through the court, wandering like a bird, pecking at this and that, murmuring a tuneless little song to herself. She paused by the three.

"What have you strangers to do with our basilikos? What has he to do with you? Who is wearing a crown of roses? Will you have him for your Great King, fine lords, will you?" Her laughter pealed, sudden and shrill.

Artabazos said gravely, "One day he will be a great king, of that I am sure."

Alexander said: "I shall tell Lanike about Kyros. She doesn't know. She thinks Persians are barbarians, but that's because she doesn't know. My mother told me that I'm a bit of a Trojan, Artabazos. I'm the great-great-great-great-great grandson of a Trojan princess. So perhaps the blood of Kyros is in me, too."

Chapter 5

"I am Alexander"

It was his birth month – he was nearly seven at last! He gave away his toys – the soldiers, regretfully, to Arridaios, knowing they would soon be broken. The only one he kept was Balios, his wooden horse named after his father's famous racer and still his bedtime friend.

He had been shown his new room; it was near his father's in another wing of the palace. His clothes were there now, in the big chest of cedar wood, which had a picture painted on the lid of Herakles wrestling with an earth giant.

Under the pillow of the bed was a hollow where precious things were kept. His brooches and arm-rings were there and a little sharp dagger. His father had shown him the bed-box, given him a gold arm-band to put inside it, and the dagger. He had warned him always to check that the knife was there before he slept, and shown him how to keep it sharp and how to use it. His mother had not yet given him a special gift to mark his growing up. Perhaps it was nothing for her to celebrate, because he was going into his father's world of men, but he would always love her best. He would tell her so tomorrow.

He was lying in his small bed looking round the room, where the nursery lamp flicked spots of dancing yellow light over familiar shadowy shapes. In the next room Lanike slept with his sister Cleopatra. He could hear soft, breathy snores. Tomorrow night he would sleep in a man's bed, alone in the dark. He drew a deep, steadying breath.

He dreamt that he was Icarus, standing on the top of a high cliff. Far below the sea stretched, sparkling and shimmering so that when he looked down it hurt his eyes. When he looked up the sky was an infinite, impossible space of blue, in which the sun revolved like a bubble of gold.

His father was fastening his wings to his shoulders, they were heavy and wobbled. The king fastened the arm-straps and gave him a push. He opened his mouth to scream, "I'm falling, I'm falling!" and then a warm wind rising from the cliff got under his wings and lifted him. The wings were strong, he lay on their strength; he was soaring through blue space, the soft air flowing past him. He wanted to see his father, to be sure that he was following behind. He half turned his head and could see only the lifting, fluttering flight feathers at the edges of his wing. He called, "Father!" and the sound was very high and clear. It went ringing round the lucent dome of the sky, like the sound of a clapper in a bell. The sun was hot on his neck and shoulders. He looked up. The golden fire-ball blazed. He could fly right up into it, he could be absorbed into the sun and be one with that radiance. He called again, to share the joyful discovery – "Father! Father!" high and ecstatic, ringing round the sky – "Father!"

"Alexander!" The harsh, angry note in her voice shattered the golden fragments of his dream. The round blaze of the sun became a clay lamp held close to his face. His mother was leaning over him. Her fingers pressed painfully into his shoulder. "Alexander, wake up!"

He struggled up, confused and aware of a loss as his dream drifted away and reality became dark and solid around him. He and his father had been going together into glory, now his father was out there alone, going alone. When he knew it for a dream, the loss seemed even greater.

His mother bent over him. She was angry. What was wrong? It was the middle of the night. "Alexander, wake up! How quickly you fall asleep. Come, get up. You and I have something special to attend to."

Still dazed from sleep, he sat on the edge of the bed and groped for his clothes. "What time is it?"

"It's early yet, halfway through the first watch. You must have fallen asleep the moment you lay down." He had called out "Father!" as she approached the bed to waken him. She had meant to do so gently, but that glad, dreaming cry had sharpened a knife of jealous anger. She must heal the wound or tonight's purpose would be lost. Sitting beside him on the bed, she kissed him and then stood up and displayed her robe, spreading the skirt with one hand. "Look, do you see this?"

Fully awake now, he gazed in pleasure and admiration. He loved beauty in all things, but most of all in her. "It's the robe you wore when you married Dionysos." It was cloth of gold, stiff with purple embroidery: dark leaves and flowers sprang from intricate, spiralling stems, curling across its shimmering surface. Her cloak was her hair, unbound, rippling to her waist, darker gold than the robe. The lamp flame, held low, cast unfamiliar shadows across the upper planes of her face, lighting her white throat, the curve of her upper lip, her brilliant eyes, and glinting on the gilded leaves of the ivy wreath twined in her hair. "Are we going to the shrine?"

"Of course, where else? You will not come there again. You must take leave of the god and ask his blessing. Never lack courtesy toward the gods, Alexander."

In her reception room her women were waiting, wearing the thin, flowing robes in which they danced for the god. Soft, spotted skins of fawns dangled from their shoulders, and they had wreaths of ivy in their hair. Phoebe and some others carried the sacred snakes in ivy baskets, and they all held wands tipped with pine cones. By torch light they made their way through the palace gardens and into the sacred grove.

Here, in a clearing with soft pine needles underfoot, was the altar of the god. Behind it, on a pine branch, the queen hung the mask that travelled in the bridal car for their ritual marriage at winter's end. It was an old mask and showed a black-bearded Dionysos, a much older and sterner image than the picture of the beautiful boy riding a panther across the palace floor. The fire was kindled with pine branches, and a black kid sacrificed. Its blood darkened the ground. The women had brought jars of wine; they dipped silver ladles with goose-head handles and poured libations to Dionysos, then they all drank. Olympias flung a handful of incense onto the flames, and as the sweet blue smoke rose up, wreathing round the mask and drifting through the torch light to disappear into the mystery of the dark, she invoked the god:

"Holy one, twice born,
begotten of the serpent and of fire,
Divine Child, bringer of gladness, lord of the vine,
life-giving, death-defying, Lord Dionysos,
accept our offering,
be gracious to us
and to Alexander, my son,
may his offerings be pleasing to you always."

She put her hands on her son's shoulders. "This is the last time for you here, Alexander. Tonight we dance for the god and for you. In future, when you may no longer be here in person, come in your heart, whenever you see our torches among the trees, and know that we shall invoke Dionysos in your name and he will listen."

The music began, the flutter of hand-drums and the soft shrilling of pipes. The women began to run with little steps, round in a circle, then turning, circling the other way, winding and unwinding, linking hands. As they danced they sang the story of the god. They sang of the secret child in the cave with his mother, of the young god hunting in the forest with his women companions, and his gifts to the earth of wine and honey. They sang of his death and rebirth, his wanderings across the world in divine madness, accompanied by raging worshippers, and his return in triumph, his companions transfigured by happiness, even the wild beasts tamed, lions and leopards walking in his procession.

The queen led the dancers. Transfigured by the wine god, she whirled and swayed, tossing back her hair, treading the earth with bare feet. She poured her snakes from hand to hand, they spiralled her arms and wound about her body as though they also danced, their fire-bright scales glinting among the purple flowers of her robe and the shadows of her hair. The drums beat faster and the women's song ended in shouts which shredded the dark, shrilling through the listener's head as though a knife point touched the bare nerve of a tooth: "Euoi Iachos! Euoi! Euoi! Euoi!" So, men said, vixens screamed in the woods in winter.

The queen staggered and drooped, Phoebe gathered the snakes into their baskets. Olympias came with uncertain steps to where Alexander stood and sank to one knee before him. Her eyes, heavy-lidded as though with sleep, gazed upward into his, she breathed audibly with open mouth and her speech came as though the words weighed heavily: "Alexander, remember who you are."

The firelight on her gold ornaments fractured into splintered stars, a dazzling blur. His eyes ached from the wine, the torch light and the need for sleep. He felt a long way away, and stupid, afraid of what he did not understand. "Who am I?"

"You are not his." What did she mean? Did the god reject him?

"Not Philip's. You are not his. You are mine and the god's." She seemed to awaken. Her voice was sharper. "Do not forget when you call *Father*! You are not his!"

"I am no-one's!" he cried. Something bound within him by iron bands burst free. "I am no-one's!" He turned to the altar and lifted his hands to the black-bearded mask. "I am my own self. I am Alexander. That's who I am."

The god in the mask looked on unmoved, but overhead came a sudden clap of thunder. With no more warning, the drenching rain came down. The ground steamed in the warm night. Then the torches spluttered and died. With shrieks and gasps the women gathered up the snake baskets, covering them with their fawn-skin cloaks, and stumbled towards the garden in the dark. There were sharp cries as a low branch scratched someone's face and another slithered on a patch where thick dust had instantly become mud. The warm rain poured down their faces and plastered their hair to their shoulders. Alexander blinked as it beaded along his eyelashes and he felt it dripping from his nose and chin. As he grasped his mother's hand to guide her forward, he began to laugh; he could feel her laughter quivering through her arm into her fingers, and hear little gasps of merriment breaking from her lips as she squelched after him. He stumbled and splashed on purpose, making more of it, laughter rising through him, a welling fountain as clean as the rain. Half way across the garden, some Pages came, running and slipping and splashing, to meet them with torches under a canopy.

The women's rooms were full of noise, light and laughter, and the smell of wet cloth; the floor puddled and muddied; the steam rising from basins of hot water hurriedly brought by sleepy servants; the girls wringing out their hair and exclaiming over scratched and muddy feet and torn dresses. The queen stood in the middle of her room, flung back her head with its shining weight of dripping, sea-dark hair, and laughed.

Alexander ran and sprang into her arms; they clung together, both soaking wet, each feeling the laughter pulsing in the other's body. He looked at her sand-dark, seaweed hair, her glistening arms and shoulders, her gleaming face, and the drenched wedding robe clinging to her body in fine wrinkles – "Mother, the sea-goddess. You *are* the sea-goddess!" It struck them both as wonderfully funny, they gave themselves up to great surges of laughter, which were also a gift from Dionysos.

Alexander slept late the next morning. When King Philip and Leonidas came to the queen's rooms to fetch him, he was still abed. Her eyes mocked them in silence:- "See, I have stolen something from you. He is not here, waiting and eager, and the dreams he had last night were mine, not yours."

Philip had a war waiting for him in the north that could not be put off. The summer winds that would prevent the Athenian fleet from sailing were due, and he was about to reckon with the powerful Greek city of Olynthos, and the smaller cities in league with her, who, afraid of his growing power, had broken their treaty with him and were making a separate peace with Athens. He had settled disturbances at home, in Thessaly and in Epiros, and was now ready to march north, but the boy must be seen to first.

In Epiros he had found the man he needed to take charge of Alexander.

Leonidas was a prince of the royal house, an uncle of Olympias. She could hardly object to such a choice – but she would have no influence over him. He was a cold, stern man, one to be neither charmed nor intimidated, especially by his own niece. Philip himself felt uncomfortable with him – he was depressing company at supper – but he admired the way that Leonidas had brought up his own sons to be hardy, self-reliant, and respectful. He was an educated man who had travelled in the south and lived for a time in Athens. He would raise the boy as a Greek whom the Athenians would not be ashamed to acknowledge; he would toughen him and teach him to endure hardship, and, above all, he would dampen the emotional fires kindled by Olympias, the dreams and passions and religious fervour that, in Philip's opinion, should be smoked out of the boy's head like a nest of wasps.

Alexander was getting washed and dressed, he had not yet met his great-uncle. Hellanike was cross and hustled him, unhappily aware that this was the last time she would do these things for him. Although thankful to be rid of so demanding a charge, she knew how empty the rooms would seem after he had gone. She combed his hair for the last time. Alexander hugged her and went to meet his uncle.

The reception room was silent when he entered it. Philip stood staring out through the colonnade at two magpies clacking over a stolen bone in the courtyard. Olympias sat in her chair of state, her fingers gently caressing the heads of the gilded leopards on the arm-rests – one could imagine that they purred. The unknown great-uncle, tall, upright, with a long, hard face and bushes of grey hair above his ears, stood rubbing a finger from side to side across his chin, watching them both, taking their measure. He turned the same calculating gaze upon the boy who darted into the room and stopped, casting a swift, appraising glance at each in turn. Philip presented them to each other. Used to affection from the soldiers, Lysimachus, Artabazus and the womenfolk, Alexander came to his uncle confidently and lifted his face for the expected kiss of welcome. Leonidas looked down at him from his height. "You rise late, Alexander. Soldiers are up and about their duties before sunrise."

Flushing, Alexander glanced towards his mother and, since she did not speak, apologised. "I overslept. I'm usually up early. I'm sorry if I kept you and Father waiting."

Philip answered: "Your uncle will excuse you this once and so will I. But from today your life will be different. You will begin to conduct yourself as a man." He spoke to his wife as well as his son, although he looked at

Alexander. "Your uncle does not wish to be called a tutor. He will be known as your governor. Address him as sir. You will obey him as a soldier obeys his commander. When I leave he will stand as your father. All matters will be decided by him, he has my authority. I expect you to behave well, to make me proud of you. Let me hear a good report when I return."

Alexander fastened on the part of this speech which most interested him. "When do you march, Father? Are you taking Kebes' squadron? He wants very much to go. Will you lay siege to Olynthos?"

Before Philip could reply, Leonidas said sharply, "Attend to your father, Alexander, and do not question your elders in that bold fashion. Boys should be silent unless asked to speak. Put your hands behind you. And do not stare at me. It is ill-mannered. Look down, if you please."

After a startled moment, Alexander complied. It was on his lips to say, 'How can boys find out if they don't ask?' but it seemed wiser to be cautious for the moment. His parents were at war and he was like the bone the magpies quarrelled over. He could feel the hidden anger in the room. His mother spoke for him. "Take care, between the two of you, when you set yourselves to muzzle a lion. You are training a prince, not a peasant; a soldier, not a slave. There is a fire born in him that you will not quench, Uncle. If I thought that you could I would die on your spear before I gave him into your care" She came to stand beside her son and laid her hand on his shoulder. "I do not fear for him," she said. "He will remember who he is." Her hand pressed lightly. She looked down as Alexander looked up, his eyes guarded, cool. 'Not theirs,' said his inward voice. 'Not yours, not his, not theirs. I am Alexander. I am myself.'

The king said peaceably: "No-one doubts your love for him. You have given me a fine boy, Olympias, he is a credit to your years of care. Now let him go." And inwardly he asked himself: 'Why do I have no more sons than that fool, Arridaios? Do I believe that she has cursed me? The people believe in her witchcraft. And what has she taught this boy? His eyes are guarding something. Has she set him against me already?'

"You train horses," she said. "Do not be less wise in dealing with your son."

Leonidas proposed that he and Alexander go riding to get to know one another. Philip had told him that his son, although small, was strong and capable beyond his years. His first sight of Olympias's child had been something of a shock – a disturbing beauty – brilliant, devouring eyes, a full passionate mouth, a white skin and a mane of dark gold hair. Nothing of Philip's squareness, darkness, robustness, steadiness. Far too much like his mother, all light and fire, and – he would not be surprised – dreams and fancies, and a temper. Quick, eager movements, impetuous speech, restless – and reckless too, he'd be bound.

He was therefore not entirely surprised to see his great-nephew in the stable yard leading out a horse that was too big for him, and, by the shaking of its head and stamping of its hoof, far too spirited. "It's all right, Uncle, I always ride Xanthos. He has the fidgets because no-one took him out yesterday. He needs a gallop." The head groom confirmed that this was the prince's usual mount. "He has a way with horses, Sir. Lysimachus the Arcanian taught him to ride and *he's* the finest horseman in Pella. As he's not here today, I'll ride with you, if you wish."

As they passed through the town, Leonidas acknowledged that the boy could manage the horse. By word and touch he guided it, side-stepping and head-tossing, past yapping dogs and children playing, a file of guardsmen marching from the barracks, and street sellers shouting their wares. A woman's blue scarf, blowing down the street and twisting like a snake, caused the animal to caper, turning a complete circle, but Alexander steadied it and set it off again at a quiet trot. On the soft ground beside the river, he shouted that this was the place for a gallop, struck the horse's sides with his heels, and was off, the groom pounding after him. Unprepared and left a length behind, Leonidas, on fire with anger, followed.

Led by Alexander, they leapt a wide stream with high banks, thundered in a shower of flying clods along the river meadows, putting up flights of shrieking birds, cantered round a stand of silvery wind-tossed willows, and came to a walk. Alexander was flushed and exhilarated, his eyes brilliant, his hair fluttering in the wind. "Isn't he a good horse, Uncle? The best they've ever let me ride. Chiron said he was too big for me at first. Chiron has a book by Xenophon all about horses. It teaches you how to train them. I want to train a horse of my own. Chiron will help me. He helps me train my dog. We're teaching her to track hares. She's called Bia. What are the names of your dogs?"

"Alexander!" He had waited to catch both his breath and his temper while the boy ran on. He put out a hand and seized the prince's bridle, gripping it so that his knuckles stood out. Staring at him in surprise, Alexander, with a slight frown, eased the horse. "Don't! Be careful of his mouth." Furious, his cold blue eyes on fire, Leonidas glared at him. "How dare you! Hold your tongue! And listen, if you ever do anything like that again I shall thrash you!" The boy stiffened. His own eyes paled with anger and widened in surprise. "Why? What have I done?"

Leonidas drew two heavy breaths and refrained from lifting his hand to strike the defiant face. "You will learn not to answer back. And to follow where your elders lead. It is time your father sent for me. And whoever this man is who has had charge of you, I shall have words to say to him. He has imposed no discipline at all. Does he think no better of you than to let you run wild like a farm boy?"

It was now Alexander whose face flushed scarlet and who glared at his uncle with hot and angry eyes. "He's my friend! He's my greatest friend! He's taught me everything I know that I care about. I would die for him and so would he for me. My father loves him and he's my mother's friend too."

Now Leonidas did strike him, first on one side of the face and then the other. Emotional, hot-tempered, untamed – it was as he had supposed. He would have a strenuous time bringing this one under the bridle. His mouth set in a grim line, he would set about the task with some relish.

The groom, who had withdrawn a few discreet paces, flinched at the sharp sound of the blows and involuntarily let his horse step forward. He was fond of the child, who would talk horses to him by the hour, getting under his feet when he was busy, asking a hundred and one questions. The boy did not cry, though the blows made his eyes water. He blinked rapidly lest his uncle should think he shed tears; his skin had paled, the red finger marks showing plainly. If he had had a dagger he might have used it, but the sudden action had set the horse side-stepping; he controlled it and the groom, taking this as an excuse, came up beside him and used his own mount to steady the other. It gave Alexander time to control himself; he sat astride the quietened horse, proud, hurt and unyielding, but hearing his father's words: "This man is your governor. You will obey him as a soldier obeys his commander."

Leonidas said: "I am prepared, Alexander, to overlook this impudent behaviour on this one occasion, since I am persuaded that you know no better yet. Also, I should be sorry to be forced to punish you on our first day together. However – mind this! – I shall not tolerate anything of the kind again. You will learn to behave as a boy should before his elders, speaking only when you are given leave to speak, and certainly never putting yourself forward in such an insolent manner as we have seen today. We will return to the palace. I shall ride in front of you at a steady pace. You will follow and your groom will ride behind us. You will not speak a word until we reach the stable yard, and then you will wait – respectfully – to discover what my orders are."

Alexander's impulse was to salute, but he guessed, rightly, that this would be interpreted as a mocking gesture. He said, "Yes, Sir," as a soldier to his commanding officer. They returned, in a seething silence, to the palace.

In Alexander's room, Leonidas looked about him with critical eyes. He removed a blanket of scarlet wool from the bed. "This is unnecessary, especially in summer. You must learn, Alexander, to live like a soldier." Alexander did not object to this. He had anticipated a harder life and looked forward to being tested. His father and his men could march thirty stades a day in armour in summer heat and winter cold; they could endure sickness, wounds, short rations, discomfort and hard labour without complaint, and he did not mean to be less capable. He had been impatient to get away from nursery coddling and fit himself for the life that Philotas, Ptolemy and other friends were already living. If Leonidas had been a man to inspire love he would have followed him passionately, however hard his regime – indeed the harder the better – as one who could help him become all he wished to be. As it was, he would still obey him, but he would do it from pride and self-respect.

Leonidas was examining the contents of the clothes chest. He lifted out cloaks and tunics of fine, creamy wool and white Egyptian linen, stuffs imported from Athens before the war, others woven by the queen and her women, dyed saffron or blue, with contrasting borders. "These are too fine for a boy of your age, Alexander. Showy clothing encourages a boy to think too much of himself. I will provide you with garments that are modest and hard-wearing."

"May I speak, Sir?"

"You may, certainly."

"My mother made these."

"Your mother may keep them for state occasions, when no doubt your father will wish to see you dressed according to your rank. For everyday you will wear one garment of plain, serviceable cloth. If you wear a tunic you will do without a cloak. Only invalids and old men need both. And you will go barefoot."

Alexander loved bright clothes. The soldiers were proud of their uniforms, their cloaks in squadron colours, yellow, purple, white; white plumes and horsehair crests on their bright blue helmets. He thought men would fight well, looking like fighting cocks. He could not understand how drab clothing would help to make him a better soldier. But he said nothing and was careful, when he looked at his uncle, to give nothing away by his eyes. He saw that they were going to be at war, and that victory would lie, not in getting his own way, because he had to obey this man, but in not showing that he cared.

Leonidas moved to the bed-box and lifted the lid. "Your brooches and arm-rings may remain here for the present, unless your mother wishes to take charge of them too, but do not wear them without my permission. What is this?" He lifted out Balios. "A toy?" Colour flooded Alexander's face and throat. "It's Balios. Father's race horse once. He won the Games."

"You are now too big for toys." He tucked Balios under his arm.

"Please!" Alexander held out his hand. "Let me. I'll give him away to someone."

"Then see to it today."

"Yes, Sir."

Chapter 6

The King's Supper

By the evening Alexander was missing Hellanike. Leonidas had been gone for some time about his own concerns, and his father had said he should go into supper with the men. It was growing dusk and from the balcony outside his room he saw one or two Companions and a steward strolling across the court towards the dining hall. It must be time to dress and go.

He supposed that Leonidas would rate this as a festive occasion – his first supper – and chose a white wool tunic with blue borders. He hesitated over an arm-ring. He would have liked to have worn his father's gift, which was in the shape of the lucky knot of Herakles, but his orders had been specific – not without permission. He poured cold water for a bath. Only women and children used warm water in Macedon. His father had demoted a general caught taking a hot bath.

He was trying to scrub between his shoulder blades when Ptolemy and Kassander arrived. They both served as Royal Pages now and had been sent by the king to wait on him and bring him into supper. Ptolemy splashed him and rubbed him down energetically, but Kassander showed a sulky face. The other Pages had laughed at them, calling them nursemaids, and he resented the task, especially as he disliked Alexander. Ptolemy had threatened to punch his head if he used his spiteful tongue to spoil the boy's first day out of the nursery, and Ptolemy was older and considerably bigger so he said nothing, but mooched about doing nothing either.

A boy did not recline on a couch at supper until he had killed a wild boar on his spear, although he might sit on the foot of one if a man invited him to do so. Kassander had only recently killed his boar, having failed at the first attempt. It was a raw subject with him. Cheerfully unaware, Alexander remarked on it:" The huntsman told me you killed this time and it was a big one. I'm glad." Cocky, patronising little whelp! Behind his back Kassander spat into the bath water.

The sentry outside the door saluted, and Lysimachus appeared. "Your father has given me the privilege of taking you into your first supper."

"Oh good! May I sit on your couch?" He would prefer that to being too close to his father.

"Indeed you may, like Phoenix and Achilles."

"What do you mean?"

"Phoenix used to take Achilles into supper when he was a child. He complained that Achilles spilt food on his clothes. Look, do you see how fine I am? A new robe." It was blue, draped elegantly around him, leaving one bony shoulder bare; his full beard and moustaches, badger-patched with grey, had been neatly barbered. "This is how they dress for supper in Athens. You'll see when the Ambassadors come. Your father wants us to show them how Greek we are so I'm practising. Are you ready? Are you wearing no jewellery?"

"Leonidas said not. I wanted to wear Father's arm-ring."

"Oh, I think tonight... it *is* an occasion and it will please your father. We must go to your mother first. She has a gift for you."

Of course she had. He should not have doubted her.

Olympias swept him into her arms – he pulled gently away. She forgot he was now a man. "What have you been doing all day? Tell me everything! But what a bruise on your cheek! How did you come by that?" It was where Leonidas's ring had struck his cheekbone but he told her he had banged his head on the stable door. "So you rode with him. A joyless man. But we shall find ways... Look, I have something for you." Her gifts were a gold clasp for his shoulder and an arm-ring in the shape of a snake coiled about a large red garnet. He thanked her but told her that Leonidas had said a boy should not make himself too fine. "Perhaps, Mother, I shouldn't wear them all tonight."

"So, will you prefer your father's gift to mine? Alexander, he is only your tutor – or governor – or whatever he calls himself. Such men are servants. And do you think your father will be pleased if you go to your first supper looking like peasant? It would be an insult to him. If your uncle objects tell him that you wore them because the queen your mother desired it."

So he wore them all. For perhaps the first time he was glad to leave her, although he would never have admitted the thought. As they crossed the court Lysimachus said: "I am going to change my name. Achilles is growing up. Chiron is not needed anymore."

Alexander gripped his hand. "I do need you! What do you mean? Where are you going?"

"Did I say I was going anywhere? You leap at my throat before I've finished. Chiron was a boy's tale. You are going to become a man and go to war. I would rather be Phoenix now."

"The man who took Achilles into supper."

"Yes, Achilles' father chose him to help train his son when he was young, and when he went to war, Phoenix went with him."

"You'll come with me when I go to war."

"If the gods are willing and my legs still able to carry me."

"Of course they will. All right, be Phoenix then."

Lamps glowed on the painted walls of the dining hall, which showed the twelve labours of Herakles. Opposite the porch by which they entered was a picture of the hero fighting drunken centaurs. He had shot one through the knee with an arrow, and the magnificent man-horse had sunk to the ground like a sacrificial bull before the altar, his mouth twisted open to spew out a dark cry of anguish. "The end, you see, of Chiron," said Lysimachus, pointing.

"Did *Herakles* kill Chiron?" Alexander was dismayed.

"He wounded him accidentally. The arrow was poisoned, but Chiron was immortal, he could not die. He lived, suffering from his wound, until the god released him." Sadness settled quietly inside the boy and became part of the strangeness of the day. "Zeus set him among the stars. In winter when the skies are clear I will show him to you."

Alexander had been into the dining hall many times, but never when the lamps were lit for supper. By day it was cool and dim, the only light coming in through the porch and the colonnade; it had then the air of an empty theatre waiting for the actors. This was the first time he had seen it warm and glowing, the men lying robed and garlanded upon their couches, while servants and Pages strode about, carrying three-legged tables, dishes of food, and vessels of bronze and silver for mixing the wine. It was like entering a busy hive which previously he had heard buzzing only from the outside as he hung over the nursery balcony, long after he was supposed to be in bed. The men were used to conversing on the hunting field and drill ground; their voices were loud, their laughter louder, and the king's loudest of all.

Philip sprawled comfortably across his cushions, propped on one elbow; his face shone with heat and good humour. First among his pleasures was to eat, drink and laugh with his Companions and guest-friends at the day's end. Lysimachus took the prince to his father, who kissed him and told him to enjoy himself.

Alexander glanced towards his governor, who had been given, for one night, a place of honour next to the king. The man's face was set in hard lines and told him nothing. It would be difficult to guess what thoughts went on behind those cold blue eyes, unless they were fired by anger. Alexander was glad that he was to sit with Lysimachus.

Another uncle sat at the foot of the king's couch, the brother of Olympias, a boy thirteen years old, also called Alexander. Philip had brought him back from Epiros, too, to enter service with the Royal Pages. Ptolemy had said that he was going on the Olynthian campaign; the king was taking him young so that he could train him to rule in Epiros as Philip's ally. Looking at him, Alexander wished the years away. It would be *forever* before he himself had grown and could ride off with the army. They were having all their great adventures without him, there would be no lands left to conquer. If only he could change places and be that Alexander! His young uncle was a handsome boy with an alert, laughing look, the fair skin and dark gold hair of his family. He might have been an elder brother of his sister's son, but he had the large bones and sturdy build that was to make a bigger man. The king loved him.

Philip was talking about his campaign against the city of Olynthos. Rumours of his death during a recent illness had sparked a rebellion. Two of his half brothers had made a bid to seize the throne and, when this failed, had taken refuge with the Olynthians, who had broken their treaty with Philip.

"They've done well out of their alliance with me," said the king, "and the sensible men among them know it. Didn't I give them all the territory of Potidae to settle their landless immigrants? I know how to reward friendship. Now they'll see the other side of the coin, unless our supporters can get them to break off negotiations with Athens and hand over my treacherous relatives. If they do that I might turn my blind eye to their broken treaty. If not, they'll find that Philip of Macedon is a good friend but a bad enemy."

"Could we trust them again?" asked Antipater, on the other side of the king. He flourished a meat bone as he spoke. "They've swung back and forth between us and the Athenians for years, siding with whoever offers them the greatest advantage or frightens them most at the time. If you take the war further east that's a dangerous gate to leave unbarred behind your back" He chewed meat off the bone.

"I shall begin negotiations," said Philip, "by giving them a demonstration of what it would mean to break faith with me again. Offer terms of surrender to the smaller cities first. Attack those who refuse and make examples of them. Then confront Olynthos. Meanwhile my stators are marching in and softening up the opposition." A look and a grin passed among the generals.

"What troop is that?" Alexander asked Lysimachus, surprised that there was one he hadn't heard of. "Are they skirmishers? But Olynthos is a city."

"Stators – gold coins –" said Lysimachus. "Your father means that he is paying men inside the city to take his part, rewarding those who vote for friendship with Macedon and against the treaty with Athens."

"An expensive business!" added the king, draining his wine cup.

"Philip!" called one of the Companions. "Have you kept back enough to pay the troops?" There was a general shout of laughter. Leonidas remained unmoved and Atarbazos glanced at the king enquiringly. Evidently they did not know a joke which everyone else shared.

Artabazos was there as a guest of the king. He sat upright in a chair of state; Persians did not recline when eating as the Greeks did. Alexander thought that he looked more regal than his father, with his long hawk-face and hooded eyes, sitting tall and straight-backed in his lavishly embroidered clothes, picking food in a leisurely manner from the dishes set before him, while Philip and his Companions grabbed, chewed and swallowed energetically as they talked. Alexander copied the Persian, eating tidily.

The king was leaning forward to explain the laughter to his guests. "It was a time – frequent enough before we won the silver mines – when the treasury was empty. The troops hadn't been paid for some time. I was having a work out on the wrestling ground – just finished a bout with the champion – streaming with sweat – not a stitch on –"

"And covered in dust," growled Parmenion. "He'd had you down twice."

"Once, once!" retorted the king.

"Twice!" said Parmenion. "He knocked the breath out of you with a flying tackle and then –" Philip shied a hunk of bread at him. "Hold your tongue and let me tell the story. We called a truce after I half-throttled him. There I stood, naked and covered in dirt –"

"And out of breath," added Parmenion, chucking back the bread, which the king caught. Alexander leaned forward eagerly, hoping they would shy it in his direction. He was good at catching and throwing.

"When half the infantry, so it seemed, surrounded the place," said the king. "The ring leaders stood round me shouting, demanding their back-pay and making more noise than the Illyrians driving off a flock of sheep. I got up on a bench where they could all see me –" Philip stood up on his couch, taking an imposing stance, one hand to his breast, the other stretched out to command silence.

"Just like that," said Parmenion appreciatively. "Like a statue of Zeus. With a bloody nose."

"Soldiers!" The king's voice rang out, commanding but also cheerful and friendly. "Soldiers – I said – you've a right to demand your wages. I know you have a genuine grievance. But that's why I'm here, limbering up, getting fit to fight the barbarians and win enough to pay you many times over. Then I clapped for the next bout, and plunged headfirst into the pool and the champ dived in at the other end."

"And the two of them went on tussling in the pool," said Parmenion, "splashing and pulling each other under, while the men were laughing at first in spite of themselves, and then left standing round wondering what to do, until they gave up and went."

"That's right," said Philip, sliding back on his couch and raising his cup. "I had no more trouble from them after that."

Most of the company had heard the tale before, but they laughed and applauded, and Alexander of Epiros raised his cup to him. Artabazos smiled gravely. "One more of your successful stratagems, King of Macedon. And who is your barbarian?"

"Ah!" said Philip. "To us, anyone who isn't Greek. But the southern Greeks call us barbarians, too." He gave Artabazos a charming smile.

"You didn't get away so easily from that old woman this morning, Philip," called one of the Companions.

"No, by the dog!" exclaimed the king, raising his empty cup to be refilled by one of the Pages.

"Who was that?" asked someone. "What happened?"

"At the Court of Justice this morning," answered Philip. "Too many long-winded cases and by mid-day there were still half a dozen more to be heard. I had the secretaries waiting with the day's correspondence, the chief engineer wanting to check his orders for the siege train, the land commissioner to settle the grants for the marshes we drained round Philippi, and enough business of that kind to keep me busy until supper time and beyond. So I sent the last suppliants away. Told them to come back tomorrow. But everyone knows we're ready to march north at any time. This old woman wouldn't go. She came after me, shouting out her

Chiron on Mount Pelion

trouble. "I've no time, Granny," I said. "Not today." "Then give up being king!" she said.

There was another general shout of laughter. Artabazos looked concerned. "Ah, she was old," he said. "Maybe her mind was confused. Did you spare her punishment?"

"Punish her?" cried the king. "What for? She was right. I sat down and listened to her. Heard all their cases and settled them all. Couldn't deal with one and not the others. The Court lasted the better part of the afternoon. The engineer and the land commissioner have to wait until tomorrow. It will delay our departure, may the dog take her, but she was right. It's the king's job to dispense justice and if he can't find the time to do it, he'd better give up his claim to be king."

Artabazos shook his head. "In Persia, Philip, I trust she would have been treated kindly and her life spared if she had thrown herself at the Great King's feet, although she offended greatly. But the Great King does not dispense judgement in public himself, and no-one but his courtiers could come so close to him."

Philip laughed. "You won't find any Macedonian, man or woman, throwing themselves at my feet, and if they did, I wouldn't want to lead them. The Macedonians are a free people."

A cheer went up, empty cups banged on the tables and boys' feet stamped on the floor. A group of young men leapt up to dance. They were led by Philotas, Parmenion's son. He was big, bold and flamboyant. The younger boys idolised him and Alexander thought him magnificent. The leader created the pattern of the dance, the others followed in a rhythmically stamping line – Philotas was a dasher only the best dancers could match. Watching them, their faces fiercely intent, their bodies proudly arched, arms linked across their shoulders, feet stamping as though they all belonged to one snake-like body, it was impossible to imagine them bowing down to anybody. It was the fighting men of Macedon who chose their king from among the royal kindred, who gave him power, and who chose to obey him as long as he was strong enough to lead them – and lead them to victory.

As the dance ended, a voice shouted, "Where are the women tonight, Philip?" "Time's young yet," answered the king. "A story first, for the boy." They had forgotten that he was there. He received kindly looks, men lifted their wine cups towards him and drank; Artabazos invoked light and good fortune to shine upon him.

The bard put on his embroidered robe and came forward with his lyre. As a complement to the king and the king's son, he recited the tale of the birth of Herakles, son of Zeus the Father and a mortal queen, who strangled snakes in his cradle, and when he was grown went out to slay the Lion of Death with his bare hands, since no weapon could pierce its immortal hide. Alexander discovered from the story that the hero had been compelled to serve a king who was mean and cowardly, but after he had performed twelve great labours for this tyrant, he was rewarded by the gift of immortality and won his place among the ever-living gods. Men gave him the title Herakles Kallinikos, Glorious Victor, for he succeeded in all the challenges the king set him. Alexander liked best the story and the painting which showed him bringing back a great boar, alive, across his shoulders, and the cowardly king hiding from them inside a tall jar.

Men and boys listened as intently as the child to the story-teller, but when he departed with a gift from the king, the noise in the hall rose rapidly and there was a rougher tone to it. Wine had loosened men's tongues and excited their tempers. Parmenion, Philotas and some others were growing heated over a wager on a horse race. Kleitos, red-faced and black-bearded, began singing a bawdy version of one of Herakles' adventures from the chorus of a comic play. He draped a scarf over his head and imitated the enticing movements of a woman, to guffaws of laughter. Flute girls and acrobats and the women who were paid companions were waiting in the shadows at the edge of the lamplight. Men were turning and calling, beckoning favourite girls to share their couches. Philip signalled to his son.

When Alexander came up, he slid an arm round his waist, tossed back the last drop of wine in his cup and held out the empty vessel to show him. It was a fluted silver bowl that fitted into the palm of his hand; inside, at the bottom, was a head, moulded in silver and gilded, of a merry, drunken old man. He had broad cheeks and a squashed-looking nose, thick smiling lips and eyes that were knowing and wine-hazy. A leafy garland dipped tipsily over his brows and the dregs of Philip's wine glistened in the deep creases of his face. "Who is it?" asked Alexander. "The teacher of Dionysos," said his father, wickedly. Leonidas sat bored, silent and sober on the next couch. Philip lowered the eyelid over his good eye and winked broadly at his son. "I could sell this to pay a few soldiers, could I not?"

"Yes, Father. Did they get their wages?"

"Oh yes, they knew the war-chest wouldn't be empty for long. Has it been a good day for you?"

"Yes, Father. very good." He had drunk a cup of well-watered wine and felt loose and warm and happy. He leant against his father's knees. "I'm glad you listened to the old woman. Did you give her what she wanted?"

"Oh, she blessed me in the name of half a dozen gods. I should do well this year!"

"But what did she want?" He had forgotten that boys should not pester their elders with questions. Leonidas was frowning.

"Her summer grazing rights. A landowner had turned her flocks off the pastures where they were accustomed to graze when her husband was alive. I ordered rights to be granted her in perpetuity."

"Does that mean forever?"

"Yes."

"But this summer is half over."

A spark of amusement glinted in the king's good eye. "The landowner was ordered to pay her a fine of two milk goats to compensate for her losses. Does that satisfy you?"

"Oh yes! I'm very glad, Father."

"Good. Then off with you to bed."

Philip kissed him and as he passed Parmenion the general put out a big hand and patted his shoulder. Leonidas gave him a steely look, noting the forbidden arm-rings and the immodest, searching stare.

Herakles had had to serve a mean master. Alexander armed himself with the thought. Nothing came easily, even to heroes and the sons of gods. Everything had to be earned and paid for, and not all battles were fought with swords. There were different kinds of courage.

As he lay alone in the dark in his unfamiliar room, after Lysimachus had gone, his fingers moved gently over the smooth polished wood of Balios' face and neck, where much bedtime stroking had worn away the paint. He knew now to whom he would give the horse.

He was woken by his father's voice, thick and loud, in the passage outside; then he heard a man's laugh and a girl's soft giggle. There were uncertain steps, someone stumbled, and Ptolemy said, "Take my arm." The Pages were helping the king and his companion to bed. A door closed and there was silence, apart from the sentry's footfalls passing to and fro. Last night she had said, "You are not Philip's," and then it had rained and he had not asked her what she meant.

Alexander dreamt that he was lying in a meadow among asphodels, pansies and bell flowers, where the big green grasshoppers were shrilling. He half closed his eyes against the brightness of the sun; the white circle shimmered, resting on the mountain's dark shoulder. Out of the haze of light came a boy, a sword at his side and a spear in his hand, a king's son and already a warrior. His voice rang out and echoed among the rocks: "Chiron, Lord of the Mountain, come forth!"

From a dark cave overhung by ferns dripping moisture, to the chime of trampling hooves, came a mighty creature, part man and part horse. The sun shone on a face like the one moulded in silver below the handle of the largest wine vessel in the king's hall: a face with broad cheeks; far-gazing, wise and kindly eyes; hair and beard flowing in deep waves. In his hand the centaur carried a lyre of burnished tortoiseshell, he did not touch the strings but the wind seemed to release their music as it passed softly over them. When he spoke his deep voice floated into the music and the wind: "Achilles, dear child, be welcome!"

Alexander seemed to be both himself, the watcher, and Achilles, the sun-bright boy. The boy's longing belonged to both of them. He spoke and listened to the boy speak. "Chiron! From my father I learnt to throw the spear and wield the sword. Now he sends me to learn your wisdom. Teach me music and song, the skill of healing, the secrets of mountain and forest, wind and stars. Chiron, show me the meaning of my dreams." And Chiron said: "I will teach you as much as you can learn. Come, I have the care of many king's sons." He put his hand on the boy's shoulder and together they went into the cave, to the quiet trampling of the centaur's hooves.

Alexander turned in his sleep and sighed. It was dark night. A pale sickle moon hung in the sky. From the black mouth of the cave came a terrible anguished cry and the music in the wind was turned to weeping, lamentation for broken dreams and a beauty that would never come again. Against the moon-grey sky stood up the black shape of a man; he wore a lion skin like a cloak upon his head and shoulders and in his hand he carried a bow. But when he turned, and the pale moon touched his face, it left a shadow in one eye socket where the sight was gone. Alexander, lying with Balios a hard lump against his shoulder, slept and did not feel the tear which slid down beside his nose onto the pillow.

He woke in the morning before it was light, and when Leonidas came soon afterwards to rouse him, he was surprised to find the boy's room empty.

Alexander stood in a glimmer of fading torch light before the statue of

Herakles, in the round room encircled by tall, slender pillars at the end of the inner court. This was the shrine where the king, when he was at home, made daily offerings to the family's gods. The statue of Herakles was taller than a man, bearded like the king, wearing the gilded lion skin over his head and shoulders. Its upper jaw rested on his forehead and its forepaws were knotted across his chest – this was the luck-bringing knot of Herakles, a charm against death. The hero leaned on his club and gazed out across the garden court with wide-staring sorrowful eyes, a fighter who had known bitter grief, who had earned his immortal glory through danger and hard labour – Herakles Kallinikos.

The altar fire glowed dully. Soon people would come to revive the embers, ready for the king's sacrifice at sunrise. Alexander added fuel from a heap nearby and blew upon the flames. Then he took Balios and offered him to the hero-god, dropping the wooden horse into the heart of the fire. He stood for a long time, watching the wood blacken and burn, making his silent vows.

"Alexander!" The harsh voice of Leonidas called from the courtyard. He turned to obey. When King Philip came at sunrise the wooden toy of childhood was a heap of charred flakes in the centre of the flickering fire.

Chapter 7

The School of Leonidas

Alexander slept beneath a scarlet blanket and a wolf skin rug. His breath stirred the long grey hairs of the pelt drawn up beneath his chin. Frost glistened on the wide stone window sill and the smell of frost crept into the cold, still room.

A crack of lamplight widened as the door opened and Leonidas came in. He frowned at the wolf skin on the bed. The queen's doing no doubt. One of her people had come during the night and spread it over her sleeping son. Unjust to scold the boy. He pulled it from the bed and folded it under his arm. "Alexander, wake up!"

He must go through the bed box and the clothes chest. The last time he searched he had found a fur-lined cloak, red leather boots and a flask of oil. He had punished Alexander for the sticky honey cakes found crammed into a jewel box, but the other luxuries he had given to the boy's former nurse to return to the queen, requesting her to keep them until he should ask for them. His niece's fury was quenched by his cold courtesy; he did not flare and fight back as Philip did.

"Alexander, wake up!"

The boy roused himself with difficulty. It was natural for him to stay awake, lively and talkative, far into the evening, and to sleep late in the morning. (Lanike had never been able to get him to bed, and later in his life his generals would cluster anxiously round his tent on the morning of a great battle while he still slept.) Last evening he had been reading late by the light of a forbidden lamp, now he slid from bed with half-shuttered eyes, and searched for the neck-hole of his tunic. Leonidas was holding out a pair of laced boots. "You may wear these. A cross-country run this morning. Leave by the north gate and where the road forks take the left path and follow the cattle track to the freedman's farm. Return across the drill field to the west gate. Ptolemy will go with you. He is waiting in the outer court."

Ptolemy was trotting back and forth to keep warm, blowing on his fingers. He was growing into a big-boned, gangly young man. He greeted

Alexander with a shout and a slap on the shoulder. They ran off together, jogging along deserted streets, setting all the watch-dogs barking. The eastern sky was lightening. Their breath smoked before their faces, the cold stung their throats. The gate sentry saluted and opened the postern to let them through. "Off to the war, basilikos? Tell the general to send one over with my name on it." Parmenion was still in the north, with a strong holding force to watch Olynthos, the king had gone south to deal with an outbreak of trouble in Thessaly, Antipater was regent of Macedon and Ptolemy had been assigned to his staff.

As the runners approached the farm, a cacophony of half-wild dogs whirled round them, leaping and barking. A herdsman offered them beakers of new milk, warm and frothing, which they drank gratefully.

On the way back, faint shadows appeared on the frosted grass as the air brightened. Then the sun sprang up and their shadows, jogging beside them, stretched to a ludicrous length. They saw the shapes of their heads crossing the next meadow, and laughed. The leaves and grass sparkled with moisture, set free from night's icy shackles.

They came home ravenously hungry. Ptolemy said: "Will he feed you? I'll keep a bowl of porridge for you if you can make it to the guard room before lessons." Alexander nodded. "Thanks." He went to splash in cold water – he disliked to have sweat dry on his skin, even in winter – and pulled on a fresh tunic before going to breakfast, a meal supervised by Leonidas. The porridge bowl was small and the bread and cheese doled out sparingly. Alexander felt that he had had enough only to tantalise his stomach, not satisfy it. "May I have more bread, please?"

"You have had sufficient. More will make you lazy and you have work to do. Would you overfeed a horse before exercise?"

"But I'm still hungry."

"You must get used to spare meals. Soldiers learn to live on plain rations in the field."

"May I go to the stables before lessons?"

"You may. Do not be late."

"No, sir." His flying feet took him first toward the stables and then by a roundabout way to the guardroom. "I'm starving! What do you have?"

The porridge had all gone, but Ptolemy found him bread, cheese and an onion. He wolfed the bread and cheese, not risking the onion, in case Leonidas smelt it on his breath. "Why does he starve you?" asked Ptolemy. "I see no sense in that."

"To make me tough, ready for campaigning in winter," said Alexander, and made a rueful face.

"In winter you need a good lining to your stomach," said the steward, himself the father of four lusty sons, "and by what I've seen of your father's men they know how to put it away, summer or winter. Come at supper time. I'll save you some stew."

"If I can." From his mother he might get cakes later in the day, and from Doris in the kitchen a hunk of new-baked bread. He enjoyed the challenge of getting there, or to the mess-room in the barracks, without being caught. After breakfast there was no other meal until supper, and that would also be moderate, leaving him hungry at bedtime.

As he darted away, the steward shook his head. "A growing lad needs his food. You boys keep an eye on him."

Outside the room where they were taught – mathematics and Greek this morning – the boys chosen to share his lessons were running and leaping for a ball. Alexander sprang into the pack. When there was a break in the game, they gathered round and gave him their offerings. Lame Harpolos brought a boiled egg, Nearchos a piece of honey comb, the others nuts, dried apples and dates. They had a place for storing what couldn't be eaten straightaway behind a loose stone in a wall. Sometimes in summer ants had discovered their hoard.

"Isn't Herakles your ancestor?" asked Harpolos, himself a prince of a highland tribe.

"You know he is."

"Well, you know what he did. Broke a chair over his tutor's head. There's a picture of him doing it on my father's wine bowl." The boys put their hands over their mouths and laughed the way they did at rude jokes.

"And he killed him," said Alexander, "although he was a son of the god Apollo. But that was his music teacher, and I like mine. Besides, they sent Herakles off to be a herdsman after that, because he was unteachable. I know how to get the better of Leonidas."

"How?" they demanded eagerly, expecting something outrageous.

Alexander smiled at them with his eyes, his mother's secret, confiding smile. "I know," he said, "but I can't tell. It's my mystery, the way things are between us and the gods. If you watch, you'll see who's the strongest."

With the perception of the young, who do not go by outward appearances, they realised that he spoke what they knew to be true.

Leonidas might appear to be cold, stern and in command, but there was something in Alexander he could not touch. When they stood face to face, it was from Alexander that the strongest force was felt, like Herakles the hero-slave before the mean king he had to serve. Leonidas sensed it, too, and it made him harder.

In the weeks between his father's departure and the coming of the school masters chosen by Leonidas, and with them the boys who would share his lessons and become his friends, Alexander had fought a fierce and lonely battle and won. He needed love – perhaps even more he needed to give love – but he taught himself to expect and want nothing from Leonidas. He was often hungry, cold and acutely miserable, but he showed nothing of this. He obeyed orders, held his tongue, kept his thoughts hidden behind a clear, straight look, and was cheerful in the company of the Pages, the soldiers, or Lysimachus. Lysimachus saw, but could only help by being there when needed. For one whose temper was hot and quick, breaking in sudden storms over as quickly as they came, this restraint had sometimes to be released in hard, dangerous gallops and violent exercise.

And then he discovered that he need not fight a defensive battle; he could attack. He could do this by not merely accepting and enduring his uncle's regime, but by choosing it of his own will and by setting his own challenges higher than those of his governor. This set him free. Leonidas lost the power to tyrannise over him. *"I am not his. I am my own and the god's. I am Alexander."* With joy he found this to be true.

So when snow flurries blew down from the north on a bitter Thracian wind and Leonidas told him that he might ask his mother for the fur-lined cloak – "Thank you, sir," replied his nephew, "but I do not need it until the weather gets colder." When Leonidas commanded him to run twice round the practice track before breakfast, he ran three fast circuits – the last one for himself and Herakles – breasting the wind, his brilliant eyes alive with laughter and the joy of effort, finishing breathless and triumphant, to the fury of his governor, who lacked any tactical sense and allowed himself to be goaded. "You are always excessive, Alexander, it is a form of showing off. If I ask you to run the track twice, I mean precisely that. No less and no more. Learn to be moderate in all things."

But moderation was a virtue unknown to the royal house of Macedon and unlikely to be practised by the son of Philip and Olympias.

Chapter 8

Dragon's Breath

Hephaistion rode across his father's land to the place where he hoped he might see the dragon. At the end of the sheep pasture the land fell away steeply; at the foot of the cliff a tumble of fallen rocks and boulders formed cracks and caverns half hidden by bushes where such a creature might have its lair. As he approached in the early mornings he sometimes thought he saw wisps of smoke rising above the cliff edge, and half-believed that when he crawled to the edge and peered over he might see the scaly serpent stretched out on the rocks, warming the night-stiffness from its wings. This would settle the question – were there such creatures – or did they exist only in legends, where Jason stole a golden fleece from a fire-breathing dragon and Bellerophon fought the three-headed Chimera from the back of his flying horse? He needed to know. But until now the vapour had proved to be threads of mist drawn up by the early sun, and all he had seen was a big green lizard scuttling under a bush when he dislodged a rattling stone.

But today might be different! He felt an expectant shiver through his bones. It would be today! He slid from his mare and tethered her beside an empty sheep-fold, going forward warily on foot, listening, and looking for the drift of the monster's rising breath. Curlews called across the lonely uplands, then suddenly the mare whinnied. Hephaistion tensed and crouched, the nerves tingling at the back of his neck. Several things happened at once. A dog barked. A hand appeared, grasping an outcrop of rock, followed by an arm and a tousled head, as a boy levered himself up and scrambled over the edge of the cliff.

The boy stood with the sun and the wind behind him, blowing his hair into a fiery golden halo round his head. Hephaistion saw a barefoot farm urchin in a rough, torn tunic, dirty, with a long, blood-stained scratch on his leg. He was younger and smaller than Hephaistion, but he spoke first, briskly.

"I'm glad you've come. I need help. My dog's fallen among these rocks and hurt her leg. I can't get her up by myself. May we use your cloak to make a sling under her belly?"

The first surprise was that he spoke Greek, not Macedonian. He couldn't be a farm boy. Someone's slave perhaps? But he spoke as though to a friend and an equal, and clearly he did not expect a refusal. His voice was light and quick and had a touch of authority, and there was nothing hesitant in his manner. He was holding out a hand for the cloak. Hephaistion's straight brows drew together as he puzzled over it, even as his fingers automatically unfastened the shoulder pin.

"Thanks. My name's Alexander. What's yours?" He turned to lower himself over the cliff edge. "I'll lead, shall I? I've been down once already. It's not hard." He had slung the cloak across his shoulder. Hephaistion called his own name into the wind and followed, his feet feeling for, and testing, each narrow ledge or unsteady boulder before he trusted his weight to it, and scanning the rock for the best hand grips. How he had come to do this so readily he did not know. Below him, the boy's small sun-brown hands moved surely from hold to hold, and his voice came clearly, pausing when he stopped to look for the best way down. "We were tracking hares. Phoenix chooses this month for training young hounds. Bia went after a fox. He had his earth just below the cliff top and she went over."

The dog was half-leaping and scraping at the rocks below, whining and barking, trying to reach them. "Down, Bia. Sit. *Sit!* Good girl. Steady." His foot feeling for the next ledge dislodged a stone. His voice came punctuated by pauses as he searched for a safer hold. "She's not usually so – ill-behaved – but she was excited – at being out." Another pause, then Hephaistion heard a note of triumph and laughter:" She's a young dog – and she's been confined too long – like me." Alexander had reached a flat boulder beside her and she flung herself at him. A few moments later Hephaistion came down to join them and received his share of grateful caresses. The hound was a fine one, Hephaistion recognised the pure Castorian breed. Enviously he stroked her smooth, bony forehead while she tried to lick his hand. Then they turned their attention to the problem of getting her up. They made a sling of the cloak and slid it beneath her. With their waist cords they tied the ends and shouldered the cords, passing them across their chests. Bia stretched her head forward and uttered a sound between a whine and a yelp as they hoisted her from the ground. "Lie still. Down, Bia. *Stay.*" Alexander admonished, softly. They waited until she was calm, balancing her weight as well as they could between their slightly unequal heights. She was a heavy dog.

It did not occur to Hephaistion to do anything other than make the climb, but he felt a nervous, doubtful flutter in his stomach. Alexander was coolly scanning the rocks above them. "It's not so far. It will be easier if we go up *that* way. But she mustn't get frightened and fidget." Hephaistion glanced down over his shoulder at Bia gazing up at them with mournful, apprehensive eyes. Alexander spoke to her again, reassuringly.

"Don't let the cradle swing and throw us off balance. We'll look for the safest ledges and holds, decide, and then try to move together. Take it slowly." At the back of his mind, Hephaistion was aware that he was working under the direction of a stranger who was younger than he was and below him in rank, but he hadn't time to let his surprise at this come to the surface. They were too preoccupied for it to matter.

Together they clambered up the steep fall of boulders, somehow managing the shifting weight of Bia between them, shouting advice: "Watch out! This rock wobbles!" "Put your foot there, no, look, *there*!" and sweating under the strengthening sun. As they came panting to the top and, with one last effort, hoisted Bia high enough to scramble onto a flat, warm slab and collapsed beside her, laughter that had been quivering in Hephaistion's stomach ever since he knew they were going to triumph, forced its way up like a fountain and burst joyously from his throat. Lying beside Bia on the rock, fondling her with one hand and rubbing his sore shoulder with the other, he laughed up into the flushed face of his companion, knowing that something had happened to change his world as surely as finding a dragon would have done. Something was new inside himself, the world was a surprise, his whole body felt surprised and different. His first burst of laughter was soon over, blown away on the wind, but his body still quivered with it silently, and with the joy of surprise.

Alexander smiled at him tolerantly and knelt, bending over Bia. Hephaistion watched his small, competent hands feeling her up and down in a business-like fashion, while she tried to lick them. "It's all right," he said briskly. "She's not much hurt. Cut and bruised and pulled a muscle here, perhaps. It hurts when I touch her, look, and she's scraped the skin off this leg, but nothing's broken." With one of his quick, certain movements he ripped the hem from his tunic and began binding her injured leg. "Thank you for helping," he said. "I'm sorry, there's blood on your cloak. And she probably wet it, too."

Hephaistion remembered that this boy was younger than he was and dressed like a peasant. He felt the need to assert himself and sat up. "You are on my father's land," he said abruptly. "Do you know that? Where are you from? I know all our people."

Unabashed, the boy met his eyes, smiling. "Oh, are you the son of Lord Amyntas? I saw him once at supper. He's one of Father's Companions. I'm with the army – Alexias' squadron – on manoeuvres. Our commander asked your father's permission to use his land."

Hephaistion stared. "Who's your father, then?"

"King Philip," replied Alexander. "Don't let it bother you." He stood up. "She'll do now. Good girl, Bia." He patted her. "Where did you tether your horse? Oh, I see. I'll race you to that sheep fold."

They arrived breathless almost side by side, and flung themselves to the ground to lie panting in the lee of the stone wall. Hephaistion's fingers had touched the wall just in front of Alexander's. Alexander turned his head and looked at him with respect. "You didn't let me win!" he said. He was an exceedingly fast runner and proud of it because Achilles had also been 'swift-footed'. He could race boys much bigger and older than himself. Hephaistion wouldn't have won if the limping dog hadn't blundered against his legs and almost tripped him.

Hephaistion propped himself on one elbow and blinked at Alexander in blue-eyed astonishment. Beads of moisture glistened along his fair eyebrows and trickled beside his nose. He had put everything into his running because he liked this boy. "Of course not!" he said. "Why should I?"

"Well, some boys do, because my father's the king."

"But if I'd done that, you wouldn't really have won, would you?"

"No, I suppose not."

"Then what are you complaining about?"

"I'm not complaining."

"You are. You said I didn't let you win."

"I'm glad. Do you think I like boys who let me win? I want to be *really* the best, because Achilles was. Do you always argue?"

"Yes!" said Hephaistion, laughing, and flopped down again. His mare lowered her head towards him and blew, ruffling his hair. They lay flat on their backs on the stony, nibbled pasture, looking up at the clouds fleeing across the sky. The sun shone warmly through the blue gaps between, but there was a sharp bite in the wind as it flowed past them down the hill. Hephaistion, looking at Alexander's bare arms and legs and his torn tunic, offered to share his cloak. "If you sweat and then lie about, you'll get chilled. It's as bad for us as it is for horses." But Alexander refused. "I don't feel cold, thanks. I'm used to it now."

"Why do you wear those clothes if you're the prince? I thought you were a farm boy till you spoke."

"My governor's orders. It's because I'm training to become a soldier. But I'm allowed good clothes on feast days."

"Training to be a soldier! How old are you then?"

"I was eight in Lion Month"

"I'm nine and a half. But my father says I'm big for my age."

"I shall grow a lot when I'm older. Some boys do, so Phoenix says. He says it's the same with puppies. Suddenly they get big. And boys do when they're twelve or so. My friend Ptolemy did."

"With puppies it depends on the breed. And you can tell if they're going to be big, my father says, by the size of their feet, and boys by the size of their knees. Are yours big?" They compared the size of their knees. Hephaistion's were broader and bonier. "But I'm nearly two years older," he conceded. "It's hard to tell. I expect you're right. Is your father big?"

He had once seemed enormous, a Cyclops casting a giant shadow. But lately his son had noticed that there were other men who were taller. He answered, "Fairly big. He looks bigger than he is, I think."

"Mine's tall," said Hephaistion. "So is this a kind of uniform, then?"

"Yes, exactly!" Alexander was pleased to find him so perceptive. "Nearly all the boys wear it now."

"Which boys?"

"The one's who share my lessons. Their fathers are Companions or my father's guest-friends."

"My father's a Companion."

"Yes." Their eyes met. "Do you want to come, too?"

"Yes. May I?"

"I'll ask my mother. But she will say it's all right. When I want something she knows when it really matters. And with my father away this is for her to decide, not Leonidas."

"Is Leonidas your governor?"

"Yes." Alexander pulled a face. "He's strict, but it's his job. He teaches me to be a good soldier."

"I don't know if I want to be a soldier, but I'd like to come if I can. I'll have to ask my father. Do I have to wear clothes like this?"

"You don't have to. Nobody does, except me. But most of the boys do, to be like me. My special friends do."

Hephaistion decided immediately to be a special friend. That this boy was both younger and smaller, or that he was a king's son, did not concern him. He was Alexander and Hephaistion had fallen under his spell.

The boys who shared his lessons had done so, too. They were soon pestering their parents to allow them to dress as he did. Met by a barrage of pleas, all beginning – "Alexander does...." or "Alexander says...." their high-born mothers gave in and let their sons go to court dressed as peasants. These school friends would be the Companions of a future king, and their fathers did not object to them following a court fashion, particularly one that would encourage hardihood and self-discipline. So, within a month or two of Leonidas opening his school, nearly all his charges were running about in grey homespun like a pack of young wolves. At first, the boys simply wanted to be chosen for Alexander's team or as his partner for exercise, but as his star shone for them each wanted to deserve his friendship even more, and to be like him. Bare feet and a single rough garment tied with a cord became the insignia of his Companions and a mark of status – Alexander's uniform, as Hephaistion had said.

A trumpet sounded, not far distant in the hills. Alexander sat up. "I have to go back or I'll be missed. That's the guard change."

"You came from the army camp?"

"Yes, just over that hill. Not far, but they don't know I'm out alone. Leonnatus thinks I'm with Alexias's squadron, and Alexias thinks I'm with Leonnatus."

"What are you really doing with the army?"

"Oh, I've been sent to watch and learn, and so I have done. But they won't let me *do* anything useful and Bia gets into trouble, too, when she's bored. She needed exercise. The school's closed for the festival days. Leonidas wants a holiday, too, but he doesn't believe in holidays for me!" He said it laughing, not knowing that Leonidas had sent him away so that he wouldn't spend any free time with his mother. Her anger had scorched anyone who came near her, but left her uncle unmoved.

Alexander was on his feet ready to leave, but waiting to give proper thanks. Hephaistion, not wanting to lose him yet, said: "Let's ride there. Whitefoot can carry us both."

"No, they'd see us coming. They have look-outs posted. They're acting as if they were at war in hostile territory, but I know a secret way to get in and out." He paused. "Thank you for helping. I might not have been able to get Bia up alone, then I would have had to fetch someone and Alexias and

Leonnatus would have been in trouble, too. So you see it was a good thing for us all that you came along."

"For me, too."

"Yes? Well, come to the camp tomorrow. I'll tell the guards you're coming. I'll show you everything. When you've seen the horses and heard the men talk you'll want to come with us when we go to war. We'll spend the day with Alexias' squadron. They have the best cooks! They make a fine mutton stew – from your father's sheep, I suspect!" He laughed and ran off, Bia limping after him.

Hephaistion stood looking after them. In the hills he had not found a dragon's lair, but he had felt the scorch of dragon's breath. A cleft in a rock had opened a way into another world, glittering with danger and the promise of adventure. He stood as though gazing through it, feeling as the heroes did when called to go with Jason in search of the dragon-guarded fleece of gold.

Alexander, who ran without looking back, was conscious only of a deep and satisfying delight. Something he needed had been found, some missing part of himself. *"I am Alexander – that's who I am...."*

Now he had a Companion who was Alexander, too.

Hephaistion

Ptolemy

Chapter 9

The Fall of Olynthos

The golden summer slid away. In the north, King Philip laid siege to Olynthos. In reply to the city's last desperate plea for help the Athenians sent a relief force which, delayed by the summer winds, would arrive too late.

On a strip of muddy sand by the shores of Pella lake, Alexander and Hephaistion played out the death-throes of the city. They built its walls of sand and constructed siege towers, catapults and battering rams from driftwood and the flotsam of the beach. Alexander directed where they should be placed.

"How did men break into cities before they invented siege engines?" wondered Hephaistion, lining up a log of wood to batter the main gate of the city. "You'd think the Greeks would have used battering rams at Troy. That wooden horse was a wild idea. The men inside were in a trap."

"The gods had decided that Troy should fall," said Alexander. "But Homer tells how the Trojans breached the wall in front of the Greek ships – they flung huge stones and pulled down the battlements with their bare hands. Of course, it wasn't as strong as a city wall – a great earthwork I should think – and men had enormous strength in those days. Homer says that the stone Hector lifted to smash open the gates was so heavy that '*no two men, such as men are now, could heave it from the ground on to a cart'!*" He clasped his hands round one raised knee, gazing across the hazy blue of the lake into the far country where his mind lived most of the time just now. He recited:

"Then Hector seized the mighty stone,
broad at the base, but sharply pointed at the other end,
and lifted it as lightly as a shepherd lifts a fleece,
before the gates he came and stood and braced his legs apart
and raised the stone and leaned into his throw.
The stone bore through, the gates fell open with a mighty groan,
the doors were smashed to splinters and the bars gave way.
Then glorious Hector, like the fall of night,

his body armoured in the glare of bronze,
leapt through the gate with two spears in his hand,
and no-one could have stopped him but a god!' "

Watching him as he recited was like watching the flame burn higher and higher inside a lamp. As he sprang up raising an imaginary spear and his voice rang in triumph, a boy gathering shells at the water's edge looked up and waved with an answering shout.

"How much of that poem do you know by heart?" asked Hephaistion, grinning.

"Oh, just some of the best parts. Phoenix has been reciting it to me since I was little. My mother, too."

They were studying *The Iliad,* Homer's story of the Trojan War, in school now and Alexander could read most of the Greek for himself, but he still liked to hear Lysimachus speak the lines as he had first heard them, the familiar voice filling his head with their splendid sound until they came on and on like the rolling swell of the sea, bringing wave after wave of pictures before his far-gazing eyes, so that he saw, not the sun-splashed leaves of the tree under which they lay, or the red glow of the fire by which they sat, but the dusty plain of Troy where the warriors went out daily to meet death and conquer fear – men who loved life but valued fame and honour more. These men were as real to Alexander as his father's Companions.

He brought his mind back to Hephaistion and the reduction of cities. "Men scaled the walls under fire," he said, "and so they must at Olynthos, once they've opened a breach. Achilles' friend Patroclus tried to climb into Troy along a buttress once, but the god Apollo pushed him down because it wasn't time for the city to fall." He regarded their sand city. "Shall we change this into Troy? This can be the Scaean gate..."

The boy who had been gathering shells came up, dragging a toy cart from which his trophies – shells, stones, feathers, a dead starfish – spilled out as he jerked it over humps and tussocks. Alexander beckoned him. "You make a road, Arridaios, a straight road from the city gate – here – to the sea, over there, that'll be the harbour." For a moment the younger boy gazed earnestly into his face, then at the track pointed out to him. His lower lip hung wetly open, his blue eyes showed his mind searching – first for understanding, then considering the task offered him – whether Alexander was bringing him into their game or pushing him out of it – and finally deciding to do it. He got down to scraping and patting the sand, a long ribbon of saliva dribbling from his mouth, chuckling, and calling every few moments: "Is this a straight road, Alexander? Alexander, come and look. Is this a good road?"

"Yes, it's a very good road. Like Father's. The Trojans bring their supplies along it in wagons." To Hephaistion he said: "I wonder we never hear in *The Iliad* of the Greeks attacking the Trojan's supply lines. They had all those ships! Ten years to take a city! My father will take Olynthos before the grape harvest."

"Look at the road, Alexander!"

"Yes, it's a good road. Drag your cart along it to the city, like the Trojans bringing corn and wine from the harbour. Or the Olynthians," he added to Hephaistion. "Father must take their harbour first."

Arridaios crouched by the road, uncertainty growing to panic in his eyes. "With corn and wine? Alexander, with corn and wine?"

"Load your cart with shells and the tops of those rushes and pretend they're sacks of corn and jars of wine."

Relief made Arridaios double over with laughter, his body jerking about as though all his joints had been loosened and an invisible giant hand was shaking him like a doll. It could be seen that he and Alexander were half- brothers; they both had something of Philip's sensuous mouth and pugnacious chin, but Arridaios also had Philip's broad face and heavy build and, although he was younger, he was as tall as Alexander. He watched his brother with the same absorbed devotion that Bia showed when trying to fathom his wishes.

Alexander was sweeping a branch across the sand to smooth it. "Down there the Greek ships are drawn up on the beach; we'll build the wall in front of them. This is the plain where they fight" – he swung round, stretching out his arm, and chanted the magic words of Homer's spell, bringing it all to be:-

" *'a wide, windy plain where once green barley*
 rippled like the waves of the sea under the shadows of passing clouds,
 now beaten bare and brown, breathing a dark fog of dust,
 under the feet of men and horses and the wheels of war chariots.' "

He shouted to Lysimachus, who, not far off, lay reading in the shade of trees, where their guards and servants were playing at knuckle bones and dice, and their horses dozed, brushing away flies with their lazily swishing tails. "Phoenix! You are Zeus, watching from the mountain top, weighing the fates of Greeks and Trojans in your scales."

"I hope I am not required to hurl thunderbolts!" Lysimachus murmured, lowering his scroll. "Well, if I can do it lying here. Who is fated to win today – the bronze-clad Greeks or the horse-taming Trojans?"

Hephaistion was frowning. "It's something I don't understand. If the gods decide the fate of men, what did it matter if a fighter was brave or not, or strong, or well-trained – he would die if it was his fate."

Alexander said, "The gods didn't decide, they couldn't save their own sons if it was their fate to die."

They moved into the shade of the trees to talk, and the servants gave them water.

Lysimachus said, "Achilles fights to win everlasting fame, and, in the end, savagely, to avenge the death of his Companion, Patroclus. Hector fights to defend his city, but they both know their destiny, to die before the gates of Troy. All that mattered then was to meet it with courage. Who is the bravest warrior in *The Iliad?*"

Alexander said, without hesitation, "Achilles! The perfect warrior!"

"The fiercest, certainly," said Lysimachus, looking at Hephaistion for his choice, which was unexpected. "Hector," he said after a pause, "because he was afraid, but he still fought Achilles."

"Ah!" said Lysimachus, "so you think courage is not to feel no fear, but to overcome it –" He broke off to brush away an irritating cluster of horse-flies.

"Diomedes," said Alexander, "wouldn't leave the battle after he was wounded, and still went after the Trojans when the others were in retreat. He was the youngest, too."

"The courage of a fly –" began Lysimachus.

They stared at him – "The courage of *a fly!*"

He held out his arm, allowing a persistent horse-fly to settle, drinking his sweat. He flicked it off; it came back; he swatted it again. "As the poet says,

'the courage of a fly, which, however many times a man brushes it away, returns again and again to bite and draw blood!' "

The boys exploded into laughter, flicking at the flies with leafy twigs. Arridaios leapt up and began waving his arms and laughing, although he had not understood. Suddenly, he became rigid. He swayed and his eyes rolled to show the whites. Alexander sprang forward to catch him as he fell. The child lay twitching on the ground, his arms and legs jerking. His servants scrambled to hold him until the fit had passed to prevent him from hurting himself, and slid a strap between his teeth so that he should not bite his tongue. The two boys watched uncomfortably. Although used to these attacks that afflicted Arridaios, Alexander was always disturbed by them. He did not remember when he had first become aware of rumours that the queen had used witchcraft to make sure that this rival to her son could never become king.

The lake at Pella had an outlet to the sea. Merchant ships bobbed like fat ducklings past the boys' playground, plying to and from the busy harbour, which was hidden from the beach by trees on a curve of the bay. From the sea a warship came gliding in, a sleek trireme, her sail furled, her banks of oars rising and falling like glossy wings, shedding bright water. They ran to the water's edge and cheered. King Philip had only a small squadron of warships, but his captains had recently inflicted irritating losses on the proud Athenian fleet.

"She's come from the north. There must be news! Let's go!" A few moments later, Alexander and Lysimachus were heading the gallop back to Pella, while far behind the servants followed, one astride a mule with Arridaios, recovered but heavy with sleep, leaning against his shoulder.

Kebes, now a young cavalry officer, had been given the honour of bringing Philip's dispatches from Olynthos. He was with the Regent a long time, and when he came out, found Alexander waiting for him. They had been friends since the boy was four. They sat on the steps above a stone lion and Kebes answered all his questions.

The great city of Olynthos had fallen to the Macedonians. Philip had defeated the league's army in the field. Then the harbour, through which supplies and reinforcements reached the Olynthians, had been betrayed into his hands, leaving the city at his mercy.

"They sent to ask our terms," said Kebes, "and your father replied, 'The north hasn't room for us both, me in Macedon and you in Olynthos. One of us has to go, and I've decided that you shall.' They gave us some hard fighting after that." He described the assault in which he had led his troop through the first breach as the walls began crumbling under a barrage of stones, undermined already by fire and saps. "We had heavy losses. Philip was like a boar baited by dogs. Now he's destroying the city. It's being wiped out and the people sold into slavery. All but the Athenian troops we caught there. He's sending them home ransom-free – don't ask me why. And his friends, of course, those who supported his cause or spied for him – they're spared. And the cavalry commanders." His brisk young voice hardened suddenly, turned sour. "*They're* being given grants of land. I've heard that one of them is getting a high command. If they're admitted to the Companions there are those of us who won't drink with them – so we say – but the king won't go as far as that. He must know how we'd feel about it." He picked up his helmet and stood up. "I must go, Alexander. The queen sent for me and I haven't reported to the duty –"

Alexander, also on his feet, grasped his wrist. "Wait! What's this about the cavalry commanders? The Olynthians? What happened?"

"They surrendered, both of them, gave up their men with all their arms in the field without a fight. Five hundred of the best horsemen! Saving themselves and leaving their city to its fate. A thing unheard of! That decided the outcome beyond doubt, made Philip's victory certain. The commanders took his bribes. How can they live with that shame? I'd rather die a thousand deaths than suffer disgrace like that." He strode away, leaving Alexander staring after him, his skin growing tight and cold, his eyes pale with shock and anger, ice-grey.

When Lysimachus came looking for him at supper time he was not to be found. The palace was swarming like a cheerful ants' nest whose foragers have found a store of honey – Olynthos was a rich city. Only in the queen's rooms was there fretting and disquiet. Her women went about in nervous silence, fearing the moment when the brooding storm would break. Rumour had travelled with the ship of Philip's latest love.

In the evening there was to be a special supper to celebrate the victory and to honour the king's couriers. Leonidas had decreed that Alexander should be present. At first, no-one was much concerned that he was missing. It was a holiday and boys have no idea of the time when climbing trees or out with their dogs. But after the sun went down, when the torches flanking the doors were lit, anger and alarm caused Leonidas to send out search parties, first about the palace grounds, then into the city. Lysimachus went to the stables. Alexander's horse was in its stall. The grooms had seen nothing of him. Nevertheless, Lysimachus called for his own mount. As he left the yard, the Wise Woman scuttled across his path, out of shadow into shadow, like a pale spider trailing grey cobwebs. Her arms and head were bare. Her appearance was so sudden that he almost knocked her down.

He rode out of the city and along the lake shore. The boy was there, where they had been that morning. Before Lysimachus saw him, neat round hoof prints in the sand showed him that he was on the right track.

The mule was tethered under the trees. The Wise Woman's robe fluttered from the branches.

Alexander looked over his shoulder. "Oh, it's you." He was still taut with anger. His voice burned with it. The sand city – whether Troy or Olynthos – had been knocked to pieces, the towers and the high mound pushed down, the walls kicked and stamped on. There were deep footprints all over the sand where he had pounded it.

Lysimachus dismounted. "Alexander, what is it?" There was no reply. "What's the matter? Tell me."

"No. I can't. Go home. Leave me alone."

"You know I can't do that. Leonidas is angry. He has sent Pages out searching for you. He's waiting to go in to dinner. It's to be a celebration of your father's victory. Tell me what brought you here."

"No, I won't. Stop asking me, or we shall quarrel." There was a brief silence. Then Alexander twisted round and looked up into the man's troubled face. "Well, I'd better come, I suppose. For you, not for him." He stood up.

As they rode back, Lysimachus said: "It would help if you could tell me something. He will punish you. I'll help you if I can."

"It doesn't matter. I don't mind."

"We'll go to your mother. I will say you have been unwell."

"*No!* We will not!" His anger flared fiercely. "Stop telling me what to do. If you must help, please take the clothes back to the Wise Woman. Don't let anyone know I had them. They're all afraid of her, but it's better if no-one knows." He added, with a sudden, reluctant grin, "They smelt horrible. I rode out of the gates at sunset with the country people going home. It was a good disguise. I bent over and coughed a bit, like this. I tied rags round my feet."

"Leonidas will ask how you left the city."

"I won't tell him."

But next day he told it all to Hephaistion. They lay under an apple tree in the garden, cooling off after exercise. Their mornings were spent learning music, poetry, mathematics and Greek; their afternoons in running, wrestling, athletics and weapon training. Alexander had worked that day with an even fiercer energy than usual, hurling his light javelins into the target to quiver on impact like bees' wings; flinging himself at his partner in wrestling as though he was Herakles tackling his mountain lion. Now he had, for the moment, spent his anger. He lay on his back with his hands clasped under his head, gazing up through leaf patterns at the drifting sky. Hephaistion leaned against the tree trunk, chewing a hard, green apple, and watched him, knowing he would soon tell.

Suddenly, Alexander rolled over and thumped his fist on the ground. "He did it! My father! He made them traitors! They betrayed their people. He said once that gold opens more gates than battering rams. He paid them to do it. He promised them land – horses – slaves – honours – and they surrendered!"

"Who did? What are you talking about?" Hephaistion had not been at the supper and knew only that Olynthos had fallen.

"The cavalry commanders. They gave up their troops in the field, betrayed their men and their city. And he'll pay them for doing it, call them his friends. They'll live rich –"

"And die dishonoured," said Hephaistion. "They'll get no good of it. Traitors never do."

"He made them traitors. I'll never do that – never! If I'm besieging a city as rich as Troy, as strong as Athens, if I'm fighting an enemy as powerful as the Great King with all his armies, I'll never use gold as a weapon. And if any man betrays his friends to me, he'll die on the spears of the Companions, like any other traitor."

There was a loud silence. "He is the king," said Hephaistion. "And he had to win."

"Not this way. Our men are brave enough to win by arms alone, our siege-craft the best there is. Olynthos would have fallen. He said a year ago, 'my stators are marching in!' I didn't know what it meant until Phoenix told me."

"Perhaps this way saved lives."

"How can you say that? You approve of what he's done!"

"No, don't be stupid. I'm suggesting why he might have done it."

"Achilles would never have done it. Nor destroyed Troy. He's wiped out Olynthos. No-one will live there again. And they were brave."

"Troy was burned."

"Achilles was dead by then. It was burnt by lesser men, men who wanted only to seize the spoils and punish the Trojans. Those men didn't care for honour. Neither does my father. Kyros would never have done it."

"Who's Kyros?" Hephaistion was growing uneasy.

"A Persian king. The first and the best."

"*A Persian!* What are you thinking of?"

"Artabazos told me about him. Never mind. I'll tell you sometime" He stood up. "I hate him for what he's done."

Even to Hephaistion he could not say: "He dishonours my mother, too. He betrays her. *He* is a traitor." Tears gathered behind his eyes, his face flushed stormily with the effort of holding them back, his fists clenched at his sides. The day before, when he had taken his horse to the stables, he overheard jokes about his father which he understood by now, and laughter which stopped as soon as the men saw him. He went to his mother's rooms to fetch his clothes for the feast, going from the noise of the stables, the wind and sun of the sea-shore, into the brooding silence of this closed kingdom. Sometimes his little sister Cleopatra danced in the doorway with outstretched arms, laughing – "You're a boy! You can't come in! Boys can't come in!" and trying to catch him. Today she lay curled up on the lion skin on the floor, her arms clasping its shabby head to her chin, watching silently from this refuge.

Olympias sat in her chair by the window. She did not turn or speak. He stopped. She knew he was there. Cleopatra looked sidelong at him and said in a flat voice, "He's here." He went forward then. "Mother – ?" He felt himself shiver and held himself hard. "Mother –" She had been weeping but he thought it was with anger, there was a dark flush on her cheek bones.

She pulled him to her. "You at least are mine. You are mine and none of his! He would take you from me if he could. He would leave me *nothing!*" She pressed her face against his hair, holding him so tightly that her gold necklace hurt his ear and her perfume stifled him. He twisted to get away; she gripped him harder. "Alexander, a woman whose husband betrays her has no-one but her sons to protect her. She cannot fight like a man to defend her own honour. You are all I have. Don't listen to the lies of those men he puts between us; they are paid to speak them. My uncle is his tool. He brought him here to make me suffer through his harshness to you. He has made my brother his lackey – Alexander is too young to realise it. If it were not for you, my darling, I would return to my own in Epiros. Here, where I am called queen, I am nothing. I am laughed at. There, I would be myself again, and no man would mock me."

"No, don't go away, Mother." He struggled free. He did not think that she meant it. She was queen; when the king was away she carried out the morning sacrifice for the people, and quarrelled continuously with his regent, Antipater. Fighting, trying to mark the men with her claws, setting up her own network of spies and informers, guarding her mystery as the priestess of Dionysos, this saved her from madness – Alexander understood the stifling boredom of the women's rooms. And by now he also understood that a new love of the king's, a new wife, brought also the possibility of a new heir, another son to supplant hers, her only source of power.

"No! No, I stay for your sake. You shall have your rights, though he would take them from you if he could, because you are my son. Well – he has no other, apart from that imbecile. He hopes, but, by the Mother, he shall have none." She was fierce and hard again. "Let him take a new wife every year, let him rut like an old goat, they will give him only daughters. I know what he swore to me on Samothrace, in the House of the Mother. The Old Gods are not mocked and I have kept faith with them." He found himself shivering.

Now, in the warmth of the late afternoon under the apple tree, he was hot and shivering again. Hephaistion was staring at him in concern. He swallowed the burning lump in his throat and masked the tremor in his voice with anger. He repeated loudly and passionately what he had said a moment ago. "I hate him!"

"Oh, hush!" Hephaistion was deeply shocked. "It's god-cursed to hate your father."

"I'm not his. My mother said so." Still not certain what she had meant by this, he repeated it as a charm to cut him free from Philip as it did from Leonidas. Hephaistion, seriously disturbed, threw away the apple core and pitched forward to grasp his knee. "You mustn't say that either! It disgraces your mother. Don't let anyone hear you say that. Leonidas would half-kill you. Don't you know what it means? Of course, the king is your father."

Alexander gave him a strange, cold look and pushed away his hand. "Of course I know that. But I'm not his. I belong to myself and to the god. That's all."

Chapter 10

Commander and King

"Well, I hear good reports of you," said Philip genially, warm with success. Olynthos had been a rich prize. The war had more than paid for itself. He had been dispensing gifts to his friends and rewards to those who had earned them. One of his agents from southern Greece had just departed the richer by twenty slaves. He had a gift for the boy, a set of light hunting javelins in a leather holster worked with gold. "Your governor tells me you can handle these. Later you may show me how often you can strike a moving target. Maybe we'll go out together, we shall be here some days, it won't be all business" – they were in Dion for the god's annual festival coupled with Philip's victory celebrations – "I'd like to see how you shape in the field."

He waited for appreciation. The javelins had slender, finely honed blades and the holster, of gilded leather over wood, was embossed with a vigorous design of fleeing stags attacked by griffins. "There were men in Olynthos famed for such work. I had these made for you, the right length and weight. They balance well. You should be able to bring down small game – fawns and foxes, maybe wild cat."

He was met by a closed look. "Thank you, Father." It would be uncouth to refuse the gifts – he would take them with cold courtesy and not use them. The king frowned, hurt and angry. Arridaios had run into his arms, been picked up and swung round, shouting, and had carried off his gift, a Thracian cap made from a fox's scalp, howling and barking with delight, thinking it was the mask of a wolf. The little daughters had kissed him for their dolls and scent bottles. What was the matter with this one?

"What's biting you? Don't show me that sulky face. Is this the way you've been taught to greet your father?" His mother had put him up to this! Philip's jaw tilted for battle, his one fierce eye sparked fire; his temper, damped down, still smouldered from that morning's quarrel with Olympias.

Angry at being spoken to like a naughty child, Alexander also flung back his head and glared hotly. Father and son faced each other, Philip with hands on hips, Alexander with fists clenched by his sides, each challenging the other with thrusting chin and pugnacious, pouting lip. For a moment Alexander blazed and Philip smouldered; then the king tipped his head back further and his laughter roared. "The cock and the bull! Hah! We make a comic spectacle! Come, boy, what is it?"

He ruffled his son's hair, planted himself on a silver-legged stool, set his hands on his knees and prepared to get to the bottom of things. Tousling his hair had robbed Alexander of his fire and dignity; he looked merely cross. Philip put out his considerable charm, turning on his son the smile that had a surprising quality of sweetness in such a ruthless face and had disarmed many an opponent. "Come!" He held out a conciliatory hand. "You are angry. You have, I suppose, a reason. May I know what it is?"

"Yes, sir." Alexander took a deep breath and ignored the hand. "They betrayed their people, the Olynthian commanders. You offered them bribes. You made them traitors."

"Ah!" Philip put both hands back on his knees and regarded his son thoughtfully. "They were prudent men. They knew they were fighting for a lost cause. They saved themselves. It made no difference, you know. I would have taken Olynthos in any case, but more would have died – on both sides."

"Would you have done what they did?"

Philip considered the question. "No. But as a general I've many times decided to withdraw and cut my losses. Heroes come to grief and get killed, you must have learnt that by now. And like as not their people perish with them. Which book of *The Iliad* are you reading? Think of Hector outside the gates of Troy, challenging Achilles. If he'd stayed inside the walls he'd have lived to defend his city. Better still, if he'd been prudent and withdrawn his men the day before the Greeks counter-attacked he'd have saved his army from destruction. You'll be going to the theatre during the festival: you'll find that most of the tragic plays are about heroes destroying themselves and their kin."

The boy was aflame with indignation. "How can you say that, Father? You're a spearman, you lead your men. I've heard Kleitos and Ptolemy tell how you got your wounds –"

"The obligation of a king. Someone speaks of that in *The Iliad* – one of the Trojans' allies – how does he put it? –
*'Our people made us kings and gave us rich estates
now let us show that we are brave men and fit to lead them.'*
But I don't waste lives, my own or anyone else's, and when you're

in command neither should you. I'm prouder of the cities I've won by diplomacy than those I've conquered."

"By trickery, by teaching men to be traitors!"

"You may call it that. Or you may say by helping men to see where their best interests lie. And some citizens think it no bad fate to be ruled by Philip of Macedon. One thing I've learnt – that there is almost no-one money cannot buy, or nowhere there isn't someone who can be bought – and I'd rather pay in gold than in blood. But there are as many ways to take a city as there are to win a woman – you'll learn them in time." Philip stood up and went over to the window and stood, leaning on his forearm, looking out. "To work from inside, building on advantages, strengthening your own party, undermining the opposition, exploiting its weaknesses, this takes as much skill and energy as undermining the walls and battering your way in from outside, and I find it more rewarding. Why blame me for using men's greed anymore than for striking where the wall is weakest? In the end a campaign that captures men's allegiance is a greater victory than one which enslaves their bodies."

"Why did you destroy Olynthos, Father? Why wipe it out?"

"Well, not for revenge. That would be your mother's way. What a ruthless general she'd make! No, they broke their treaty, harboured my enemies and gave me some hard fighting, but I didn't wipe them out through spite. When you're a commander, never let your passions over-ride your judgement. See what it did to Achilles. I'll give you better reasons for the sack. One – to make certain the league can never rise to power again; it was the Olynthians who drove my father out of Pella the year I was born. Two – to pay for an expensive war. The sale of captives alone has done that and we took valuable booty. There's good land, too, where Macedonians can settle. Three – as a warning. I want the Athenians and others to note that Philip is a good friend but a bad enemy."

"But you sent the Athenian troops home free, without even a ransom!" He was too interested to allow himself to resent the slight on his mother.

"Athens is the place where reputations are judged, even now, although the days of her greatness are over." Philip turned back towards him and stood, dark and solid against the light, strength and vitality flowing from him, filling the small room with his presence and power. "Take notice, Alexander, that not all my friends are won by golden promises. There are men who see in me their natural leader, a king who can bring unity and peace to the rival states of Greece, who can settle their quarrels and lead them again to greatness." He walked back to the centre of the room. "What do you think I've been doing these eight – nine – years of your life?"

The child thought, and answered carefully: "Securing the borders of Macedon; keeping out the Illyrians. Moving people to new cities. Winning Thessaly. Advancing into Thrace."

"Why?"

"To make us strong and safe. To win good fame."

"So, what next?"

Alexander's fair, feathered brows drew together while he scanned his father's face, and thought. North to the wild tribes beyond the Ister? Farther east into the fastnesses of Thrace, and beyond that to the sea-gate of Asia? West into the Illyrian mountains? South, to challenge the lioness crouching on her rock? Which offered the most gain? Which presented the greatest danger?

"To the south? To carry the war to Athens?"

"Yes, the south is next. But Athens must be won, not conquered. We are all Greeks, we share our blood, our language, our gods, our belief in ourselves. Look." Philip took up a map and unrolled it with a flourish across his table. Alexander held down one end and the king stabbed at it with a forefinger as thick and horny as a blacksmith's. "Here they are, the great city-states of the south, Thebes, Sparta, Corinth, Athens. Each has had its time of power when it has mauled its rivals, and each has been mauled in its turn. Thebes." He pointed – "The Thebans counted for something in my father's day. They bred brave men and clever generals, but as dull as their cattle. Sparta. A nation of trained soldiers, the best fighting men in Greece, or so they believe. But now they won't lead and they won't follow. Corinth. Traders and seafarers, great craftsmen. They built the first warship; they still have a navy. And the prettiest women in Greece! Athens. A nation of talkers. Thinkers, too, they have produced subtle men, philosophers and the greatest poets." He paused. "The Athenians saved Greece when the Persians invaded. They sacrificed their city – the Persians burned it – and they built it up again to be the wonder of Greece. Those were her years of glory. *'An eagle in the clouds!'* the oracle called her then. Where is the eagle now? Scratching about on the threshing floor of Greece like an old fighting cock, making threatening runs this way and that, but striking always too late, cackling and crowing of past glories." He looked, not pleased, but tragic.

Alexander offered consolation. "The Spartans were brave," he said, "when the Persians came. Leonidas told me." After hearing the story he had thought better of his governor for sharing his name with the heroic Spartan king. "The Persians came with a huge army. It took them seven days to cross the sea from Asia on a bridge of boats. They marched across Thrace and south through Macedon and Thessaly, drinking the rivers dry, but the Greeks stopped them at Thermopylae."

"They stopped me there," said Philip, "after the battle of the Crocus Field. Do you know what it's like? Have you looked at the map? A path between a steep cliff and the sea wide enough for a single cart, and beyond that three narrow passes through the mountains, three gates into southern Greece guarded by forts. The Hot Gates, they call it. A few can hold it against thousands. I didn't attempt it with the forces I had then. Four years I've waited for that fruit to ripen – soon I'll shake it down with no trouble!" He grinned in great good humour. "But I interrupted. Go on with your story."

"Leonidas, the king of Sparta, led the Greeks," said Alexander, "with three hundred of his royal bodyguard. When their scouts told them the Persians were so many that their arrows would darken the sun, one of them answered, 'Good! So we'll fight in the shade.' For two days they beat back all that the Persians could send against them. The great king was in a fury of despair. Would you believe that he sat on a throne to watch the battle? *He sat on a throne!* And three times he leapt up, calling on his gods. But then a traitor showed the Persians a goat track over the mountains and they sent a crack force to take the Greeks in the rear. Leonidas sent some divisions to try and outflank the Persians, others ran away and the Thebans surrendered, but the Spartans fought on and the king and all three hundred of his bodyguard died there. They have a marker over their grave and on it is written:

'Go tell the Spartans, stranger passing by,
that here obedient to their laws we lie.'

One day I shall pass by and read it, and see where they fought!"

King Philip's brows and mouth twitched. "So you shall." The boy had lived the story as he told it, his head tilted a little to one side, gazing with shining intensity into his father's face. 'That look,' thought Philip, 'will win men to him in a few years time, they will follow him as they did Leonidas and dare the impossible.' He blew his nose to shake off the spell. As a general he suspected some details of the story, which had not lost in a hundred and thirty years of telling, and he would have thought more of Leonidas if he had managed to withdraw his forces in good order from a hopeless situation, but he could not say this to the ardent face in front of him. "Well," he said, "the Spartans were brave, and they won the land battles against the Persians, but the sea battles were won under Athenian leadership and there would have been no co-ordinated resistance to the Persians at all if the Athenians hadn't coaxed and bullied the other states into it, and then held them together by every trick and threat they could think of. The Greeks had despaired simply at the noise of the Great King's coming.

But do you see what this means? The Persians brought trained soldiers from fifty different nations, they had experienced generals and a fleet manned by the best sea-farers, supported by the entire wealth of their empire, and the Greeks, when they acted together, beat them. The Greek sailor, the Greek cavalryman, above all the Greek foot-soldier, proved superior, though outnumbered four to one, ten to one, seventy to one! All they needed were the right commanders."

"The Spartans have a king – two kings! The Athenians don't. Who rules them?"

"The people! So they say. They have a council and officers chosen by lot each year and they elect ten generals. Parmenion is worth all ten of them. All male citizens meet in an assembly to approve or change or throw out the proposals put to them by the council. That's when the speech makers get to work on them. Anyone may speak whether he knows what he's talking about or not. Some men make it their profession. I forget which of their comic poets said:

'The cicadas sit in the branches and chirp for three months of the year;
the Athenians do it for ever, talking away their lives!'"

"You despise them! I thought, just now when you were talking, that you wanted to lead them yourself."

"Oh I do, I shall!" said Philip, laughing. "I may despair of what they have become, but I don't despise them. Nor must you. We will show them a way to wipe out the shame of the past, to redeem their honour. Do you know there are Greek cities on the coast of Asia under the rule of the Great King, with Persian satraps to govern them?" He stooped forward suddenly and lowered his voice. "Who will liberate them? Philip, King of Macedon, Commander of all the Greeks? Alexander, son of Philip...?" He tilted the boy's chin with one finger and Alexander kindled at his touch. "Yes, Father! When?"

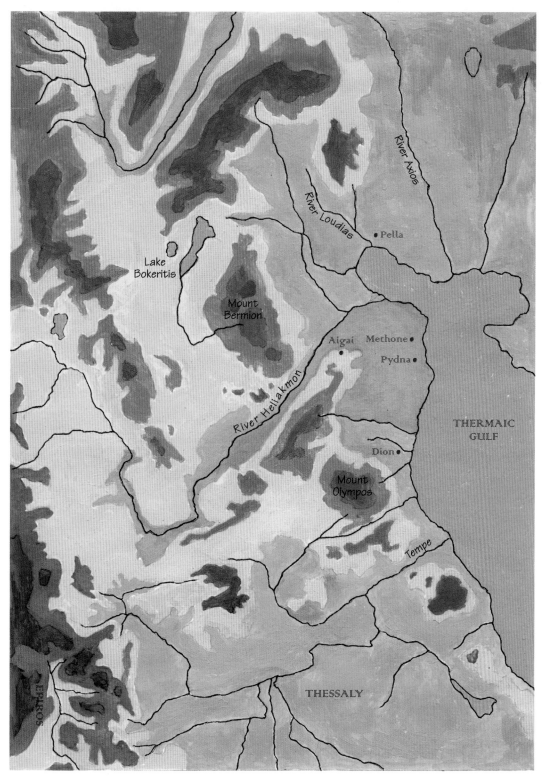

THE MACEDONIAN KINGDOM

Philip laughed. "Agammemnon and Achilles assailing Troy. Not yet. You'll have time to grow. Let the southerners get used to the idea. They've despised us, with some cause, in the past. Let them learn now what we really are. Come here and look." He led his son to the window. They looked down on the crowd in the courtyard. "There are Athenians here for our festival, and athletes, actors, horsemen, poets and statesmen from all of Greece. The games will rival those at Olympia, the plays equal any put on in Corinth. And the prizes will be something more than a laurel wreath or a jar of oil. At the end there will be a state banquet for the victors. You may attend." He looked down at his son, suddenly attentive to practical details. He had grown a little and appeared sturdy, but the delicate beauty of his face still made Philip uneasy. "Wear court dress but nothing gaudy or fancy. Make sure your mother understands – nothing pretty, keep it plain, nothing girlish." A vivid flush spread under the boy's skin. Philip went on, affecting not to notice. "How well do you play the lyre? Leonidas says your music teacher is pleased with you. Can you prepare a piece for my guests?"

He answered stiffly, "Yes, sir. I know a good song about victory at the games."

"Good. Practise it. Remember Athenians will be listening. They are judges of the arts if nothing else." And half to himself he said: "They are ready for a king, although they don't know it yet. A king trained in philosophy, that's the ideal of their thinking men now, men who see that rule by the people has failed. Let these men see your education well begun."

"But, sir, we're still at war with Athens."

"There's a truce for actors and athletes, and others whom I wish to see here have been granted free passage. But you may as well know that I've started moves towards making peace with Athens. An alliance, too, if they're sensible; we shall need their navy. But keep that to yourself, and all that I've told you today." A demon of jealousy entered suddenly into Philip, aroused by the unexpected pleasure he had enjoyed in his son's company; it gave a bite to his voice. "Do you still tell your mother everything? Don't trust her with any of this, I won't have her meddle in my affairs. She has quarrelled daily with Antipater in my absence; she could govern better it seems. She has told me his faults – at length – does she tell you mine? Eh? What does she tell you about me?"

Furious beyond words, Alexander twisted from under the king's hand on his shoulder. His first impulse was still, as it had been when he was small, to punch, to kick, to throw, but he restrained it. He was as angry with himself as with his father. He had been beguiled into consorting with her enemy – how could he have forgotten so easily? He had let slurs on her pass unheeded to keep his father talking. He, too, was a traitor, then. In a child's high-pitched voice of rage and grief he shouted: "My mother is the queen! You bring shame upon her. I don't want your gifts." He swept them from the table to clatter on the floor. "I shall leave you and go to her. You are not my father! You are *nothing!*" He stamped his foot on the word and rushed for the door.

A bellow like that of an angry bull behind him was cut short by the sight of Kleitos, as the door flew open, standing with his hand raised ready to knock and a look of quizzical astonishment on his face. With the quick reaction of a bodyguard, he seized Alexander as he swerved past. "Do you want him, Philip?"

The king stood, hands on hips, looking down at the defiant face and glittering eyes. "Don't you dare," he said evenly, "shout at me like that again. Apologise."

The mouth and eyes of his son hardened, his chin jutted. "Come," said Philip quietly, "a soldier accepts discipline."

"I am sorry that I shouted."

"Well, go to Mama. But remember what I told you. Take these." He handed over the javelins. "I don't care to have my gifts thrown back at me." He grinned. "You may draw my face on your practice sack if it gives you satisfaction. And be ready with your song. If you make a fool of me in front of my guests, I'll have the hide off you with my own hands."

He did not go to his mother. He went to the guard-room, where the soldiers called him basilikos and set up a target to let him show how straight and hard he could hurl his new weapons.

Chapter 11

The Women of Troy

The morning smelt of sharp green apples, the roadside grass was chilly with dew. They were walking to the theatre at first light, before the sun was up. Mount Olympos was a long, flat grey shadow, a little darker than the sky. When the sun leapt out of the distant sea the eastern faces of the mountain came alive; blue shadows filled the gorges and bare cliffs rising above dark forests caught the light like bronze mirrors.

Lysimachus was taking Alexander to the theatre for the first time and he was dancing with anticipation like a horse before a race.

"Can't we walk faster?"

"Nothing will happen until your father arrives. We've plenty of time. What's the hurry?"

"I want to *get* there. I hate to dawdle. You can walk much faster if you like."

"Yes indeed, but this is a holiday. Look, there's Creon."

So Lysimachus strolled pleasantly, talking to friends, and Alexander leapt impatiently back and forth across the roadside ditch. Without Hephaistion he felt bare. The Pages sent to escort them were some way behind, engaged in horseplay and sharing jokes he did not understand.

When they reached the theatre, the seats were filling up: – country folk, farmers and soldiers on the benches at the top; officials, visitors, nobles and their families on the stone tiers lower down. Behind the semi-circular hill in which the seats were set rose the heights of Mount Olympos, a gallery for immortal spectators. The audience looked down on a round dancing floor, the orchestra, and before it the altar of Dionysos, Lord of Festivals, for whom the plays were performed. At the edge of the orchestra were the carved seats of honour for the king and the judges. Lysimachus led Alexander to a place several rows up.

"You don't want to sit down there, we shall see better here. Your father has a worse view than anybody. His spearmen in the back row see better." Lysimachus had brought a rug to cushion his own seat. "Age is creeping into my bones."

"Not yet. Remember we have to go to war together."

"Oh, I won't be left behind. But you'll have to make up a soft bed for me in your tent as Achilles did for his Phoenix."

"Don't let Father hear you say that."

He turned his attention eagerly to the prospect before him. Behind the orchestra a wooden building had been erected, painted to represent a palace with triple doors between a row of columns. He scanned it avidly, searching for clues to the play they were about to see.

The noise in the theatre competed with the excited chatter of birds, gathering in autumnal flocks in the surrounding trees. Wounded soldiers from the last campaign were clambering into the block of free seats reserved for them. The royal women came, with attendants bearing cushions and shawls, and settled into the first row, protected by awnings from the sun. Beautiful Nikesipolis was not among them. She had not lived a year after the birth of her daughter, whom Philip had named Thessaloniki for her mother's country. Alexander thought of her sometimes. She had been like the pomegranate flowers, silken and golden and red, and her time had been as fleeting as theirs. None of Philip's wives had given him another son.

His mother came in an embroidered robe, her hair dressed high encircled by bands of gold, floating veils about her face. He stood up and waved and she laughed and inclined her head. Across the distance he felt the bond of shared delight. She loved the theatre. Her place was in the seat of honour as the priestess of Dionysos.

The clash of cymbals announced the coming of the god. His image was carried in procession and set up before his altar. Dionysos was Master of Revels and Lord of Festivals, he did not watch from far Olympos but came among his worshippers to share their pleasures.

Now trumpets for the king! Necks craned, some country people stood up to see better, there were cheers and applause, shouts of 'Philippos!' in many accents. The king came smiling through the actor's entrance, accompanied by senior officers of his bodyguard. He wore a long white cloak and a wreath of golden oak leaves. As he crossed the orchestra a shaft of the morning sun caught the tips of the quivering leaves. He made the offering to Dionysos, invoking the presence of the god; a soft cloud of blue smoke rose from the burning incense and threaded its way upwards through the still morning air.

All were now present: the people, the king, the god and his priestess.

The audience settled, voices hushed like dry leaves blowing away. The musician beside the altar raised pipes to his lips. As the first deep notes floated out into the silence a shiver of anticipation ran down Alexander's spine. Figures appeared at each side of the orchestra – mysterious, masked, in solemn robes – and moved rhythmically across the dancing floor, singing, to begin the play.

All that surrounded Alexander vanished: the cold, fresh morning; the people murmuring and sighing; the solid warmth of Lysimachus beside him; the whispering Pages beyond. He surrendered completely to the spell of the words flowing from the masked faces, sharing the triumph, the terror, they called upon him to feel with them. They were real; nothing else was.

When the play ended, he came back slowly from another world to discover that the sun was hot on his shoulders, that there were people around him, warm and sweating, to hear them shouting and applauding. He lifted a wondering face to meet the eyes of Lysimachus, sharing with him the mystery. The actors came on to take their bows, holding their masks in front of them. He wished they had not done this. They had been kings and gods; he did not want to know that they were men.

There were intervals when the people could walk about, greet friends, eat their bread and fruit, and go out to relieve themselves, but the plays continued all day. The last was a comedy, so deeply shocking that at first he could not believe it, and shot a startled, enquiring glance at Lysimachus, who was laughing and did not see.

The first shock came when he realised that one of the two actors wearing grotesque masks and costumes padded to give them enormous fat behinds and bellies was meant to be the god Dionysos. The other was Xanthos, his slave. They came on as travellers, Xanthos riding a donkey and carrying their luggage on a long pole. They were going down into the Underworld to bring the poet Euripedes back to life because Dionysos said all the best poets were dead and nobody could write good plays anymore.

Dionysos wore a lion skin over his yellow robe – he was pretending to be Herakles because he thought that would frighten the fierce guardians of the Underworld. But it was Dionysos who was frightened when the porter at the gate roared angrily at him:

"You scamp, you utter rogue, you scallywag, you're here again!
Last time you stole our watchdog, three-headed Cerberus,
you seized and choked and off you ran with him. But now we've got you!"

He ran off to summon a snake with a hundred heads and other monsters to tear him to bits. Alexander heard his father's laugh roar out when Dionysos messed himself in fright. He was a great coward. He changed places with his slave, grabbing the luggage and making Xanthos put on the lion skin, but before the porter came back a maid appeared who gave 'Herakles' a different welcome:

"Herakles! Darling! Back at last! Come in.
My mistress, hearing you'd arrived,
at once put loaves into the oven, made pea soup,
pots and pots of it, and cakes and rolls,
and barbecued an ox. So do come in."

So Dionysos hurriedly claimed the lion skin back from Xanthos.

"Dressing you up like that was just a joke
Pick up these bundles here and be yourself."

This was a mistake. They'd hardly changed places before some angry landladies stormed in demanding revenge – Herakles had once eaten all their bread and cheese and beef and then refused to pay the bill. They called the law officers who beat both Dionysos and his slave.

The hair prickled on the back of Alexander's neck. The actors were mocking the god in his very presence – there stood his image by the altar, watching all this, on the dancing floor sacred to him. His father had called upon the god to come among them – now he and all the people were laughing at him! What would he do?

His mother, the god's priestess – she sat watching this too. She was hidden from him by the awning – was she laughing? At one point the actor playing Dionysos ran across and begged her protection – it was crazy, the proper order of things turned upside down. Beside him, Lysimachus was laughing with his head thrown back, slapping his knees. The Pages were hooting and whistling, their arms round each other's necks, rocking with laughter.

The play ended with Dionysos and Hades, Ruler of the Underworld, choosing which poet to bring back to life. They held a competition between Euripedes and a rival poet, who stood before them to praise their own work and criticise each other's. The rival said that the rhythms of Euripedes' poetry were all alike and he could smash them with an oil can. Each time Euripedes started to quote from one of his plays the other one shouted out *"Lost his oil-can!"* The crowd enjoyed this and joined in. So –

"No man is completely happy," began the unfortunate poet, *"one who is nobly born is poor, another of low birth –"*

"*Lost his oil-can!*" roared the crowd in time with the second actor, drowning his words. The longer it went on the sillier and funnier it became, and Alexander found himself laughing with the rest.

When the play was over, Lysimachus looked down at him, smiling. "Well, what did you think?"

"I liked the croaking of frogs when they crossed the lake." He imitated the mocking chorus of the frogs' song: "*Brekekekex, koax, koax!*"

"I heard you laughing."

"Yes, it was funny, but –"

"But – ?"

"But they made fun of a god!" He looked his disbelief, astonishment and concern.

"So you think the gods can't take a joke?"

"Won't Dionysos mind?"

"Oh, I daresay it wouldn't do to mock at Olympian Zeus or Far-Shooting Apollo, but Dionysos is the Lord of Misrule. Think how men behave when drunk – wine releases them – that's the freedom of the god. And I think that what amuses us must make the gods laugh, too." He turned and looked at the evening clouds gathering round the mountain peaks. "Didn't you hear laughter up there?"

"The chorus criticised the Athenians," said Alexander as they made their way out, people standing aside for them. "Some of the things they said my father told me yesterday. And they poked fun at their generals and people like tax collectors."

"It's an old play. But the actors changed the names, brought them up-to-date."

"How old?"

"Oh – fifty years or so. It was written just after the poet Euripedes died and, we may presume, went down to the Underworld."

"*Was* he the best poet? It was silly to make him lose the contest because everyone shouted 'Lost his oil-can!' Who do you think should have won? Was he the best?"

"Oh, he didn't lose because of that. They chose the other poet because his plays made men feel courageous, but Euripedes showed them their faults."

"Do they? Why? It must be better to make people feel brave."

"Well, tomorrow you may judge for yourself. We shall see three of Euripedes plays performed – if you want to come again?"

"Of course I do! I mean, yes, thank you."

"You'll find the plays interesting. They're all about the Trojan War."

"About Achilles?"

"No, not this time. You'll see. Do you know that Euripides lived the last part of his life here in Macedon? He was a guest-friend of King Archelaus. When he died, the Athenians asked for his bones, but we never sent them back. We buried him here where he was welcome and where the plays of his old age were written."

"Why did he leave Athens?"

"Well, his plays made the Athenians uneasy, although they like to question everything. He was very unpopular there. Perhaps they grew impatient with his turning everything inside out, forcing them to look at old beliefs in new ways. Euripedes liked to make his audience think – and think hard. You'll find out tomorrow."

The following day the queen took Alexander with her. He sat on a stool of scarlet leather beside her chair, looking out from the patch of shade under the awning across the white dust of the orchestra, not yet trodden. They were separate from the crowd behind them and there was nothing now between Alexander and the actors. When the plays began he was conscious that he was watching men performing in masks; he did not lose himself in another world as he had done the day before from his seat up on the hillside.

Until the third play began. In this, Troy had fallen. The painted skene represented the walls of the ruined city and smoke drifted through the central door, now meant to be the Scaean gate. The slow beat of drums, like hard sobs of pain, proclaimed the city's end. Onto the wall above the gate came a tall figure, moving slowly in stiff robes of green and blue that gleamed with threads of silver. His face wore a mask dreadful in its cold, still beauty, in his hand he held a bronze trident. Poseidon, god of the sea. A powerful voice, deep and resonant from within the hollow mask, swept towards Alexander and engulfed him like a breaking wave.

"I am Poseidon. Troy and its people were mine.
This ring of walls I and Apollo built, squared every stone...
Now Troy lies dead under the conquering spear,
stripped, sacked and smouldering...
Now I must leave my altars,
when desolation falls like a blight
the day for worship of the gods is past."

132

He moved his hand, pointed with his trident towards a dark heap of rags on the ground beside the gate.

"Look at this pitiable, prostrate figure,
drowned in tears for a world of sorrows,
it is Hekabe..."

Hekabe, aged queen of Troy, mother of Hector, her husband and sons dead, she and her daughters captives, slaves of the conquering Greek lords.

"Farewell then, city, you had your day of glory."

When the god had departed the pipes began a low, tremulous wailing that made Alexander's skin creep. The heap of rags that was the Trojan queen stirred, and from it rose a terrible mask of age and grief under ragged locks of grey hair, shorn for mourning. The dark eye-sockets rimmed in red looked straight towards him, the downcast mouth spoke and filled him with its own pain.

"Lift your neck from the dust, up with your head!
This is not Troy. The kings of Troy are dead.
Bear what you must."

He knew that all actors were men or boys. All day he had been conscious of the men behind the masks. Now he heard only the voice of the queen of Troy. In her black agony of despair she gathered remnants of courage and royal pride about her as she gathered the smoke-stained tatters of her royal robes. Once, she had led the women of Troy in sacred songs and cheerful dances; now she called on them to lament with her, like seagulls crying round their broken nests.

The captive women came, three lines of ragged figures, three rows of masks with black holes for weeping eyes, black mouths for crying pain. They were not boys in women's clothes, they were the shorn-headed widows, mothers and daughters of slaughtered Trojans, of the men he had watched fight and die through the eyes of Homer. They tried to comfort their queen, but no words of theirs could help her.

"Here let me lie!
Here in the dust such pain as mine belongs.
I was a princess born. My husband was a king.
The sons I bore were heroes to a man.
No mother in Troy, in Greece, in all Asia
could ever boast such sons. I saw them one by one
fall to Greek spears. I cut locks of my hair
to lay on their still graves. The father of them all, Priam,

is gone. Myself, with these same eyes, I saw him
hacked to death at his own altar, his city laid in dust.
My virgin daughters, whom I cherished as choice gifts
for husbands worthy of them, were torn from my arms,
given to our enemies. There is no hope that they
ever again will see their mother, nor I them.
Now I in my old age shall go to Hellas as a slave,
they will lay on me tasks to humble my grey head,
answering the door, or keeping keys, or cooking food –
I, who bore Hector!"

Under the lament of the women which followed, telling of the night the Greeks, emerging from their hiding place in the wooden horse, burnt and sacked the city, the music swelled to a martial storm of shrilling pipes and clashing cymbals. Then it wept quietly into silence.

The gates in the centre of the wall swung slowly open. The chorus of women parted in lines on either side. Through the gates came a cart piled high with treasure. On top lay the great shield, the plumed helmet, the spear and sword of Hector, dead champion of Troy, and among her husband's panoply of arms sat his widow, gentle Andromache, with their son, Astynax on her lap. The child wore no mask. He was a little younger than Alexander.

"Where are they taking you, sad Andromache?"

From the pale mask of the woman came a voice of stone, arising from a heart bled cold of all feeling.

"The Greeks are carrying home their property."

At the sound of that dead voice, Alexander's hand sought and gripped his mother's. Living the tragedy of Troy, unaware of the breathing multitude behind him, the heat, the smell of dust, the stiffness in his limbs, yet he remembered that it was through this captive woman that the blood of Achilles had come to him.

Andromache and Hekabe lamented all they had lost:

"Once we were happy. All that is ended."
"Ended."
"My noble children, they are gone."
"Gone my home, my lovely city."
"Gone."
"All that we love, lost."
"All we have known destroyed."

Hekabe had only one comfort to offer her son's widow.
"Oh, my dear daughter,
cease mourning for Hector. Your tears cannot help him.
Honour your new husband. Win his love by your sweetness and worth,
And – who knows? – you may yet bring up our Hector's son
to light new hope for Troy."

Upon this the Greek herald came. The conquerors had held an assembly. Their leaders had decided that Hector's son could not be allowed to live. He must be thrown from the battlements. If the women protested he would be given no burial. If they put up no resistance they would be allowed to bury him.

Andromache and her condemned child were led away. A Greek king, Agamemnon's brother, entered in splendid armour:
"How gloriously the sun shines on this happy day!"

Hekabe sank to the depths of her pit of pain. The blood-stained body of the child Astynax was brought in, lying on his father's shield, and given to his grandmother. She washed his wounds and wrapped him in such grave clothes as the women could find, preparing his soul for its journey to the House of the Dead, where his father waited for him.
"You Greeks are fine fighters, but where is your pride?
Did you quake with fear before this child?"

Flaming torches were carried in, smoke lit by a red glow rose behind the walls of the ruined town; the Greeks, ready to set sail, were burning all that was left of Troy. Hekabe tried to leap into the fire. *"That is a royal way to die!"* but the soldiers pulled her back.

The women called for the last time on the gods who had deserted Troy. Did Zeus see their suffering? Did he care? Was their torment justified? Then they were led off to the ships of the victors. And in the distance sounded the gathering storm – the thunderous anger of the waiting sea-god, Poseidon.

Too stunned, too deeply moved to weep, Alexander gazed dry-eyed at the empty orchestra, at the place where the ghosts of Troy had passed, leaving their footprints in the dust, white in the sun. The red glow of the fires faded, the actors came on to receive their applause. Gently, his mother loosed her fingers from the fierce clasp of his hand. But no theatre company released its audience still in the grip of grief. Tragedies were always followed by a brief, comic farce. Alexander laughed as loudly as anyone else, laughter being close to tears.

He saw, as it ended, his father conferring with the judges. Had he known what the third play was about? How long was it since the fighting king of Macedon had read Euripides? But Philip looked unperturbed. He was laughing with Antipater over the finale to the comedy.

In fact, Philip had not been disconcerted by the subject of the play. The theme of the Trojan War, the conquest of Asians by Greeks, had seemed a fitting choice for his victory celebrations. He had not been displeased when the chorus reminded everyone of an earlier conquest of Troy by his ancestor, Herakles.

'He split with fire's red blast the stones that Apollo squared,
And laid in dust our city's life. So twice
the reeking sword has pierced the heart of Troy.'

As to the suffering of the slaves, so much the better if the Athenians and others were made aware again what such punishment of a city meant.

"Euripides wrote that play," said Lysimachus, who had taken charge of Alexander again, "after the Athenians attacked the little state of Melos for refusing to help them in their wars. They put all the men to the sword and sold the women and children as slaves."

"But was it performed in Athens?"

"Oh yes, the following year, a month before the Athenians sent a great fleet to conquer Sicily. But there was a strong peace party then as there is now, and the Athenians have always allowed freedom of speech. The play won no prizes, though."

"Was it real blood on Astynax?"

"Would you like him to tell you? We can go behind the skene and talk to the actors, if you wish."

"Yes! I'd like that."

In the wooden skene building the actors had their dressing rooms. Alexander stood among the costumes and props, the flimsy stage armour, the herald's staff and Poseidon's trident, the bronze mirrors and the wigs and masks on their stands. The painted faces of the masks were empty now and no longer terrible, the life having gone out of them. The actors, musicians and stage hands gathered round him, smiling.

The leading actor who had played Hekabe was presented to him – Aristodemus, a lean, handsome man whose face looked smooth and young but whose thick dark hair showed feathered streaks of grey. Alexander regarded him with deep respect.

"Do you feel her sorrow when you play her part? You have great courage, I think."

136

He was told that actors often experienced fear before going on and nodded, understanding. "It's the same in war. My father says Fear is the only enemy. We have to kill him first. I'm glad that the judges awarded you the prize, Father is sure to give you something splendid. Your voice sounded so like an old woman's. Is that hard to do?" He learnt that actors did voice exercises every day to improve their skills. "A good, experienced man," said Aristodemus, "should be able to take the part of a warrior, a princess, a king or an old crone, and the audience should hear every word, even when he whispers, right to the top row."

"So, that is like a soldier, too. You have to train for it and every performance is a battle and a victory." He smiled up at the tall young man who had taken the part of Andromache. This one had the liveliest face, with strong, slanting cheek bones, laughing grey eyes and dark red hair, damp and curling from having been under a wig all day. Alexander remembered the shock of surprise he had felt at the end of the play when that eager, adventurous head, like a bony young horse, had emerged from behind the pale, sad mask of Andromache. He asked the man's name. "Thettalos, Alexander, from Thessaly."

"Then you come from Achilles' country. Do you know, Thettalos, that we are descended from Andromache and Achilles' son? My mother is and I am."

Thettalos made him a graceful bow. "That is delightful. I shall remember when I play the part again. It would have eased her sorrow, and Hekabe's too, I think, if they could have seen as far into the future as this." His look was warm with admiration. Alexander flushed with pleasure and held out his hand. "I would like to see you act again. Will you come back when we are at Pella? Is there a play about Achilles? I hoped there might be one today."

"There is," said Thettalos, "but this is Aristodemus' company, Alexander. If he will put it on for you I shall be very happy to play in it." Aristodemus smiled and said it would give him pleasure, too. "Then I will see you again in Pella. If you come from Thessaly you must enjoy riding. So do I. So we will ride together. Now I should like to talk to the boy who played Astynax."

The child was drawn forward and presented. He was the son of the third actor and had been in several performances. The two boys stood for a moment looking at each other and then Alexander said: "You played dead very well. I was close, I would have seen if you had moved. Your wounds looked real. Was it blood – or dye?" Astynax had washed himself clean by now. The wardrobe man offered to paint a wound on Alexander's arm to show him how it was done and he was delighted. "My father had a sword cut just there."

He walked home with Lysimachus feeling as though he had lived a hundred lives in one day. He was considering whether he would like to have been born an actor's son rather than a king's. "I could play Astynax," he said. "I can lie absolutely still for a very long time." He sprang across the roadside ditch and lay sprawled on his back on a flat, hot white stone. "Imagine this is Hector's shield." His head lolled to one side, his eyes closed and his lips slightly apart. "My dear boy, come on! You can't lie about here." A fly buzzed above Alexander's face. He did not stir. "Alexander! I have things to do before supper. I shall go and leave you here."

"You daren't!" said Alexander out of barely moving lips. "Lift up my arm as Hekabe did and let it go."

With a sigh, Lysimachus raised his arm and let it drop; it flopped limply back onto the grass. "You see!" Alexander leapt up, triumphant. "I didn't twitch even when the fly tickled me. I'd like to be an actor. They travel everywhere."

They walked on, past Philip's vineyards where there were new slaves still wearing wooden collars.

Alexander said: "But I wouldn't do the first part as that boy did. He hung round his mother's neck. And his father's sword there on the cart! I'd cut the hand off the first man to touch me!"

"Oh no!" said Lysimachus, laughing. "Actors can't please themselves in that way. A play is directed, either by the author, if he's alive, or by one of the leading actors. Aristodemus directed this one. He tells the others how he thinks the parts should be played, they must all work together or the meaning of the play could be lost. Actors, you see, are like soldiers in this, too, and have their general."

"Well!" said Alexander, "I wouldn't want to play him if he has to do as he's told and cry when he would rather fight."

He had had the same difficulty a year ago at the beginning of his music lessons. Learning the first notes on the lyre, enough to put together a simple tune, he had added more dramatic ones of his own.

"No, no!" exclaimed his teacher. "Where did you find that? That's not as I showed you."

"I'm making up my own."

"Well, don't. You must play the tune as I set it down."

"Why? Why can't I play as I like? Why must this note-" he plucked it – "come after this note –" he plucked again – "if I don't want it to?"

"Well, I suppose basilikos may play as he wishes, but if he does he will never be a musician. How would you regard a soldier who said, 'Why must I step off on my right foot and march and counter march in time with the others? Why can't I walk about as I please?'" He won a reluctant chuckle in response. "You see? Now let's begin again."

He loved music, now that he better understood the playing of it; it was worth learning to do well, that was the due of the poets and musicians who had composed the songs – unfair to give them less than one's best. He loved his teacher, who was good-humoured but cared about what he taught and demanded excellence. And his teacher delighted in him; he had a high, clear, true voice and a sensitive touch on the strings. His best was becoming very good indeed.

For the victor's banquet he learnt a new song. His mother refused to take any interest in it, since it was prepared for Philip, but she had made him a tunic with blue borders. After two days he had washed off the painted wound reluctantly. His mother had cried out when she saw it and he would have liked to cause a stir at supper. His father would not have been deceived, but he might have laughed. He described it to his young uncle Alexander when he came to tell him that the king was ready. In fourteen months the Epirote prince had grown taller and heavier and his face was changing, as though his clear-cut boy's beauty was melting and being remoulded into the stronger features of a man. He had killed his boar and reclined upon his own couch at supper.

Alexander sat at his father's feet. Eating, always a serious business in Macedon, was over. The tables were being taken out and great silver jugs of wine and mixing bowls were carried in. The guests were given garlands, a steward brought Alexander a wreath of myrtle leaves. Strangers smiled and raised their cups to him. It was much quieter than the usual Macedonian feast. He supposed it was because of their foreign guests.

He was sorry not to see Thettalos present, but only leading actors were eligible for prizes. The heralds began announcing the victors. He applauded loudly when Aristodemus received his crown. The actors sat near the king, who liked their company. They were the liveliest of his foreign guests, talking and laughing freely, peddling scandalous and entertaining gossip, even discussing politics, while others were far more cautious, conscious that they were dining in the lion's den. But actors were protected by Dionysos, whose servants they were; they went practically everywhere and saw everything and were used to partying with all kinds of people. They were often used as diplomats and ambassadors. Philip had asked Aristodemus to take his proposals for peace to Athens.

Each victor had been invited to choose a generous gift from the king, and these were now being handed out with ceremony – chased silver bowls, arm bands of twisted gold set with garnets, cloaks with embroidered borders, bridles entitling the receivers to horses from the royal stud. This was in the tradition of kings whose glory and fame rested on feats of arms and spectacular guest- giving. Philip was enjoying himself.

Alexander thought of Agamemnon and Achilles awarding gifts and prizes on the plain of Troy – bronze armour, prize-winning horses, copper cauldrons and tripods.

He saw that tonight his father was also an actor, playing the part of a gracious ruler and generous friend, and doing it convincingly. He reclined on his couch with dignity instead of sprawling; he refrained from shouting to his Companions across the hall or from allowing Macedonian expressions into his speech. In good Greek, with scarcely a trace of a Northern accent, he was conducting a lively conversation on horse breeding and training with those nearest to him, and the Pages hurrying to refill his wine cup found it more often raised to emphasis a point he was making than to show that it was empty.

The herald, checking his list, bent to the king's ear. Philip looked up and looked round the hall enquiringly. Several couches away, Satyrus, the comic actor, reclined in silent gloom, his chin resting on his hand, his long face creased in melancholy, ludicrous beneath his festal wreath. He had played the slave of Dionysos in *The Frogs,* a part for which he was famous, and had won the prize for comedy. The king hailed him. "Satyrus, what's wrong with you, man?"

"Lost his oil can!" shouted someone down the hall, to a gust of laughter. Everyone stopped talking and sat up to look, expecting a witty answer. Satyrus made none. He waved his hand in a gesture that said, 'carry on, never mind me,' and returned to his dejected pose. Smiles and expectation grew.

"Satyrus, you've chosen no gift, I hear. Why is this?"

The comedian shook his head and sighed.

"Why not?" pursued the king, enjoying his new role as comic's feed. "Do you think we don't wish to honour you? Have we offended you?"

Slowly Satyrus sat up, looked round and saw that the eyes of all were upon him, and said – playing straight now – "Philip, I want none of the things the others have asked for." He paused. "And what I do want you may not wish to give."

"Why, what is it?" asked the king, laughing. "The throne of Macedon?"

"No, king," replied Satyrus, perfectly serious. "Nothing it wouldn't be easy for you to give, but I'm afraid to ask it."

"Afraid!" Philip was on his feet. "Afraid? A guest under my roof, eating bread at my table? Ask, man. Whatever it is, I'll grant it. After such laughter as you've given us, who could refuse you anything?" There was a ripple of approval.

"Two of your Olynthian slaves."

The hiss of indrawn breath from the Athenians present was distinctly audible. Popular comedian Satyrus might be, but they would not forgive him for this. Philip, astonished, paused to consider how to answer and still maintain the atmosphere of goodwill he had worked hard to create.

"Let me not be misunderstood," said Satyrus. He had achieved the dramatic effect he wanted. He knew the incident would be remembered and talked about. He explained that he had seen among the prisoners from Olynthos the daughters of a man, now dead, who had once been his guest-friend. If Philip would give the girls to him, he would set them free, provide them with dowries and find them husbands. The hall exploded into applause, swiftly checked. All looked to the king.

Philip, also greatly relieved, spread wide both arms. "Is that all? My dear man, your request is granted. Why did you doubt it? But for yourself, choose something more. Such generosity itself deserves reward." This time the applause was loud and continuous. As Philip sat down he saw his son, glowing and applauding vigorously with the rest, but whether his own part or that of Satyrus, or both, he could not tell.

It seemed the right moment for the victory song. The boy sang with passionate conviction and perfect control, his voice high, clear and true, his hands moving with certainty across the strings. The guests were enchanted; warm with sentiment already, they were overwhelming in their applause. His father, seeing another opportunity for goodwill, took him by the shoulders and kissed him. They applauded that too.

As he made his way out between the couches, smiling and showered with praise, Aristodemus leant towards him and said gravely: "A fellow artist.

That was quite splendid. I shall tell Thettalos what he has missed." It was better than all the applause and his father's praise. He went straight to share his triumph with his mother.

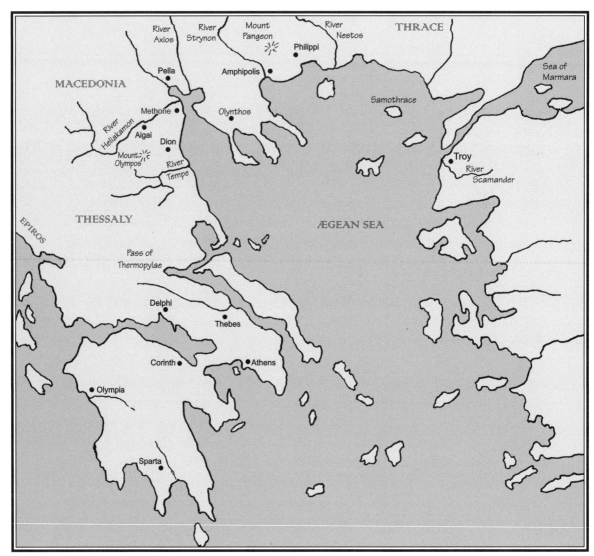

CITIES AND RIVERS OF GREECE IN THE TIME OF PHILIP

Chapter 12

Demosthenes

When he saw the secretaries and the messenger with his letter bag leave, Alexander ordered his dog to 'stay' and ran up to the king's book room. The door guard nodded him in. The man behind the great table littered with scrolls and writing tablets was Antipater, who stood up to greet him. Alexander noticed the courtesy. These two liked each other.

"He's growing at last," thought Antipater. The boy was still compact and sturdy rather than tall, but he had grown in the last year and the childish beauty of his face was being moulded into stronger features. His skin was reddened by the wind, he wore no cloak and his feet were bare on the winter stones. 'Leonidas is a hard man,' thought the general, 'but he's doing the boy some service. The heir to Macedon can't be soft.'

"What happens?" the boy asked, unconsciously echoing the question of the two-year-old long ago.

"The Athenians are ready for peace. They are sending an embassy to agree terms. Ten of them."

"Ten?"

"Ten!"

"Why so many?"

"They don't trust each other. They'll report on each other's conduct when they get back – so none of them will give away too much."

"Do we know any of them?"

"Aristodemus ..."

"The actor ! Good! Is Thettalos with him?"

"No... Aeschines – he's been trying to work up an alliance of the southern states against us but nothing came of it... Demosthenes – he's no friend of ours either. He calls your father a barbarian." He quoted from one of Demosthenes' speeches – "'*Who is Philip, is he not our enemy? Is he not a barbarian? Is he not anything that you like to call him?*'"

"Is Demosthenes a soldier?"

"No, he's one of their speech makers – the one who makes the most noise. I'm told the people listen to him. The others … Cimon, Philocrates …"

The two exchanged a look. Antipater saw that the boy knew these were Philip's agents, in his pay. He named the other five Athenians, but little was known of them, except that they were of the party that genuinely wanted peace.

"When do they come?"

"They're on their way, having a rough journey it seems. There were storms at sea, so they landed in Thessaly and asked Parmenion for safe conduct through our lines."

"Will Father be back in time?"

"If not they'll have to wait. But yes, he was at Philippi yesterday."

"I should like to hear them."

Antipater laughed. "*All* of them? Well, speak to your father. It's time you saw how these things are done." He paused, wondering whether to say, 'Be careful how you talk to them. These men are politicians, out to take advantage.' He knew the boy's readiness to offer friendship, his eagerness to talk, to question. But, wary of seeming to patronise him, he contented himself by saying, "Demosthenes has a nickname, I hear. They call him Snake-bite," and trusted Alexander to draw the right conclusions from this.

Demosthenes edged his mule into the ford, drawing up his legs from the splash of icy water. Aeschines plunged past him, his horse's hooves splattering him with mud. The wind attacked them viciously. Demosthenes huddled in a thick cloak, his hat brim pulled down over his ears. Aeschines rode upright, bare-headed, letting his cloak blow back from his shoulders. 'Acting the part of a soldier!' thought Demosthenes. 'Last night at supper he began every other sentence with the words – '*when we were on campaign*' – or that's how it seemed. But I doubt whether his martial airs impress these Macedonians.'

King Philip's herald rode in front of the party; behind came the guards provided by Parmenion. The roads were deep in mud. A harsh wind blew across the Thessalian plain from distant mountain ranges white with snow. They had left spring behind in Athens. There, poppies and anemones sprinkled the hills like drops of blood, the pale wings of cyclamen flickered in the shade of woods, and the scent of violets drifted above the flower sellers' fields. Here in the barbarian north it was winter still. At night wolves howled at the edges of the forests, and one morning the tracks of a bear were seen by the rubbish tip of an inn. In the glens the huge, half-wild dogs of herdsmen rushed upon them down the hillsides. The travellers were glad of their military escort.

At the end of their journey the Macedonian Boar awaited them in his den.

A sudden, sharp pain gripped Demosthenes in the stomach. He blamed the chill, or the fish they had eaten last night. He longed for a soothing bowl of curds, honey and wine; for a clean, comfortable bed; for a long night's sleep undisturbed by the snores of fellow travellers. He shifted his bony frame on the mule's bony spine, the damp cloth laid across its back affording little comfort. But, despite the miseries of the journey, his spirits lifted from time to time as he felt the excitement of an untried soldier going into battle. He was going to win for his city, not a humiliating peace, but the prize she most longed for. Her citizens would honour him. Schoolboys would learn his name with those of the great leaders of the past.

The prize was Amphipolis, that vital northern city, once an Athenian colony, commanding all the roads into Thrace and the only crossing place on the River Strymon, and guarding the coast along which the corn ships must pass from the east on their way to Athens. Philip had captured it in the second year of his reign, and agreed to return it to Athens in exchange for a city they held in Macedonia. He had not kept his word. But now, thought Demosthenes, the bully had over-reached himself. He was anxious for peace. Very well, let him pay for it with Amphipolis. Athens also needed peace, but Demoshenes would win it for her in a way that would make it seem a triumph. He would be his city's champion. These thoughts made his endurance of the trials of the journey seem heroic, and subdued his creeping fear of Macedon.

The travellers stopped for the night at yet another depressingly comfortless inn. The actors in the party lodged together, sharing the same supper tables and the same dormitory. Demosthenes attached himself to them. They were used to travel and knew how to obtain the best of whatever there was.

"Why does he hang around us all the time?" demanded Aeschines, as he and Aristodemus hung their sodden cloaks to dry beside a sullen brazier in the porch. "It must be perfectly plain that we don't care for his company."

"We must put up with it, I suppose," answered Aristodemus. "We can hardly say to his face that we don't want him. He's not feeling well tonight. That may keep him quiet. If he reminds me once more that it was thanks to *his* good offices that I was chosen for this embassy, and that *he* proposed I should be compensated from the public funds for my lost earnings, I may be in danger of tipping the soup bowl over his head."

"His face is enough to sour the wine. He can't laugh. He won't drink. And he uses that snake tongue to smear suspicion on anyone not present. According to him, half the members of this embassy are in Philip's pay. And when he's not attacking his colleagues, he's boasting of his achievements. Yet what has he done? You were the one who brought Philip's peace proposals to the assembly. It was I who went from state to state hoping to work up an alliance against him. Demosthenes talks."

"Persuade him – for his stomach's sake – to take unwatered wine tonight. It may improve him."

"Oh no! A man of his temperament? He will grow maudlin and end in tears. Still, that may be preferable to his boasting. And if he babbles in his cups we may learn something of interest. It would be amusing if the snake should turn and bite himself. How do you suppose he will do in Pella? You know Philip. Demosthenes declares he will wipe the floor with him."

"Philip may surprise him. He may surprise you all."

The following day they passed through the beautiful Vale of Tempe, the wooded hillsides clouding softly with the promise of breaking leaf, and crossed the river into Macedon. The peaks of Mount Olympos were hidden in cloud as they rode by its long blue walls. Demosthenes glanced that way with little interest. He felt some curiosity, certainly, in seeing the famous mountain, but it was long since any educated Athenian had believed that the gods built their palaces on its summit. Rain was still falling, but they had left the mud behind. A wide, paved road, wet and shining, led them into Dion, and the holy city of Zeus offered them a gracious welcome. It was well furnished with guest houses, provided for the important visitors who came to the festivals, and they found themselves lodged in real comfort for the first time on their journey, well-fed and tended by well-trained slaves.

"This is hardly as I imagined Macedon to be!" remarked one of those who had never travelled north before. Aristodemus smiled. Full of well-being, they reclined in the dining room of the largest guest house. The actors and senior members of the party were lodged there. The others had joined them to decide how to proceed on their first meeting with Philip. It was a fine night, the rain had drifted away, and a full moon shone in a nimbus of soft, furry light. Slaves lit the lamps, set out the cups and mixing bowls for the wine, and were dismissed.

Cimon blinked across at Demosthenes under spidery brows. "I've heard you say often that Macedon is a country from which it's impossible to buy even a decent slave," he said, "But these fellows have excellent manners, neat, quick and quiet – don't you agree?"

"They're not Macedonians." Demosthenes' harsh voice sawed across the pleasant murmurs of conversation. "Not Macedonians, nor Thracians. We should be on the look out for Greeks, for Olynthians, and arrange ransoms where we can. Do any of us believe that Philip released every Athenian he captured?"

Cimon hurried past this unwelcome suggestion. "But that is not the purpose for which we came, agreeable though it would be if such matters could be taken in hand during our embassy – where practicable, of course. No, the matter of first importance is to decide, now that we have crossed the borders of Macedon, what line we should take when we appear before Philip. There are ten of us, I assume that each man wishes to speak and that each has some idea of what he wishes to say. We may hold slightly different views among ourselves, but we must, I think, agree to a general policy. It will not do to contradict one another before the Macedonian, nor to repeat ourselves so that we tax his patience. The first thing, then, is to decide the order in which we shall speak and then the point at issue which each will deal with – or so it seems to me."

This useful information Cimon intended to pass on to Philip.

There was a wary silence. Certainly each man wished to speak, not only to influence the king, but to be able to report to those at home how well he had represented their interests. Each was jealous of his reputation; there was bound to be rivalry over the order of speaking.

Demosthenes had no hope of speaking first. He was neither the oldest, the wealthiest, the most aristocratic or the most experienced in diplomacy. But he saw that he could claim to be the youngest with every appearance of truth, and even of modesty. He would speak last – as a lawyer he knew the value of having the last word. The others would prepare the ground, he would bring all to a triumphant conclusion. His mouth twitched into the semblance of a smile. He proposed that they should speak in order of age. He did not speak again until they had all claimed their places and he found them looking at him.

"I am thirty six," he said. "I will speak last."

"The same age as Philip," said Aristodemus. "May it be a good omen."

They began to divide the matters for discussion between them – the causes of the war, previous treaties between Athens and Macedon, the treatment of Olynthos, the protection of Athenian colonies in eastern Thrace, the inclusion of their allies in the treaty. Again, Demosthenes kept silent until they had done and turned to him. Then he said he would deal with any matter they had omitted, including Athen's claim to Amphipolis. Cimon looked doubtful.

"Do so, by all means. The matter should be raised. But Philip will say that Amphipolis demanded independence from Athens fifteen years after the colony was founded, and that when the Macedonians attacked and she applied to Athens for help, none was forthcoming."

"No help was sent," said Demosthenes, "because Philip had made a secret agreement with our ambassadors to give up the city in exchange for Pydna. That was our first experience of his double dealing. He took Pydna himself a year later and denied any promise to hand over Amphipolis."

"I've heard of the secret agreement, of course," said Cimon, "but since it *was* secret, there's no evidence to prove it ever existed. Philip will claim right of conquest and I'm afraid he'll have the better of us."

Demosthenes drained his wine cup. It was gentle wine, smooth and delicate. He drank little as a rule, a mix that was hardly more than coloured water, which amused his rivals, but heavy wine disturbed his stomach and soon made his head spin. Tonight, however, he felt in command of himself and the world. He was surprised at how easily everything was falling his way. He did not usually regard himself as a lucky man.

"I promise you," he said, "that I will close Philip's mouth. I will leave him without a word to say for himself. He did not take the city from us in time of war; he took from the people of Amphipolis a city that did not belong to them. Therefore he cannot claim right of conquest. Philip renounced all claim to Amphipolis when he needed to secure our neutrality in the first year of his reign, just as his brother did before him and their father before that."

Aeschines leant over and refilled his cup. "No, no! Don't water it down. This can do you no harm. Ambrosia, fit for the gods. It must be imported. When did Philip's father take this stand? I've not heard of it before..."

Later, he helped Demosthenes to bed. His rival was somewhat unsteady on his feet and unusually garrulous. He was still boasting of the impact his speech would make. "The most powerful piece I've ever put together.

Look! Look, here it is!" He fumbled, thick-fingered, with the laces of a bag, and drew out several scrolls. Two rolled away across the floor and were retrieved by Aeschines. Kneeling, clasping the scrolls on his lap, Demosthenes tapped one against the others. "All here. Every scrap of evidence. Nothing omitted. Unanswerable! Every point hammered home. Nothing relevant to the case omitted. All hammered home. Not a word to say for himself – you'll see! I have it all by heart –"

He began scrambling the bundles together and pushing them back into the bag. "Let me help," said Aeschines. "You'll take them by storm, I can see. We shall all applaud. Now to bed. It's a long ride tomorrow."

Two handsome boys came swiftly across the palace forecourt. Both were barefoot and plainly dressed. Demosthenes quickened – Olynthian slaves? But Aristodemus broke off his conversation and turned, smiling: "There's Philip's son!"

The taller boy had cropped, curly hair; a proud, firm mouth and an air of cool assurance. He might have been a well-born Athenian. Demosthenes' eyes narrowed as he searched him for faults he could take pleasure in. The younger boy, with whom the prince was arguing, had the untamed look one might expect in the offspring of these wild highland lords: a mane of heavy, bright hair; an eager, demanding face, and an almost violent energy contained in his rapid walk and gestures.

But it was this younger boy who came straight to Aristodemus and took him by the hands. "Aristodemus! I'm glad to see you! Why haven't you brought Thettalos?"

"I am honoured to be here, Alexander. Thettalos would make an excellent ambassador but he is engaged to perform at Delphi. He sends you his greetings. May I present some of my colleagues? This is Aeschines, secretary to our council, who used to be an actor in my company."

"Used to be! Why are you no longer? If I had not to be a soldier, I would like to be an actor."

"I enjoyed my profession, son of Philip, but I have been called upon to serve my city in other ways, as a politician –"

(*'Ha!' thought Demosthenes, 'Let him speak the truth. He was no good as an actor.'*)

"– and as a soldier."

"A soldier!" The boy's face kindled. He could be seen swiftly to appraise Aeschines' appearance – an upright carriage, a vigorous, direct manner –

"Were you a spearman or a cavalry man?"

"A spearman."

(Demosthenes: 'He had no choice. He couldn't afford to maintain a war horse.')

"So is my father. Where have you seen action?"

('Fighting the rebels Philip encouraged. Let's see him wriggle out of that.')

Naming the latest battle in which he had distinguished himself, however, did not seem to disconcert either Aeschines or Philip's son. "I should like to hear more about it," said Alexander. "The reports my father received were conflicting. Perhaps we shall meet at supper." He turned to the other members of the delegation. When it came to Demosthenes' turn he felt anger at being presented formally to this boy who looked barely ten years old. A dark flush mounted to his cheeks, noted by the boy's wide grey eyes. It would have been a disturbingly searching look to receive from a grown man, let alone from a child half one's height. Demosthenes glowered, aware of his hands and arms dangling, his hands feeling too large, as he had not done since the first days of his public speaking. He lifted them to tug at the neck of his robe.

"Welcome to Macedon," said the boy coolly. "You have not been here before. Are we as you expected?"

He must know of the speeches, the virulent attacks upon Philip – "*the man is a bully, a barbarian, he is anything you like to call him.*" Aeschines had also made harsh speeches denouncing the aggressor, yet here he stood, beaming like a foolish, fond uncle upon Philip's precocious son. Well, Demosthenes was not going to pander to this princeling. The crease between his brows deepened, his fingers clenched tighter on his robe. He lied: "Exactly as I expected."

The boy's brows lifted slightly. Was it amusement that flickered across that vivid face? "Ah, barbarians! But perhaps your opinion will change." He turned slightly and slid his hand over the smooth haunch of a perfectly modelled marble horse, one of several fine statues that graced the courtyard.

The wealth of decoration lavished on the palace at Pella had filled Demosthenes with bile. He had hoped to find it vulgar, but it was vigorous and superb. The pediments and friezes were cleanly carved and richly coloured. The paintings in the public rooms were as fine as the famous painted porticoes in Athens. In every room the heroes of Greece wrestled with their fate, aided by gods and goddesses. The colours of these masterpieces glowed; the great figures leapt and rode and ran and overcame monsters and fought the sea with an energy that left one breathless just from looking. Aeschines declared, walking beside a chariot race depicted along the wall of a corridor, that he could hear the pounding hooves and almost felt compelled to run alongside. Aristodemus, watching three large, naked young men, as splendid as the painted heroes, leaping for a ball in the stable yard, sighed and said that Macedon made one feel old.

Paintings and mosaics of the god Dionysos and his ecstatic followers were everywhere. It was said that the queen of Macedon worshipped the god extravagantly. Aristodemus had once been presented to her after a performance and said that her conversation was graceful and well-informed; none of the other ambassadors had seen her, but they had heard tales of her snake-worshipping and witch-craft, and cast hopeful glances towards the inner court whenever they passed it. The rose trees were bare now, and the fountains dry, and all they saw was the Wise Woman, more than ever like a mouse in a furred cloak, peering back at them

Meanwhile, Demosthenes turned his eyes from the sculpted horse and allowed himself an open sneer. Very much put out by his companion's lack of courtesy, Aristodemus hurried on to the remaining introductions. They were interrupted by an elderly Macedonian who appeared among a pack of playful young dogs. "Achilles! Where have you been? I've been ready since dawn."

Alexander apologised while the dogs leapt round him with swaying tails, uttering impatient little yelps. "I'm ready now. Have you met the ambassadors from Athens? You remember Aristodemus, he —" He broke off, staring at Demosthenes, who was pressed against a pillar, holding back from the questing nose of a panting dog. "Do you not like dogs?" An incredulous note, restrained by courtesy, crept into his voice. "You're not *afraid* of him, are you? Here, Warrior, here! Phoenix's dogs are very well behaved, even the young ones." He checked the dog again, took leave of the visitors, and went off with the elderly man, linking arms with his fair companion, who had not spoken except to the animals, but who had laughed silently when Demosthenes drew back from the thrusting hound. He reminded Demosthenes of the handsome, confident boys who had mocked him when he was a spindly youth and given him a vulgar nickname.

Ever since he had crossed the borders of Macedon, there had lurked in his mind the tale told in Athens that Euripedes, their great poet, had perished in his old age at the court of the Macedonian king, savaged to death by a Companion's pack of dogs. The fierce shepherd dogs encountered on their journey north had reinforced his fear. He twitched nervously at any sound resembling a whine or a growl, or a scrabble of claws on the pebbled floor behind him. The confidence with which he had set out from Athens, the certainty of triumph he had anticipated at Dion, were ebbing away from him among the chilly splendours of this vast, alien palace. Why had he come to this hard, mocking northern land? Might he not have done better to have stayed at home, rejected the peace, continued to denounce Philip? No, it was the bitter truth that Athens had no allies who would support her. If she fought on she would fight alone. The times were past when her citizens would go out willingly to fight, and there was no money in the treasury to hire troops. Philip, if rejected, would bring his armies south. Athens had stopped him once before at Thermopylae, but it had cost her half a year's revenue to do so. There were states at war in the south ready to invite Philip to come and settle their quarrels. It was this that gave urgency to their embassy. Athens needed the peace.

But she should not be humiliated. The peace could not be an admission of failure. From it they must snatch a triumph, the recovery of Amphipolis. This was what he had understood and the others had not. Aeschines had smiled when the dog came for him. He had ostentatiously stepped forward and fondled it after the boy called it to heel. Let him smile. Demosthenes' turn would come.

What had the older man called the boy? Achilles. Was that how he liked to see himself – *'brilliant Achilles, beloved of Zeus?'* Let him beware. The gods dealt severely with men, or boys, who presumed on good fortune. He imagined Philip in chains, and the boy put up for sale in the market place.

Chapter 13

The Embassy

"Well, you've met them, I hear," said Philip. "What do you think of them? Which of them can be bought?"

Alexander's lips shut in an angry line. Philip gave a bark of laughter, his hard eye mocked. "Don't be so delicate, boy. I've two agents among them, as you must know. You're not a fool. Well then, of the others, who can be won over? Who is susceptible to charm? We need friends in Athens. You've done well, I gather. Aristodemus is quite fulsome in his admiration of you."

"I like Aristodemus."

"You like his performances. He's an actor, not a politician. Takes a great many words to say nothing. But very gracious and does no harm. The others?"

"Aeschines has been a soldier. He was commended for bravery at the battle of Tamynae. I asked him to give us a first hand account."

"I'd like to hear it. He's made some hot speeches against us. Can he be won over?"

"He smiled a lot. He despises Demosthenes."

"Ha, fierce little Demosthenes. He carries weight with the people, I hear. What did you make of him?"

"He was afraid of the dogs. It angers him that we're better than he supposed."

"You will come in during supper," said Philip, "and entertain them. Leonidas has spoken to your music master. He tells me you have several pieces well prepared. This time I want you to debate as well." He turned to Leonidas, who had accompanied the prince to report on his progress, the king having just returned from Thrace. "He won't shame me, I take it?"

"He has learnt to speak in public, to set out an argument. He is quite proficient."

"Good. Choose an opponent who'll play up to him, feed him the right lines."

Alexander flushed. "I'd like Hephaistion, son of Amyntas," he said. "We often dispute together. But he won't play up to me. When you wrestle do you want your opponent to give way to you, offer you the best holds? Does that make for a good match, Father?"

Leonidas made the sound of exasperation that seemed to come from him with every second breath. "Alexander, how often must you be told not to –"

Kinder laughter brightened the king's good eye as he waved the rebuke aside. "You'd better know what you're about. These are Athenians you have to impress. The world's talkers. Show them what a Macedonian boy can do. A great man died last year in Athens. He said there would never be a truly just society until kings became philosophers and philosophers kings. Discuss with your friend the nature of a just man in a just society. But remember, we'll have spent the day listening to tedious speeches. Make it lively and don't go on too long."

The sun, slanting between the columns of the portico, laid pale stripes across the pebbled patterns on the floor. One shaft reached to the foot of a massive, marble throne, carved and gilded and filled with shadow. Empty, it seemed to breathe power, power invested in one man. The eyes of the ambassadors were drawn to it in unwilling fascination.

Announced by a herald, the man himself approached. It was the first time some of them had seen him. As Alexander had once said, he seemed bigger than he was. He walked, limping slightly, along the shaft of sunlight, and took the seat of majesty. When Demosthenes had first seen Philip's head upon a silver coin, he had said it was a natural conceit for any monarch to portray himself as Zeus the Thunderer. Now he was annoyed to discover that the likeness was a true one. Philip wore white and purple, a gilded diadem on his dark head. He greeted the Athenians in Greek with the barest trace of a northern accent, and invited them to sit.

The Companions who accompanied him ranged themselves in two groups at either side of the room. The generals wore parade uniform. The civilian lords were resplendent in court dress: tunics and cloaks of amber, purple, blue; knee-length boots of dyed leather, embroidered and fringed; gold arm-rings and heavy, intricate brooches and finger rings. The Athenians wore plain robes: long tunics, a length of blue or white cloth draped round them and over one shoulder – or both if the wearer felt the cold. Not one of them wore any ornament. To the Macedonians they looked like poor, plain schoolmasters, to the Athenians their hosts appeared as over-dressed pirates, gaudy in their loot.

The stern-faced man who came in with the prince, though, was obviously his tutor, and severely dressed. His charge might still be taken for a slave boy but for the way his keen gaze searched the delegate's faces. Many of them felt resentment at the presence and scrutiny of this child. Philip's good eye also flicked shrewdly along the line of speakers. He signed to the herald, who announced the first.

Demosthenes had stilled his griping stomach. He waited with an unusual sense of calm. It was all unreal. Briefly, he reflected that events never matched one's expectation of them. Philip was not the king he had imagined. He sat easily in his deep throne, attentive to each speaker, thanking each one graciously when he had done. Demosthenes listened fitfully – he had promised to pick up and deal with any points the others overlooked, but he knew he would not make much show at this; he relied upon his prepared speech and Philip's response to it to eclipse everything else. The presence of the boy irritated him. He tried to keep his glance from moving in that direction.

The eighth speaker was called by the herald. The king gave away nothing as he listened. How little they knew this man! He could take his decisions in secret, no-one knew his intentions. In Athens all was public. The cold clutched again at Demosthenes' stomach. Whatever they said to Philip he could decide – instantly – what action to take. There was no-one he need consult. He could summon armies, raise taxes, wage war, make peace at will. What Philip replied to them they must report back to the assembly, six thousand or more citizens must decide how and when to act upon it. It was hard to conceive of so much absolute power in one head, one hand.

And suddenly, now, another realisation came to him. Never before had he practised his art upon one man. He saw the present speaker addressing the king across a space the width of a shop counter. When he had tirelessly rehearsed his speech in his mind during those cold, painful rides, those restless flea-bitten nights, he had envisaged – he knew it now – the platform on the hill in Athens, the vast crowd of faces looking down. His gestures had been matched to them, his voice to the open air, his force to the factions who would heckle or cheer. Panic throbbing in his chest, he began revising the manner of his opening paragraph, adjusting his style to this one room, this one listener. What would serve? Could he simply modify his voice, limit his gestures? He had never displayed any charm in personal conversation. He decided simply to be grave and moderate in manner – but then how would he drive home the dramatic climax of his speech? If he did so in the forceful manner he had planned, would he now appear to be simply shouting in Philip's face?

While he wrestled with these thoughts, he forgot to listen at all. Aeschines had been called. His own time was almost upon him. With bitter envy he watched his rival's easy stride forward, his graceful stance, and heard the rich voice perfectly modulated to the occasion. At first, when Aeschines began to talk of former relationships between Athenian statesmen and the royal house of Macedon, and about past treaties, he was not concerned, even when Amphipolis was mentioned. This was paving the way for him. But it was not a passing reference. Aeschines took up the whole question of Athens' historical claim to the territory of Amphipolis, he dealt with it at length, he left out nothing, even the legend that the land had been the dowry of an Athenian queen in ancient times. Fear and fury washed through Demosthenes in a scalding flood. He felt his skin burn and freeze and burn again. It was unreal, as in a dream, a nightmare. He would wake and find it was not so. But the melodious voice went on. And a new fury seized him. Aeschines had stolen the subject of his speech but he had not Demosthenes' purpose or skill. It was a mere shopping list of grievances, hastily conned and beautifully spoken. Even the order was lost. Demosthenes could have wept for his great climax, the compelling sweep of his final declamation, when Philip would see that he had been led to the point where no treaty could be signed that did not include Amphipolis. Now a less skilful huntsman had set up loose nets from which Philip could escape.

It was all lost. How could he begin again, repeating all that Aeschines had just said, albeit differently? And now a greater fear took possession of him. Of what would he speak? There must be matters still untouched, but he had scarcely listened, deep in his own thoughts. In any case, he could never improvise.

The herald called his name. Sleep-walking, he moved forward. Philip tilted his head a little, wary, as before a wrestling bout, assessing this thin, white-faced man who led the opposition to him. He had heard that Demosthenes had promised to 'stop his mouth.' But his adversary did not come out fighting. He did not even meet his eye. Demosthenes raised a hand that trembled slightly and passed it across the side of his head, his customary opening gesture. He was not sure how to pitch his voice, if he began too high they would all laugh – inwardly now, openly later.

He opened his mouth and began; the first paragraph of his speech was general and would serve; he willed the gods to send him inspiration to follow. His voice was too low, indistinct. Philip leant forward, surprised, to catch the mumble. For the first time in years Demosthenes' tongue tangled with the syllables, bringing back the stammer he had overcome when he first began public speaking. Trying to master his confusion and force his lips to frame words distinctly, he forgot the words.

Philip, astonished and disappointed, was also compassionate. Sweat dampened the man's brow, his bony shoulder gave a nervous twitch. The fierce eyes glared in desperation, misery, fury, helplessness. Philip reassured him. "Take your time. This is not the theatre. You have had to wait too long. We can wait while you collect your thoughts." He motioned to one of the Pages in attendance, made a drinking gesture. The boy brought a cup of water. Demosthenes swallowed, hearing the murmur of the Athenians behind him, seeing from the corner of his eye movement and whispering among the Companions, the prince speaking into his tutor's ear. "Now!" said Philip heartily. "That's better. Just a momentary lapse. Don't let it put you off. Begin again."

Demosthenes managed half a dozen words, then his jaw became rigid. He tried to force his lips, his tongue to move – "cl...cl...cl..." His mouth was empty; the stammer had returned. His mind was empty, too. He made a hopeless gesture with his hands and returned to his seat. There was a moment of complete silence. Then the herald's voice checked a rising hum of comment. Philip thanked the ambassadors, invited them to rest and be refreshed. In the afternoon he would give them his answers.

The delegates withdrew to an anteroom where food and wine were served. Very little was said until the servants left, and then Demosthenes lashed out at Aeschines with all his pent-up fury. In clumsy ignorance, in spite, in rivalry, he had thrown away any chance there might have been for Athens to achieve an honourable peace, to regain the best of her northern possessions, to reassure her allies. Aeschines, in polite bewilderment, as though mystified, asked whatever could he mean? He thought it had been agreed that they should make Amphipolis one of their conditions for an alliance.

"And what chance is there of that now?" demanded Demosthenes. "Philip will laugh. Have you forgotten the state of Athens, the poverty of the treasury, the hunger of the people for peace? Did you think of Athens when you planned this, when you made this show of yourself, blabbing on and on in that fruity voice and goading Philip with every word into defying you rather than winning him over? Don't you know his reputation for being stubborn when defied? I would have led him into the net. We must have this treaty, we all know that, however reluctant we may be to appease the King of Macedon, but we could have had it without shame. Now Philip will be more inclined than ever to take what he wants, seeing that he can get away with robbing us of our own."

Aeschines turned to the other delegates. "Do you understand what he is talking about? I do not." He shrugged his shoulders and shook his head. "I'm afraid you've not been well..."

Demosthenes thought, 'He's in Philip's pay. Why didn't I think of that before? He's been offered bribes. Philip knew the greatest threat came from me. Traitor! I'll be revenged. Athens will be revenged.'

King Philip was an accomplished speaker, he had a natural gift for words and a ready wit, and he had been primed by Cimon and Philocrates. His reply to the ambassadors was courteous and very much to the point. He answered each man in turn, he seemed to have forgotten nothing that anyone had said, and dealt in order with every point that had been made. The Athenians were impressed, they admired his force and brevity, his command of language. Having taken their measure, he put out all his charm; each ambassador felt that his contribution had been properly valued. Aeschines received a comprehensive and flattering reply to his speech, unaware that Philip and Parmenion had laughed over it during the interval. "Amphipolis? That's ancient history! Where have these men been for the last ten years!" But the king had nothing to say to Demosthenes, judging it best to leave him to lick his wounds. He then complemented the ambassadors on the moderation and clarity with which they had presented their case, and expressed the hope that if they conveyed his answers with the same skill to their people in Athens, a lasting and satisfactory peace between them might be achieved. He proposed that, their work being done, they gratify him by attending a dinner in their honour; he looked forward to the pleasure of their company and the opportunity to further friendship between them.

Philip raised his cup to pledge his guests. Custom demanded that the Athenians reply. There was a challenging glint in the king's eye: this was the third round of such pledges and the meal was scarcely underway.

Philip II

Alexander

The Macedonian lords downed their cups and watched their guests in the manner of lions circling a cattle herd preparing for a kill. Philip's laughter gleamed in his dark beard. Let the southerners show what they were made of; they had ducked the fighting, made a poor showing as speakers – now let them see whether they could match the despised northerners in their cups.

Aeschines replied for the Athenians. Philip had been at work on Aeschines, laughing with him, and showing a flattering interest in his family and career. Aeschines had been encouraged to speak of his uncle and his brother, both army commanders, of his own distinguished service as a young cadet, and of the wreath of honour awarded to him by his officers for his bravery on the field of Tamynae.

Alexander came in with Hephaistion in time to hear the end of this tale, and when he discovered what they were talking about, ran to the foot of his father's couch and slid on to it, his eyes fixed on Aeschines' face, his mouth already half open to form his first question. Leonidas, whom Philip was careful to set at a good distance from himself, could only hiss and frown, but Philip nodded to his son indulgently. He did not mind the boy showing off a little before the southerners.

Alexander glowed in the light of the lamps, his mane of hair garlanded with gold leaves, a deep flush from the heat and pleasure showing brilliantly through his pale skin. Aeschines, who had sons of his own, answered his questions with charming courtesy. Demosthenes, watching them, felt a surge of hatred so intense that he longed for a day when he could destroy them both.

Their talk turned to the theatre. Aeschines was asking Alexander which plays he had seen. When he mentioned *The Frogs* Aeschines exclaimed, "Then you have seen the friend of Demosthenes here, Satyrus, in one of his most famous roles. Demosthenes does not act himself, but he enjoys the company of actors – do you not, my friend? He finds them helpful to his profession, since we all study the art of speaking to an audience."

Alexander glanced wonderingly at Demosthenes, whose couch was below a wall painting of Herakles bringing the three-headed dog of the Underworld to his royal master, who cowered in fear inside a huge earthenware pot. Some remembrance caused a spark of laughter to light his face but it was quickly extinguished.

"Did you enjoy *The Frogs*?" asked Aeschines. "Demosthenes' friend would be interested to hear your opinion of his performance."

"I expect not," said Alexander. "I saw him at supper after the plays and everyone was telling him how good it was, so he knows. I was surprised that they made fun of the gods, but I laughed, although it was silly. It was so silly that we couldn't help laughing in the end."

"What was silly?"

"The contest between the poets. I'd have chosen Euripedes for the best, because his plays make people think, Lysimachus says, and *The Trojan Women* made me think. But the other man kept shouting out *'lost his oil can!'* when Euripedes was reciting and that spoilt his chances. It was cheating and he shouldn't have won, but, as I say, we couldn't help laughing."

"Lost his oil can?" repeated Aeschines with satisfaction. "It's curious, isn't it, how a catch phrase such as that will take hold of an audience? Why do you think it has that effect, Demosthenes?"

To their mild surprise, the king and prince saw Demosthenes' face darkly flushed, his scowl pronounced. He did not answer, but turned to lean on his other arm and wiped his nose. He was a strange man! His one cup of wine stood untouched on the table beside him. He had not lifted it to salute the king when Aeschines pledged him and neither had he put on the festal wreath a Page had brought him. Both actions were an insult to his host. The Athenians did not admire this defiance. They were embarrassed by it. Demosthenes enjoyed their discomfiture. He was planning a speech to the Assembly in his head: 'When others drank with Philip and flattered him, I did not... ....' Did the boy know that the catch phrase *lost his oil can* had been shouted at him by the crowds when he first began public speaking and could not control his stammer? Had they colluded together to mock him, Alexander and Aeschines? They were smiling at each other.

Philip, judging that his son had held court for long enough, asked him to sing for the pleasure of their guests, and Hephaistion slid down from his father's couch to join in. Their performance was generously applauded, although the Companions might have preferred a more robust ballad to the ode which the boys' music master had chosen to please the Athenians. The song was followed by a recitation which Alexander thought appropriate to the occasion. It came from *The Iliad* and told how the goddess Athena inspired a young Greek warrior, Diomedes:

"The grey-eyed goddess made straight for Diomedes
and found the prince standing by his horses and chariot,
cooling the wound a Trojan arrow had made in his shoulder.

Sweat had made it smart under the broad strap of his shield.
He held up the strap and wiped away the dark clots of blood."

Athena encouraged Diomedes to attack Ares, the war god, who was helping the Trojans, telling him not to be afraid, she would stand by him, taking the place of his charioteer.

"So she herself, the angry goddess, stepped into the chariot,
beside brilliant Diomedes, and the oaken axle groaned aloud
under the weight of a dread goddess and a mighty warrior."

Athena made straight for Ares, caught the spear he flung at Diomedes, and pushed it harmlessly away across the front of the chariot. When Diomedes cast his bronze spear, Athena leant upon the weapon and drove it into the belly of the war god, between the leather flaps of his armour.

"Then Ares the brazen bellowed with a sound as great
as nine or ten thousand men might make in battle,
when they roar with the fury of the war god.
And as a column of darkness rises from the clouds,
when, after a day of heat, a whirlwind springs up,
so Diomedes saw Ares the brazen go up through the clouds
into the wide expanse of heaven."

Having driven off the war god with Athena's help, Diomedes met an ally of the Trojans, Glaucus, prince of Lycia, on the field of battle.

"Now Glaucus and Diomedes came together
in a space between the two armies, eager to do battle.
The first to challenge the other was Diomedes of the loud war-cry.
'Tell me who you are, good friend, if you are a mortal man.
Never before have I seen you among the warriors.
Yet now you stride out in front of all the others,
full of courage, daring to stand up to my far-shadowing spear.'"

Glaucus gave his name and an account of his family, and Diomedes discovered that their grand-fathers had been guest –friends.

"He spoke, and Diomedes of the loud war-cry was gladdened,
he drove his spear deep into the bountiful earth and offered him
gentle words of friendship. 'Now, since from far-off times,
your family have been guest-friends of my people,
I will be your friend and host in the heart of Argos,
and you will be mine when I come to your country.
So let us avoid each other's spears, even in the thick of the fighting.
There are plenty of the Trojans and their allies for me to kill,

those whom the god sends me, or those my swift feet can overtake,
and there are many Greeks for you to slaughter if you can do it.
But let us exchange our armour so that others may know
that we declare ourselves to be friends from our fathers' days.'"

As a complement to the visitors from Athena's city, celebrating the rout of the war god and the sealing of a pact of friendship, the piece could hardly have been better chosen.

Aristodemus and Aeschines certainly appreciated it. Alexander's recitation had been faultless and charged with feeling; Hephaistion had played the lyre and recited the speeches of Glaucus. At the end they clasped each other's shoulders and exchanged the wreaths on their heads in token of the armour exchanged by the warriors.

Philip wondered why he felt so irritated. Although he had not asked for a recitation, it was well thought of and well done and seemed to have pleased his guests. It should have pleased him. But when Alexander stood under the flaring lamps and lifted up his head to watch the war god ascending like a whirlwind and his voice rang with the thrill of victory, Philip had felt something bite like a snake into his heart. This fiercely shining child became suddenly a stranger, but a stranger with something remembered about his face that provoked such pain and dislike that Philip was bewildered. Was he jealous of his own son? It came to him later where he had seen that rapt, transfigured face before – under the flaring torches in the hall of Samothrace. Had he loved her once? She was now a stranger to him, a dangerous stranger. Were the whispers true – had she cursed his big, beautiful Arridaios? Had she cursed his seed, so that his wives bore him only daughters? She had had this boy until he was seven. He wondered how successful the hard regime of Leonidas had been in driving out her influence. Was this boy he had fathered his son or hers?

Alexander and Hephaistion were half way through their debate by the time he came to himself. Their idea of the qualities of a just man owed more to Achilles and Diomedes than to any philosopher. They praised heroic friendship, generous guest-giving, courtesy to the old, a fierce regard for honour and the unceasing conquest of fear. "For it is a lovely thing," cried Alexander in conclusion, his voice ringing round the hall, "it is a lovely thing to live with courage, and" – quoting Achilles – "to die leaving an everlasting fame!"

The words hung in the silence for a moment, as the crest of a wave hangs before it breaks, then the applause came like the sudden rush of

water and swirled around them. Flushed and brilliant, Alexander turned
to his father, to share with him the splendour of the thought, the mystery
they lived by and shared with their Companions in the hall .

Philip, knowing his anger unjust, had to force his lips to move. He held
out their gifts, knives with silver handles and scarlet leather sheaths.
"The singers' fee. Thank you on behalf of our guests. You may go." Taking
the knife without feeling it touch his hand, Alexander stood, the colour
draining away under his white skin, his eyes, pale and wide, searching
his father's face. It told him nothing; it was the face of a king who had
dismissed a servant who had dis-satisfied him. Conscious only that he must
not cry in public for the spoiling of something splendid, Alexander executed
a curious, stiff little bow of thanks and walked from the room, unaware of
the praise and pleasantries that the diners tossed to him as he passed. He
had hold of Hephaistion's hand and, when he let go, the marks of his nails
left four red crescents across its palm.

Chapter 14

'The Boar Grunted and the Piglet Squealed.'

"So," said Satyrus, "you came face to face with your barbarian. What did you think of him? Aeschines was impressed, I hear"

"The boar grunted and the piglet squealed," said Demosthenes. "Neither impressed me."

"Ah, you met the beautiful Alexander, the new Achilles. A clever little brat, isn't he? Didn't he charm you either?"

Demosthenes sneered. "His father would have done better to have kept him out of sight with his daughters. Philip can sire only girls it seems, apart from one imbecile. Macedon will be torn apart again as soon as Philip falls."

"So the Macedonians seemed less formidable in the flesh than by report. And you did not succumb to Philip's generosity? I hear that his guest-gifts, as usual, were extravagant."

"The others flattered and crawled to him and held out open hands. I did not. I was thwarted in my purpose; I would have made Amphipolis a condition of this treaty if it hadn't been for that traitor Aeschines. He's in the Macedonian's pay. I'm sure of it. Vain fool! His time will come. I can wait. But now we must have peace, before Philip marches south to force the pass, and I shall do all I can to achieve it."

During the journey back to Athens from Pella, Demosthenes had partly restored his position among the delegates. He had been pleasant to them all, hinting at favours he might do for some of them. He had referred to his breakdown before Philip with forced humour and had even excused and praised Aeschines' failed attempt to press the claim to Amphipolis.

"Indeed, I understand how it came about," he said one night over supper. "Your first experience as a diplomat abroad – over-enthusiasm – your tongue ran away with you. Meaning only to introduce the subject, in your anxiety to do your best for Athens, and the stress of unusual circumstances, before you knew it you had covered everything and left me nothing to say. It did not have the effect you – we – desired. Philip made short work of your arguments, nevertheless you put our case squarely before him. You won't have disappointed those who chose you for this embassy. It was an excellent speech. I have nothing but praise for it, although it left me speech-*less*!" He raised his cup of watered wine. "Drink to Aeschines, friends, the master-thief. This man can steal the words out of your mouth, so watch him! I shall expect compensation, Aeschines. You shall stand me a dinner in Athens." The others smiled and drank uncertainly, eyeing Aeschines, but he accepted the pledge with a smile on his mouth if not in his eyes. Demosthenes deserved his name of snake-tongue.

Later, when they were easy with wine, he led them to give their opinions of Philip, asking if they did not think him a remarkable man? Those who had not met the king before, expecting a brute, had been so charmed by him that they were lavish in their praise. Cimon even went so far as to call him loveable! "Well!" said Demosthenes, shading his eyes by rubbing a hand across his forehead, "He has certainly won you over. According to you, the Macedonian is pleasant and easy to deal with, has a complete grasp of affairs, is a master of wit and eloquence, great company at a party, a generous host – and so on and so forth. Your tongues are ready enough to praise him here, privately amongst ourselves, but will you dare to say as much to the Athenians?"

"Why not?" demanded Aeschines. "Why not speak as we find?"

"Because, my dear Aeschines, when you find yourself on your feet before the people your courage will fail and you will tell them what you know they hope to hear – that Philip is a lout and a fool." The delegates protested. They declared that they could see no reason for concealing the favourable impression that Philip had made upon them. Surely this would help to secure the people's support for their peace treaty? What had they to fear?

"I shall be surprised," said Demosthenes, "if you all keep to your resolve. And if you fail, Aeschines, you shall buy me another dinner."

It seemed good-humoured enough and harmless. When each of the delegates rose to speak before the Athenian assembly, to report upon their mission, it also seemed sensible to convince the people that they were making a treaty with a man they could respect, a man who had qualities and values comparable to their own, and not some northern savage. So they spoke at length of the charm of Philip's personality, his wit and generosity, his 'Greekness' and his admiration for Athens. They also dealt fully with the contents of their own speeches and Philip's response to them. Aeschines, in particular, could not resist describing in detail his demand for Amphipolis and the flattering attention paid to him by the king. By the time nine speakers had had their say, the Athenians were finding the stone seats hard, the wind cold and their ambassadors the most tedious set of wind-bags it had ever been their misfortune to listen to through a long morning.

When Demosthenes stood up their interest revived a little. He could usually be relied upon for a sharp attack on someone. He passed a hand across his forehead in a weary gesture which expressed their own boredom. "All this," he said, "is mere gossip and a waste of our time. I am astonished at the behaviour of my fellow ambassadors. There is only one matter we need to put before you, men of Athens. Herald, please read the commission with which we were sent to Macedon." This was done. "Those," said Demosthenes, "were our instructions. Now," – to the herald – "please read Philip's letter." This was done also.

"There," said Demosthenes, "is Philip's reply. That is all it is necessary for me to say or you to hear. Now you have to consider his proposals."

He stepped down. A wave of laughter and applause greeted this admirable brevity. As it died away, Demosthenes stepped back onto the platform adding with a flourish, "And if you want to hear my impressions of Philip, I will tell you. My fellow ambassadors admire him greatly, it seems. I do not. Is he handsome? In my opinion, Aristodemus is better-looking. Can he hold his wine? Our Philocrates can hold more. Has he a good memory? So have many others. Aeschines is impressed by his eloquence, but take off Philip's purple robe and hang it round another man's shoulders and I dare say Aeschines would be just as impressed by him."

Waiting until the laughter subsided, ignoring the impotent fury of his rivals, Demosthenes then proposed that safe conduct be granted to Philip's herald and the ambassadors who were coming to witness the oath-taking, and that the delegates be rewarded for their services by a public dinner.

The Assembly accepted the terms of the treaty, and in early summer, in the month of Daisios, the ambassadors returned to Macedon for the peace to be sealed by sacred oaths. This time the land was smiling – crops were growing tall on the rich farmlands and little dark red poppies bloomed by the roadsides.

They found Pella throbbing like a nest of wasps. Ambassadors from all the warring southern states were there. But Philip was not. He was fighting Thracians in the north, where he had captured Kersbleptes' treasury and made him his vassal.

Chapter 15

Through the Gates

"Is he a sailor?" asked Alexander of the man he had passed leaving his father's room just as he entered it.

"What makes you think so?" Philip was lacing on his riding boot, his foot propped on a stool. The room was dim in the grey pre-dawn light, a night-lamp still burning.

"He walks as though he had a pitching deck under him. I've noticed it before with sailors. And his clothes smelt of tar and the sea."

"Ha!" Philip's good eye glinted approval. He straightened up. "Sailors are like actors or your mother's cloth merchants. They come and go and keep their eyes and ears open. Sometimes they are worth their hire."

"Was this one worth it?"

Leonidas would have sharply checked such bold questioning. Philip, in a good mood, enjoyed it. But there were Pages choosing weapons and rubbing oil into leathers in the adjoining room, with the door open. He put a hand on his son's shoulder and guided him away, towards the window. "How much do you remember of the Sacred War?"

"The Phokians occupied the temple at Delphi and used the god's treasure to pay their troops. You defeated them in Thessaly when I was four. You fought for the god!" In spite of an attempt to keep his voice cool, it was charged with some of the wonder of that day when he rode on his father's war-horse before the cheering crowds, while the god thundered overhead. His eyes shone. An emotional response always irritated Philip, reminding him of the boy's mother. Alexander responded to his father's quick frown. His chin lifted. "The Athenians stopped you at Thermopylae."

Philip grinned again, good-humour restored. "They wouldn't have stopped *you,* I suppose."

"There is a way over the mountains. The Persians found it. A goat-herd showed them." And he thought, 'I would have found it.'

"Yes," said Philip, still unruffled, "we shall see great things when you're a general. But learn the value of patience, too, Alexander. I could have stormed the pass – at some cost – and settled the business of the south then – maybe. Instead I've waited six years while the southerners have exhausted themselves. Now they are ready for a settlement and some of them may even be grateful for Philip of Macedon to handle their affairs. The Phokians have run out of temple gold to pay their troops. Their commander is a desperate man, but he still holds the pass – it's all he has left to bargain with and when the time comes he'll sell it to me."

"For what? For gold? How do you know? That sailor, he comes from him?"

Philip nodded. "For safe conduct for himself and his men."

"But where will they go?"

"Wherever they can hire out their swords."

"The god will hunt them down. They robbed his temple."

"Maybe, but the Athenians have used their temple treasures in time of war. The Phokians had to defend themselves against the Thebans, they raised an army and the army had to be paid.Then the Phokians tasted power and wanted more of it. Well, they've had their moment and it's over. I shan't be hard on them. I'll go in as the champion of the god and gratify the Thessalanians by finishing off their old enemy, but I'll save them from complete destruction."

What mattered to Philip was that he would gain entry to central and southern Greece, it would be his influence that decided the terms of peace between the warring states. He would be a power in the south. The boy appreciated this.

"They're all here," he said, wondering, "ambassadors from the Phokians, Thebans, Thessalians, all the southern states as well as the Athenians. Did you –?"

"I summoned them," said Philip, as though this was nothing extraordinary, "to a peace conference."

"The Athenians were furious. It took them by surprise. And that you were away, still campaigning in Thrace when they arrived, ready for you to swear the Peace. Aeschines told me. Demosthenes wanted to hire a ship and sail east to catch up with you."

Philip threw back his head with a roar of laughter, that caused the Pages in the ante-room to glance up. "I wish he might have tried it. And with the summer winds blowing!"

"The others refused of course. They were all quarrelling with each other."

"Well," said Philip, "they've cooled their heads as well as their heels by now. I shall hear them, all of them, over the next two days. The Thebans, the Spartans, Boetians, Thessalanians. They will all be encouraged to hope for the best."

"And then?"

Philip gave him a sudden hard look. "This is for you. Not for Ptolemy or this boy who is always with you –" He did not say – or your mother, since he had no wish for a quarrel – it would be understood. "Friendship is one thing – responsibility another."

Alexander looked steadily at him. "Hephaistion," he began –

They were interrupted by the two Pages coming into the room. The elder, a tall, handsome boy from the royal family of Orestis, had come to the age when he should leave the king's personal service and join the Bodyguard or the Companions. But he had been the king's favourite for some time, and Philip was reluctant to lose him. He aroused some resentment in the other Pages. The younger boy had not long come to court, from another highland kingdom, a kinsman of Attalus, one of Philip's most able and popular commanders. Both were called Pausanias, and that caused friction between them.

King Philip abandoned the diplomatic instruction of his son. "Well," he said, clapping the older Pausanias on the shoulder, "they've waited some time for me, these ambassadors, they can cool their tempers and work on their speeches for another morning, while I breathe some Macedonian air. Today is for Artemis and Apollo."

He turned to Alexander. "We're deer hunting in the woods by Loudias. You can come along to carry weapons. Bring your own javelin, you might get a chance to use it. The fawns are fast but tire quickly. You'll need a good horse. But remember you're there in the first place to serve, not to hunt on your own account. Let me see discipline. Go with Pausanias," he nodded at the younger Page, "and follow his lead."

Alexander, who had supposed, when he was summoned to attend his father in the dark before dawn, that he was to spend the day listening to the ambassadors' speeches, had felt a leap of joyful expectation when he saw the king in hunting dress. His hopes now realised, he would have accepted any conditions – "Yes, Father!" – and grinned hopefully at the younger Page, who did not look as though he would be overbearing. He was a dark-haired boy with deep blue eyes, whose hawk-like features were very different from the other's fleshy, flamboyant good looks.

They went first to make the daily sacrifices to Herakles and the gods.

The priest was waiting with a ram and took the omens from the steaming entrails when the king had made the offerings. They were good.

In the stable yard four other Pages had received the horses from the grooms and they were waiting, stamping and chomping against their bits. A pack of eager hounds, uttering little yelps of excitement, were held in check by the huntsman and his boy. The morning had brightened. The sun was not far off. A horse was brought for Alexander, and his father handed him his spare weapons. Pausanias had a short sword and an axe.

They rode out of the city across the morning lands. At the edge of the cultivated fields, where woods tumbled down the low hills and the river curved in a wide bend, deer came out to feed before sunrise. Sometimes hunters and farmers laid nets to trap them, but today they ran free, the challenge of the hunt was in the chase.

Approaching downwind, they halted, detecting movements in the shadows under the trees, branches which became antlers as the light grew stronger. A large herd was feeding there. A brief, low consultation, then the king raised his hand to make the dedication.

The dogs were led off to outflank the herd. The hunters separated, riding swiftly now. 'Like a raiding party,' thought Alexander. 'Phoenix says that hunting is like war.' A bird flew up from the ground before the leading horseman. The deer lifted their heads, turned to sense danger, and sprang away, leaping golden shadows in a sudden blaze of light from the rising sun. The dogs were after them in full cry; the hunters urged their horses recklessly over the broken land.

Alexander and Pausanias followed the king, riding side by side, pace for pace, their horses being well-matched. Philip had marked a king stag for his prize and the boys kept up, although the pace was a hard one. The stag was tiring; he stumbled as he tried to escape across the stony shallows of the river. The bank on the far side was high and wooded. He plunged into deeper water and turned at bay as hounds leapt upon him. The king brought him down, striding into the water and lunging with his spear below the shoulder. He grasped the lowered antlers and held hard, his other hand outstretched. Alexander was there beside him in the water, ready with another weapon. The does, scattered by the dogs, fled in different directions, and some in their panic ran into the path of the hunters. The boys brought down three of them.

At the edge of the wood they lit a fire, broke the game, sacrificed to Artemis the goddess of beasts, and fed the dogs. The king sprawled on the turf, laughing with the older Pausanias. Alexander sat beside him, hot and dirty, blood from the sacrifice on his hands, and happy. His father gave him an approving nod. "Good boy," he said. "You ride well, think fast and keep discipline. And you can share the honours, you don't grab. Good qualities in a soldier as well as a hunter. Or a friend. You can tell Lysimachus you do him credit. Next time, we'll hunt lion."

Hephaistion was waiting for Alexander when he came out of the room where Philip gave audience to the ambassadors. "I don't know how you stand it!" he said. "Another day of speeches!"

"The last!" said Alexander, laughing. "I have to see how things are done. I like to watch the men – see who are afraid of the others, guess which of them are lying – or at any rate hiding the truth. I decide who *I'd* choose to carry an embassy for *me*. And I try to guess what Father makes of them. It's hard to tell. When he thanks them, he flatters them: you can see they think they've scored with him. But he never *promises* anything. Afterwards I expect some of them realise that. And he sees certain ones separately, I think, but we're not supposed to know that."

The peace conference ended with a banquet at which the ambassadors were thanked and given generous gifts. Demosthenes refused his. Philip said the man was consistent.

The following day the boys watched from a gate tower the departure of the southern embassies. King Philip was accompanying the Athenians and Thessalians as far as Pherae, where Parmenion was still conducting the long-drawn-out siege of a rebel city – a plausible reason – perhaps – for Philip to bring his Macedonians so far south. He was taking a military escort from units of the Bodyguard and the Companion Cavalry.

"Do you think the ambassadors appreciate the honour?" said Harpolas, laughing, as they watched the tall cavalry men on their war horses, armoured and plumed, raising the brown dust in clouds as they clattered into position amid shouted commands and trumpet calls, while the diplomats, with their servants and pack mules, struggled to keep their nervous mounts steady between the van and rearguard of this aggressive cavalcade.

"So he's going south!" said Alexander, under his breath. "It's his opportunity. He's waited six years for it." He knew that waiting was something he could never do.

After they had gone Pella was not quiet. Fires roared in smithies, hammers rang in the shops of the armourers, sutlers came and went with loaded wagons. On the drill fields and in the barracks the army formed its companies and assembled its baggage train. Two days after the king left, the main body followed him south, taking a different route and travelling fast.

In Thessaly, Philip and his allies concluded the treaty of peace and alliance with Athens. The Athenian ambassadors went home. Philip and his Macedonians did not.

"He's through the Gates!" Alexander, racing up, laid his hard grip on Hephaistion's arm and led him apart from the others, who were honing their javelins beside the practice butts. They conferred, heads close together, leaning on a bridle rail in the shade of a tree. The other boys grinned and winked, and some stretched their ears, but caught only a word or two. Alexander half-whispered, his eyes alight, triumphant, "He joined the main army at Thermopylae. They're through the Hot Gates and marching on Phokis – Philotas brought the dispatch to Antipater, they let me hear the first part. You have to admit he played that game well! Not a blow struck, not a man lost. The Athenians left looking about them like men who've been robbed while they slept!" He laughed aloud.

"Hold it! You're too fast for me. What happened in Thessaly?"

"Oh – they took the oaths, Father and the allies. The Athenians went home. Father marched to join the main army. They'd reached Thermopylae by then."

"No fight for the pass?"

"The Phokian leader surrendered it to him. I couldn't tell you before. Father's been treating with him in secret. He let him go with his men, gave him safe conduct. Now Father's marching down to free the temple at Delphi. The Thebans are with him, he's asked the Athenians to join –"

"Alexander! Hephaistion! What are you doing, loitering there? On parade, both of you!" The instructor lifted his switch, pointing to the butts. They made a face at each other and ran out onto the field where the boys were at target practice with javelins.

A group of young men running by on their way to the wrestling ground paused to watch. One of them looked out of place among the Macedonians – a tall whiplash of a boy with dark hair which glinted blood-red when the sun caught it, blue spirals tattooed on his cheeks and the lines of galloping horses on each forearm.

He stood forward, watching with narrowed eyes more intently than the others. Alexander's javelin thudded into the target, a padded wooden man, at a point above the collar bone and the edge of the breast plate, piercing the base of the throat *'where life can be taken most swiftly...'*

The tattooed boy grunted, strode forward as Alexander withdrew the spear, and put out his hand for it. Surprisingly, Alexander let him take it. He weighed it in his hand, feeling the balance, grinned as he felt its lightness – the youngsters were using hunting spears – then stepped back, let out a blood-chilling war yell and ran a few steps forward to hurl the weapon. The yell brought the instructor's head round with a jerk – he had been correcting Hephaistion's handling of the launch – but before he or any of the boys could move the spear was thrown. Its point crashed into the target on the mark left by Alexander but with such force that it split the wood.

"Good throw!" said Alexander with a glinting smile as he took back his javelin.

"And you!" The boy grinned, showing big white teeth. He pointed, first to Alexander, then to himself. "King's son – and me." He raised an arm in salute and ran off to rejoin the others. It looked as though a dispute had broken out among those supposed to be in charge of him, and punches were being thrown as the instructor strode across, bellowing abuse, warning them off interfering with his charges and sending them to settle their differences on the wrestling ground.

"Who is that barbarian?" demanded Hephaistion. "What's he doing among the recruits?"

"Doesn't he know who you are?" asked Nearchos, himself a Cretan prince of ancient royal race.

"Oh I think so. And I know who he is. A Thracian from the far north –"

"One can see *that*!"

"– a chief's son from the Ardei tribe."

"A hostage then?"

"No. He asked to come. Or his father asked if he could. They are horse-taming people. They admire our cavalry. They have warlike neighbours and think that Father would be a good friend to have. And amongst themselves they are used to fostering the sons of chieftains in each other's houses."

"I bet the others don't like it."

"He's caused some fights, Ptolemy told me. He doesn't care about being beaten because only Father may punish him. As long as it's the king who strikes him he's quite proud of it, so Ptolemy says. But if he gets another pugnacious one, like Kassander, into trouble with him, then he makes a real enemy."

"Well I don't blame Kassander," said Nearchos, tossing his dark head. "A painted savage like that!"

Alexander gave him a cool, hard look and he shifted his gaze. "My Father accepted him," he said. "He chooses his Companions from among all our allies, and so will I. A man who is honourable and brave may cover himself with tattoos and be my friend. Those horses mark him out as a king's son. His people worship a horse god."

"Can he speak Macedonian?"

"Not much, Ptolemy says, but he's learning fast. I'll ask him to teach me some Thracian. It's time I knew more, now that most of Thrace is ours."

Silenced, they pursued their own thoughts as the instructor called them sharply over to continue the business in hand.

"He may be a chief's son," said Hephaistion to Nearchos as they walked to their marks, "But he stinks like a fox. Did you smell him?"

"Perhaps," said Nearchos, laughing, "Alexander will teach him to bathe."

"Is Delphi truly the centre of the earth?" asked Alexander, carefully testing the edge of the knife he was honing.

"You could think so when you're there, surrounded by the mountains." Ptolemy answered. "The priests show you the carved stone where the eagles are supposed to have landed." There was a legend that Zeus had released two eagles to fly across the world, one from the east and one from the west. They met and came to earth at Delphi.

"So it's a story?"

"It may be true. I mean that it's the centre of the earth. In one sense anyway – people come from all over the world to question the god and ask his favour. And it's like nowhere else."

"Tell me."

They were sitting on mounting blocks outside the stables. Ptolemy put down the harness to which he had been adding new silver plaques in celebration of victory. He had returned from the south with King Philip the day before.

"Well, it shines. The light's so strong, so bright. You can see why it's sacred to Apollo. And the wind comes down from the snow fields up above, clean and cold. The gods can breathe there. The sanctuary is on the side of the mountain." He leant forward to mark the dust with his awl, drawing the long slope of Mount Parnassos. "Here's where the sacred spring flows out of the rock, then a paved road winds all the way up, past the temple treasuries – the ones the Phokians robbed" – he drew the road leading up to a large rectangle – "here, high up is the big temple – they've been rebuilding it all these years since the earthquake, even during the wars – all bright new stone and gilded figures shining on the roof – then, higher up" – he drew a semi circle – "here's the theatre cut into the mountainside – and higher up still, much higher – the paved road ends but the path goes on winding up the mountain – here's the stadium where the Games are held." He drew a large oval in the dust. "It feels half way to the sky. Apollo's sky. From there you can look down on all the rest – the temple looks tiny down below – and further down past olive orchards to the sea. But you can't see the mountain peaks. They're out of sight somewhere above and beyond the great cliffs of rock rising up behind the sanctuary. The rocks catch all the light, like fire sometimes at sunset! They're called The Shiners!"

"I've heard of other mountains like that. Go on."

"After the fighting the allies wanted all the Phokian men of military age thrown from the top of those cliffs," said Ptolemy. "Your father prevented it. Imagine polluting that sacred place with the blood of vengeance. There would have been no peace!"

"So the cities of Phokis were broken up into villages and they have to pay back yearly sums to the temple. Antipater told me that."

"Yes. The Athenians called that an atrocity."

"They didn't send the troops Father asked for."

"No! Demosthenes told them that we would take their young men hostage. He convinced the Athenians that we would attack them next and the country people fled into the city. The king sent letters to re-assure them, but they sent no athletes to compete in the Games when they heard that your father had been asked to preside over them."

"Were they like the Games at Dion?"

"You should have been there. You'd have won the boys' foot race. There was no-one faster than you."

"That would have embarrassed Father," said Alexander, laughing. "He wouldn't have wanted me to lose, but if I'd won it would have looked contrived."

"Perhaps," said Ptolemy, "but I wish you'd been there to see Philip and

Parmenion being Greek! Your father wore a long white tunic and a purple robe draped over it in the Athenian style and a wreath of laurel on his head in honour of Apollo –"

"As he did on the Crocus Field –"

"Yes," said Ptolemy, looking at him in surprise. "You remember that? It's six years ago!"

"Of course."

"Well, this ends their Sacred War, as they call it. And it's your father's triumph. The gods must approve – listen to this! After the sacrifice and the dedication in the temple, your father stood up there in the stadium to declare the start of the Games, the priest put the torch in his hand to light the sacred fire – and two eagles soared up over the cliffs. The king looked up – we all did. And they came flying down the mountainside. I just stopped myself bending down – they came so low – I would have looked a fool! They flew the length of the stadium – a great beating of wings – chasing their shadows along the ground where the athletes would run. Everyone took it for an omen – the blessing of the god. Your father lifted the torch up high, saluting them and the god who sent them, before he plunged it into the fire bowl. The flame leapt up – it looked pale in the brightness of the sun – everyone was applauding, and the Games began. The first held in peace after ten years of war!"

There was a pause while they both saw it happening – Ptolemy remembering, Alexander imagining.

"So," said Alexander, "Father has what he's waited and worked for – leadership of the Greeks. Now we'll see what happens. Do you think he questioned the oracle of the god while he was there?" Ptolemy shook his head. "Not this time. He was in command – victorious. He couldn't risk an unfavourable prophecy, nor one the priests adapted to flatter him."

"You think they do that? Cheat the god? I would have asked." He frowned over this for a moment before saying, "He promised me a lion hunt. Do you think he'll remember?"

As though he were an actor given his cue, Philip came into the yard, riding with the younger Pausanias. He drew rein and they stood up to greet him. He wore the gloss of his success – military and diplomatic – and sat smiling down at them. As though he had overheard their conversation he said, "I promised you a lion hunt, boy."

"Yes, Father!"

Taking in the age and size of his son as he stood beside big, raw-boned

Ptolemy, Philip wondered why he had been so rash, and added, "As a spectator, you understand, to learn how these things are done."

"Of course, Father."

Philip looked over his shoulder at Pausanias, "You'll keep guard over him."

"Yes, Sir."

"We'll go to the old palace at Aigai. It's time your grandmother had sight of you. There's plenty of game up there in the mountains and the huntsmen know their business. You remember your grandmother? It's some years since you saw her."

"I remember. She's like Queen Hecuba."

This meant little to Philip. One of the boy's fancies. He said as he gathered the reins to move on, "She'll like you better if you're not afraid of her."

Alexander replied scornfully to Philip's retreating back, "Why would I be afraid? She's *brave* – like Queen Hecuba!"

Philip's mother, Queen Eurydike, lived quietly enough now in the old palace at Aigai, across the wide plain west of Pella at the foot of the Pierian Mountains. A princess of the Lyncestians, the leopards of that high country, who remembered when the women of her clan fought beside their men, she had survived the murders, the civil wars and invasions that had ravaged Macedon before Philip's accession, and lived now like an old eagle in her eyrie, her hunting done for her by others. Philip seldom had time or the desire to visit her, but now he wanted to share his triumph with her. She, of all people, would understand the meaning and the magnitude of what he had achieved.

Chapter 16

Lion Hunt

Storks were already flying south for the winter when they crossed the great plain a week later. Alexander, riding beside Lysimachus, half-turned to watch them pass overhead, black-tipped wings rowing the sky, red legs trailing. "Agammemnon's fleet!" he said, laughing. "They'll be flying over Pella before we reach grandmother's – cross the sea and the ruins of Troy!"

"They will. Their kind have always done so. Achilles might have seen them."

"They'll fly above his grave mound. One year I'll follow – when Father invades Asia!"

He laughed again and kicked his heels, setting his horse forward, enjoying his freedom. The king was riding ahead with his Pages and Companions. Grooms and servants followed with the baggage, spare horses and packs of hunting dogs.

The mountain barrier ahead drew nearer, blue ranges and distant peaks rising into the clouds. They could see the thick green forests covering the lower slopes. Sun and shadow picked out the walls of the city of Aigai, the gate towers, and above them the roofs of houses and the red pillars of the palace and temples.

They were passing the burial ground of the kings. Alexander and Lysimachus drew rein for a moment, under poplar trees that scattered yellow leaves over the green mounds. Here the ancestors of his house lay in underground chambers with their weapons and their tokens of royalty. "Which one covers the tomb of Perdiccas, do you know?" He did not mean his uncle, who had died fighting the Illyrians, but the boy Lanike told him had gathered up the sunlight into his cloak and claimed the kingdom for his family. Lysimachus shook his head. "No-one knows. It was too long ago." Alexander nodded and moved on. He did not ask for his grandfather's tomb.

The king's party had gone ahead. Pausanias, mindful of his charge to look after Alexander, dropped back to ride beside them. Black and white goats came bleating and skittering down through the trees, accompanied by tall, striding shepherds with yapping guard dogs running to and fro around them. The dogs hurled insults at the royal hounds, who yammered and strained at the leash trying to reach them and had to be whipped and dragged away.

The king raised his hand to the shepherds as they held back for the royal party to pass. Alexander looked at them curiously and at their fair-haired children who clustered together and stared back at him. "Do they speak Macedonian? I'd like to talk to them." He called a greeting. The children looked sideways at each other and shook their heads, but one of the older shepherds called back. "It's a hill dialect," said Pausanias, "similar to ours at home." He lifted a hand and shouted something which was understood and brought smiles, and the shepherds raised their snake-headed crooks in a friendly salute.

"We must go, Alexander. Come on. Your father's well ahead. We'll meet shepherds in the mountains. You can talk to them then. These must be the first to come down to find winter pasture."

"Goat city!" said Alexander, laughing and turning to wave as they rode away.

Aigai opened its gates, the people came out to welcome the king they seldom saw, the commander of the garrison provided a guard of honour, and Queen Eurydike came too, astride a black horse, accompanied by the staff officers of her household. As he watched her greeting his father, Alexander thought, 'So will Mother come out to meet me when I ride home victorious!'

In the outer courtyard of the palace they dismounted and Philip brought him forward. "May you live, Grandmother! My mother sends you her greetings." She gave a brief nod of acknowledgement as she put back her veil. There were white wings in her black hair and her eyebrows swooped fiercely upward like her son's. She put a strong, lean hand on Alexander's shoulder. Her eyes, still bright and sharp, appraised him.

"Your mother's face – but I see Philip there, too." She pulled gently at a thick lock of his hair. "Lion cub! What a mane! Never cut it short. Bring me the mask when you've killed your lion and I'll make you a cap from it."

"Herakles wore a lion skin cap."

"So he did. So shall you. Come, I'll take you to his shrine and we'll make an offering for you."

With her hand on his shoulder she led them in. The statue of the hero-god in the shrine was very old. He had the long, thin face of the mountain shepherds and the lion-skin over his shoulders might have been a goatskin cloak. "He was a lion hunter," said his grandmother as they made the offering. "He will send your lion to you if you petition him."

The palace was large and old; in the royal rooms there were faded archaic paintings on the walls and beautiful intricate pebble patterns on the floors, but after the noise and activity, the brilliance of Pella it seemed dim and half-deserted. Voices echoed across the central courtyard. A keen wind blew through the pillars of the high north terrace that looked out over the vast plain below. To Alexander it seemed a place the warmth of life had left, flowing away like the rivers to the east, towards the sea, the world and the sun. Here was only the burial place of the kings.

His grandmother's life, he thought, for all her vigour was nearly done. He could not guess then that she would outlive her son. Her servants, too, seemed old to him. The women who waited on her had been with her for a long time. Even the guards and grooms tended to be men retired from active service elsewhere. The noisy intrusion of the king and his Companions seemed just that, disturbing those who had been half asleep.

As he lay down that night in the room he shared with Lysimachus, Alexander heard the young Pages laughing and singing in his father's room next door. There were scuffles and thuds as they baited one another, a sudden silence when the king came in, followed by another burst of laughter at something he said to them.

Lysimachus was already asleep, breathing so heavily that he would soon be snoring.

Achilles had wanted never to grow old. He chose glory and an end to life while he was still young and strong. And a name that would live on after his death. Wasn't that best? The boy paused, feeling the weight of the dedication he would make. Then he spoke softly into the dark. "I choose it, too," he said, to whatever god might be listening. "I choose it, too. To earn my fame but never to grow old. I am his great, great, great, great, great grandson and I will be like him."

By the following night they were camping high on the wooded slopes of Mount Pieros. The men had had a good day's hunting. The servants had taken the spoils of deer and boar and one bearskin down the mountain on mule back. Tomorrow they were after prouder game. They sat round their campfires; Philip and his Companions, his Pages and huntsmen, and Alexander and Lysimachus. Away from the fires the chill of autumn crept down the hillside. Alexander held out his hands to the blaze, seeing the blood in his fingers outlining them in red. Lysimachus shifted his position. "This ground is not kind to elderly bones."

"You're not elderly. Not yet. Remember you're coming with me to war."

"Achilles made up a soft bed in his hut for his Phoenix. Will you do that for me?"

"I'll get some more bracken for you, and you can have my cloak on top, folded up."

"Boy, I'm joking. I've brought sheepskins for us. Keep your cloak. It gets colder before dawn." They spoke softly. This was still their private game, not for others to hear. But the others were talking and laughing, not listening. The younger Pausanias, on his way to join the king, dropped down beside them.

"Has it been a good day?"

Alexander nodded. "Father says we'll hunt lion tomorrow."

"The huntsmen have found tracks. They'll bait a trap – tether a goat I expect."

Alexander frowned. It seemed unfair – trying to cheat the gods. "Why don't we just ask Herakles to send us a lion?"

"Perhaps he will. Look, here is our luck-bringer!" A snake slithered swiftly through fallen leaves toward their fire. The men and the boy sat still. Pausanias said, "The shepherds honour them. Wait, it has come for something."

He rose smoothly to his feet and moved softly away, while the snake came no nearer but raised its head, swaying slightly and flickering its tongue. Pausanias returned with a shallow dish of goat's milk which he slid gently along the ground towards the snake. It stooped its head graciously, as though it would honour them by taking the gift, and sipped silently. After a moment it raised its head and looked at them, firelight caught in its eye. It flickered its forked black tongue, stooped and sipped again. They watched in silence, as though they shared a ceremony. When the dish was empty the snake turned and slid away.

"He will bring you your lion tomorrow," said Pausanias, smiling at Alexander. He got up and went to join the king. Soon afterwards they heard him singing one of his people's ballads. His voice was already a man's, deep and pleasant. When Alexander went to relieve himself he saw him leaning against the king's shoulder. The other Pausanias sat at the edge of the group, watching.

"Do you want to sleep in a hut with your father?" asked Lysimachus on his return.

"No, out here with you." There were large, round huts used by the shepherds in summer around the clearing, and empty pens where the hunters had put their horses.

"Imagine we're campaigning in Thrace!" said Alexander, vigorously drawing bracken into two heaps.

"Not too near the fire!" Lysimachus spread the sheepskins over the bracken. "Now get some sleep, Achilles, it will be another hard day tomorrow and an early start." Alexander pulled his cloak over him, and lay, looking up past the smoky light through gaps in the leaves to the starlit sky. There was no moon. "Where is Herakles' Lion up there?"

"Hard to see this month. Right over there towards the east – look." Lysimacus pointed. "You can't see the star on the end of his tail, that's below the trees. Find the Bear. Follow those three stars down to the bright one below. That's his forefoot."

"I have it!" Alexander had followed his outstretched arm and pointing finger.

"I hope the lion we find is a male with a good mane. Grandmother wants the mask. She asked me to bring it for her. Tell me again about Herakles' lion."

Lysimachus stretched out and folded his cloak around him. "It was sent by the moon goddess to punish the men of Argos. It had its den in the wood of Nemea and that's where Herakles came searching for it. He was a young man then. He met Molorchos, a farmer whose son had been killed by the lion. He told Herakles that no weapon could pierce its hide, it could only be killed in a wrestling match, but he showed him where to find the den. Herakles told him to wait thirty days; if he hadn't returned by then, Molorchos should sacrifice a ram for him. The den had two entrances. Herakles blocked one and forced his way into the other. It led deep into the earth. Molorchos, listening outside, heard the lion roaring. After a while there was silence.

Thirty days passed and Molorchos prepared a ram as a funeral offering. But then – on the last day – Herakles appeared with the dead lion on his back. He'd strangled it but then he'd fallen into a dangerous sleep – a sleep like death – and woke only on the thirtieth day. He cut off the lion's hide with its claws and wore it as a cloak. He and Molorchos sacrificed the ram to Zeus, and Zeus set the stars of the Lion in the sky to honour his mortal son."

Alexander wondered: why did they call it the Lion of Death? Had Herakles really conquered death, so that he would live for ever – like the gods? He was too sleepy to ask questions now ...tomorrow...

His eyes were closed. There was less noise and laughter from the men, no singing. One of the tethered horses snuffled softly, and another answered. Lysimachus also composed himself for sleep, wondering, for a fleeting moment, how many camp fires he might share with Alexander in the years to come, not knowing that one cold night in the mountains of Asia his young king would steal fire from the enemy to warm him.

Alexander thought he heard the roar of a lion before he opened his eyes. It seemed to come through the ground – the lion of Herakles. Then he woke fully, and knew it for a dream.

The sky was grey, a shade lighter than the tops of the trees. The men were moving about. He heard his father's cheerful voice. Hunting gave Philip his greatest pleasure. He hoped that when he passed the Gates of Death the hills and forests of Hades would be like these of Macedon, abounding in herds of deer and wild boar, in panther, lynx, lion and bear!

The king's Pages and Companions stood around eating breakfast – bread and cheese, onions and olives. Philip called to Alexander and when he came flung an arm across his shoulders. His other arm drew Pausanias close. He looked from one to the other. "If the gods approve we'll win a shabraque for each of you today! The huntsmen are looking for tracks. They found lion spoor yesterday, up there." A jerk of his head indicated the direction above them. "You'll ride with us, Alexander. Lysimachus is not a lion-hunter. His dogs are bred for small game. Pausanias, keep guard over the boy – both of you stay close to me. Military discipline today! A lion is no mean enemy. Be alert, weapons ready, but no acting on your own. This is not child's play. Await my orders."

"Yes, Father!"

"Yes, Sir!"

The king felt that he had made amends, aware that having regretted his promise to Alexander he had tried to ignore his presence, leaving him to Lysimachus, but the boy had made no trouble and behaved well. He would let him join the hunt and decide how far to let him participate according to circumstances.

He made the morning offerings to Artemis and Dionysos, and to Herakles Lionslayer. The huntsmen came in to report finding the tracks of two full-grown lions.

The hunting party bridled their horses and rode off, as early sunlight speared the branches overhead. Later, the huntsmen warned, they would have to dismount and follow the lion on foot through steep, rocky terrain.

Suddenly, young Pausanias, riding close behind the king and beside Alexander, almost lost his seat as his horse flung up and shook its head and stumbled over the rough ground. The bridle strap had broken and the bit jabbed its mouth. It took a few moments to steady the horse and Pausanias had to dismount to find a way of mending or replacing the strap. The older Pausanias grinned and cast a mocking look back at him as he rode forward to take his place. 'He cut the strap!' Alexander thought. 'A stupid trick on dangerous mountain paths. And he's no longer a boy, he's a man.' He did not look at or speak to him.

They came out of the trees onto open moorland where the horses could quicken their pace. Pausanias caught up with them, having improvised a bridle from his waist cord. In his highland kingdom he had often ridden with a length of rope for a rein, although not when lion hunting. The rivals jostled for position as roughly as they dared without drawing the attention of the king. He was riding ahead, intently scanning rocky outcrops where, at the end of summer, much of the cover was lion-coloured

The rocks became steeper, the surface scree looser. The hunters dismounted, tethering their horses and leaving two armed grooms in charge of them. Below them now the valley and the lower wooded slopes were hidden in rising clouds of mist lit by the sun. They were in a world above the world, closer to the gods. A world empty of any concerns except the starkest and simplest – life or death. They climbed upward.

A bird call, the hunter's signal. The men halted, hands tense on their spears. Among the bushes Alexander glimpsed a golden hide. Someone released the big hunting dogs. They raced up through the rocks and disappeared. Moments later their voices rose in a volley of sound that echoed round the hillside, and Alexander heard the lions roar in response.

The hunters had spread out. It was impossible to tell where the lion – or lions – might break from cover. The men nearest to the bushes hurled in rocks and stones, hoping to drive the game towards the king and his son.

Branches cracked as a full grown male lion rushed out with the hounds screaming behind him. He came in great bounds, faster than thought, his intention to escape rather than attack, but one of the men flung a spear into his side. He was heading away from the king on the far side of the ring of hunters, and the game belonged to whoever was first in its path. The lion reared up and roared, his tail lashing back and forth, and seized in his jaws the shaft of a spear badly aimed to break his charge. But a third blow finished him. He jerked upward and rolled over. The hunters cheered, but briefly, and turned to face the cover where he had been hidden.

There was no sound. But the hunters knew there was more than one lion. Cautiously, the men advanced, holding back the dogs. Philip cast a brief look behind at Alexander. "Close to me!" he ordered. "Pausanias!" "Sir!" They moved step for step behind the king.

Through a break in the bushes they saw him. He stood over the carcass he had been devouring, head lifted like those of the stone lions that guarded the gateway at Pella. The dogs had not frightened him from his kill and he defied the hunters. When they came in sight of him he gave a deep warning growl. The black tuft on the end of his heavy tail swung and thumped the ground. Philip watched the bunching of his thighs, knowing that another step or two and he would leap out and charge. He hefted his spear.

The lion seemed to lift the front of his body higher, his brown mane flowed out with the movement. His size astonished Alexander. The faded lionskin on the floor at home, the stone lions guarding the steps, bore no relation to this animal. This was Herakles' lion, promising death. The burning golden eyes looked into his own – knowledge passed between them – the conversation of death – here he met it for the first time – later he would know it on the battlefield, meet it in the eyes of a man above the rim of a shield – 'Your death or mine!'

The lion put back his head with flattened ears and opened the cavern of his mouth, showing his four great incisor teeth, his purple tongue and the red gape of his maw. Then his roar seemed to shake the ground, the hillside reverberated with the sound. Alexander felt it swell inside him, becoming part of his blood, his bones.

The king shouted. It sounded like a battle cry. As the lion gathered its body to spring he drove in his spear. Stepping aside in the same movement, he shouted again – "Alexander!" The boy leapt forward and threw all his weight behind the launch of his javelin, his movement following its flight. It struck below the shoulder. Was it deep enough to reach the heart? A quick jerk of Philip's head ordered Pausanias to follow.

With the first blow the lion had given a deep grunt and reared up; with the second it groaned, a sound that seemed to come up out of the earth; now with the third it sank slowly down, its last breath escaping in a long, deep sigh.

The Pages and Companions cheered. Alexander stood slightly stunned by the enormity of this death. *'This is what it will be like to spear a man in battle. Or to be speared.'* He had a warrior's kinship with the lion; it was not like hunting hares or deer. Philip grinned at him. "Now you've blood on your spear. You can tell your grandmother you're a Macedonian."

He came out of his trance. The heap of flesh and tawny skin that had been the lion lay empty on the ground. Now it was nothing. He answered his father. "She wants to make me a lionskin cap, like Herakles."

"The lion-slayer!" The king laughed. He was in high good humour. He claimed both animals to fulfil his promise of a shabraque for Alexander and Pausanias.

They had returned to the palace when the huntsman brought his pelt to Alexander. He ran his hand over the harsh, tawny coat. It brought back a memory. Himself about three years old, crawling over the nursery floor under his father's lionskin, growling defiance at Lanike who had come to put him to bed. His mother, coming through the door at that moment, shrieking and pretending to be frightened, running away so that he scrambled after her, trying to roar, getting tangled in the skin and laughing too much to go on. Then both of them tussling on the floor, trying to dab each other with one of the paws. It came to him then that he would give his first lionskin to his mother. He could wait for his cap and shabraque.

But when his grandmother came to find him he found it hard to tell her. It was his father's face that seemed to look down at him under her swooping brows.

"Look at this!" Her large hand slid out from the folds of her dress and showed him a coin lying in her palm. The portrait of a man was stamped on the silver, a bearded man wearing a cap made from a lion's mask on his head. She asked him, "Who is it?"

He read the letters stamped on the coin. "A-myn-tas. Amyntas. Grandfather?"

"Your grandfather," she said, "your father's father, wearing the cap of Herakles. I shall have this skin dressed and make one for you."

It could not be hurried; the skins had to be cured. King Philip had to return to Pella with his son. Queen Eurydike sent the cap after him. She had made the shabraque for his horse, lined and bound in green cloth. She did the same for Pausanias, knowing it would please the king.

Philip gave Pausanias not only the shabraque but the horse to wear it

– a fine black Nisean from the royal stable. Alexander gave his shabraque to his mother, which so angered the king that he said nothing about the horse he had planned to give his son. Olympias spread the lionskin over her bed, saying that she would dream well beneath it She would dream that she was the mother of a great king.

Chapter 17

The Sacrifice

The wounded who survived the journey were back from fighting off the latest invasion across the Illyrian border. The campaign had been a hard one. A hundred and fifty Companion Cavalry had been killed or wounded. Philip's horse had been killed under him and a spear had pierced the calf of his right leg and splintered the bone. He had not yet returned. His dispatches to Antipater showed him dealing with mopping up operations, enforcing the terms of his treaty on the tribes who had allied against him, and sharing the booty among his troops.

Alexander and Hephaistion were in the hay loft above the stables, where Bia was nursing seven scrambling puppies. Hephaistion had a pup between his knees and was making barriers with his hands for it to tumble over. Alexander had Lysimachus's fragile and damaged copy of the fifth book of *The Iliad* across his knees, unrolling it as carefully as if it had been made of spiders' webs. He read aloud:

"As he fled before him,
this man Eurypolus, running hard in pursuit,
slashed his arm from his shoulder with a blow from his sword.
The heavy arm fell bleeding to the ground
and the shadows of death and destiny covered his eyes."

He held the book towards Hephaistion. This was a ritual they had begun to practise. Their eyes met and said, "Yes, I can read this. I can look at it, know it and not fear it." "It is from the god," Alexander had said, "to know death and to be free from the fear of it." Leaning on his shoulder, Hephaistion read:

"Megeas, the mighty spearman, closed with him,
and struck with his sharp spear at the nape of his neck.
The point of the blade was driven through his jaws
under the root of the tongue. He fell in the dust
biting the cold bronze between his teeth."

War was no longer a game of make-believe, and listening to hero tales, or the accounts of returning soldiers showing their scars. The lion hunt had made it real for Alexander. And in two years they would be Royal Pages, hunting deer, lion and boar with the king, guarding his horses and carrying his spare arms into battle. In practice now they used sharp-edged weapons, short swords and javelins, but not, since they were training for the cavalry, the mighty sarissas wielded by the infantry. These were an innovation of Philip's; twice as long as normal spears, they were carried horizontally by the first five ranks, upright by those coming behind, so that a fortress of impenetrable blades advanced upon the enemy.

"Powerful Agamemnon struck his shield with his spear,
the bronze smashed clean through and was driven on
through the belt into the depth of the belly.
He fell –"

"Alexander!" Hasty steps sounded below, then Ptolemy's craggy head appeared at the top of the loft ladder.

"Alexander, Kebes came in with the last detachment of wounded."

"Where is he? Can we see him?"

"With the doctors. His hand was smashed. He may lose it."

They clattered down the ladder. Hephaistion took the scroll. "I'll put it back and catch up with you."

The barrack buildings for the sick and wounded were outside Pella, on low rising ground where in the heat of summer they might be cooled by a wind from the sea. They were built round a courtyard where there was an altar to the gods of healing, Apollo and his son Asklepios. The smells of sickness met them in the courtyard, and the distant undertones of men in pain, broken occasionally by a harder cry.

Kebes had been taken to a small room at one end of the building. The doctor's helpers had laid out instruments on a table beside him, a roll of cloth for bandaging and a flask of drugged wine. A charcoal brazier with a hot iron and pitchers of water were ready.

"He can't save it," said Kebes, when Ptolemy and Alexander knelt beside him. "Too many bones are smashed and it's turning black."

"What did it?" asked Alexander.

"A rock. They still hurl rocks in Illyria." He managed the vestige of a smile.

The doctor was approaching – not Philip – he was with the king in Illyria – and two men to assist him, sturdy army veterans, who had dealt with such things, and worse, before.

"Too many of you here," said the doctor. "Getting in the way."

"Do you want us here?" Ptolemy asked Kebes.

"No." Kebes looked at Alexander. "Go and make an offering for me."

After a moment's hesitation, Alexander saluted him and went out. Looking back, he saw Ptolemy had taken the wine cup and was giving it to Kebes, giving him also the support and strength of a fellow-soldier. Outside in the courtyard, although he could no longer see, he could hear.

On the stone altar to the gods of healing was a carving of the staff of Asklepios entwined with the sacred snakes of Apollo. The table for offerings was covered with petitions – little clay tablets or folded scraps of thin metal with names scratched on them, or the shape of an eye, hand or foot, and tiny limbs, legs and arms, fashioned from wood or clay. Alexander filled the bronze cup from the cistern and poured a libation of water. He had no wine or incense and was wearing nothing precious that he could offer. He pulled his knife from the sheath slung at his waist and took a thick lock of his hair to cut it off.

"No!" Hephaistion had come up beside him and seized his arm. "No. They do that for the dead."

"Boys in Athens offer their hair to Apollo. Thettalos told me. I've nothing else." He stood for a moment holding the knife, then held his arm over the altar and made a quick scratch in the flesh. Drops of blood spattered over the stone. Hephaistion hardly hesitated. He did the same. His blood fell on Alexander's.

"You boys, idling there! There's work to do!"

An orderly shouted at them from a doorway. An amused look passed between Alexander and Hephaistion. Alexander went to the door, Hephaistion following. As he reached the man he lifted his direct, clear gaze. "What do you want us to do?" The tone was brisk, not the voice of a slave.

Another orderly appeared at the first man's shoulder, gave him a sharp nudge in the back and said, "Alexander!"

"The king's son?"

"Yes, you fool!"

The boys grinned. "Not your fault," said Alexander. "How should you know? We have to wait for news of our friend. We can help. I like to know how things are done. What do you want us to do?"

The first orderly was too disconcerted to direct them, but the second showed them where they could be of use. They helped the slaves pound garlic and honey into ointment, wind cloth into bandages, sweep and sand blood-stained floors while they waited for Ptolemy and whatever news he would bring.

Kebes survived the operation. Alexander went to him whenever he could escape from his lessons and duties, until his brother came to take him home to their highland farm. Other men got used to his coming; some he knew already, they called to him for water, or to ease the position of a painful limb. He sat by them to hear how they had received their hurts, with what company and in what campaigns they had served, rousing them to boast a little of their exploits, to revive their hope and courage, at least while he was with them. He was their luck-bringer, their basilikos. "Kyros visited his wounded men after a battle," he said to Hephaistion, "I shall do it. It will mean more to them when I have scars of my own. I need to learn medicine. Achilles learnt to treat wounds and sickness – from Chiron so the stories say – but I think he did it in life. There's a picture I've seen of him binding a wound in Patroclus's arm. I shall ask Father to find someone to teach me. The army doctors are too busy." Out riding, he began to look for plants that he saw being used as treatments for dysentery and fever and for festering wounds. Hephaistion, reminding him that Patroclus had also treated and bound a comrade's wounds in the Greek camp at Troy, helped to collect and press them and make note of their names and their uses.

King Philip returned. Pride enabled him to defy his doctor and bestride a steady horse for his entry into the city. In one of the reception rooms he gave audience from his couch and dealt with the secretaries, agents and generals who brought him the accumulated business from the aftermath of war and his absence from his capital. Morning and evening he swung on crutches to the shrines to offer the sacrifices. Incapacity shortened his temper.

Alexander did not approach until the third day, when he judged his father had had time to deal with the most urgent matters. He came to offer congratulations for the victory, and, if he found his father in an easier mood, to ask about the battle and the settlements for peace. Leonidas came with him to report on his progress. Philip glared at them, unsmiling. "Well, boy, what do you want?"

"May the king live. Welcome home, Father. We gave thanks for your victory. Does your leg heal well?"

Philip grunted. "I've good healing flesh. Bone, too. It will mend."

Leonidas began to speak. The king stopped him with an emphatic jerk of his hand. "That'll do. I've no time now, Leonidas. I've no doubt you've all discharged your duties. I'll hear your report later. You may go, Alexander."

He dismissed them as though they were servants. Leonidas inclined his head, put a firm hand on Alexander's shoulder and they moved away. From a sidelong glance, Alexander saw that his great-uncle looked unmoved by the discourtesy. His face was always stern, but there was no frown or flush of anger. Outside the room he said with unusual kindness: "This was not a slight to you, Alexander. Nor to me. Disregard it."

"But why –"

The disciplinarian was back in an instant. "No! Do not question. I have said – disregard it. You may go to your field practice."

It could be felt everywhere, in the court and in the barracks. Something that was being talked of avidly in secret but not said openly.

"Do you know what it is?" Alexander asked Ptolemy. "He won the war. He's been wounded before. Why is he like a bear? The grooms were talking when I went to get my horse from the stables. They stopped when they saw me and started to throw dice. They wouldn't have deceived Arridaios. Well?" He had watched Ptolemy's face. "You know. What is it?"

"He's like a bear," said Ptolemy, "because we lost more men than the campaign warranted. And the king of Epiros, who Philip helped to the throne, stayed at home. He'll replace him with young Alexandros before long."

Alexander shook his head. "There's more. No-one would whisper about *that* in corners. Why am I not to know?"

After a moment's hesitation, while he weighed options in his mind, Ptolemy said, "Young Pausanias was killed. He felt responsible."

"Yes, I heard that. How was it? Junior Pages don't fight in the front line."

"They have to be on hand with spare weapons. I was often in the thick of it. But the boy rode out in front – it's the madness that comes on some men in the heat of battle. Your father's discipline controls it, but this boy was untrained – never been in a full-scale assault before – just tribal skirmishes." A distant trumpet sounded, to Ptolemy's obvious relief. "That's the guard change. I'm duty officer. I'll have to go. Give your father time, Alexander. He'll send for you in a day or two. There's a deal of business for him to catch up with."

Hephaistion, standing silent behind them, watched his quick departure and felt, like Alexander, there were things still left unsaid. So, for the next two days he also stalked the truth. And since no-one broke off what they were saying when he walked into the stable yard, or dropped their voices when he came looking for a weapon in the armoury, he had more success than Alexander.

After weapon practice the following day they galloped to a headland within sight and sound of the sea. They tethered their horses to graze and lay side by side on the turf. Alexander knew he had something to tell and waited. Because it was unpleasant Hephaistion told it plainly and without wasting time. He kept his eyes on a blade of grass he was shredding with his finger nails and said, "Pausanias told Attalus before the battle what he would do – told him he would fight beside the king. Attalus is his kinsman, the same clan. So he rode between Philip and the Illyrian spears. The king. pushed forward to save him and that's when a spear hit him too, in the leg."

"Why? Do you know why he did it?"

"Supposing that someone said I was with you for what I can get out of it? That to be a friend of the prince does me no harm?"

"Who? Kassander?" Anger came from him like a heat that could be felt.

"No, I said supposing. Oh, I suppose some of them do say it, but not so that I get to hear of it. And if I did there would be a punch-up and that would be that. I know why I'm here."

Alexander glanced sideways at him, smiling. He reached over and they clasped hands, fingers interlaced, tightening their grip. Hephaistion had no need to boast. He knew as well as Alexander that he was necessary.

"This was said in public at a dinner after they'd all been drinking. Pausanias, the older one, was jealous – said the boy would go with anyone and made up to the king for what he was getting out of it."

"So he had to prove his honour. And rode between Father and the spears of the Illyrians." Alexander paused. "Who guards their tongue at a drinking party? You'd have knocked Pausanias down and forgotten it. You or Kleitos. And Ptolemy would have doused him from the water jug."

"You forget where he came from."

"That's true." Alexander recalled the dark-haired, hawk-faced boy with intense blue eyes, passionate and proud, newly come down to the plains and to the court from one of the high mountain kingdoms where honour was fiercely defended, women who transgressed were killed and blood feuds continued for generations.

In the silence that followed he glanced again at Hephaistion and felt the weight of something still left unsaid.

"So – what else? His death must have grieved Father, but it's nothing shameful to whisper about. He was at least brave."

A dark flush spread along Hephaistion's cheek. He pulled at the grass, deciding what to say. Alexander waited.

Hephaistion had thought long and hard about this. And had known that if he did not speak someone else would tell Alexander. And maybe not someone safe like Ptolemy, but someone vicious like Kassander, or vindictive like his mother. He had decided it had better be him.

He said, "Pausanias left a message telling Attalus what he meant to do – and why –"

"He couldn't stop him?"

"Maybe he tried, or maybe he didn't get the message until after the army left. Maybe he thought it was just a boy's wild boast. But after it happened he took revenge."

He paused, and went on in a colourless voice: "It was at another drinking party. At Attalus' house. Pausanias must be stupid to have gone. The older Pausanias, I mean. If he knew they were kin. Attalus and his friends got him dead drunk. And threw him out into the stable yard and told the grooms to do what they liked with him. He came to lying in the yard next morning."

Alexander's hand felt hot in his. A gull screamed and the grass rattled. He thought, he would have heard it from someone. It was best from me.

Alexander thought, Father caused all this. How must he feel?

They rode home in silence. Hephaistion did not care to break it. It lasted until they had given their horses to the grooms and were leaving the stable yard. Then Alexander's hand touched his arm and slid down to grasp his wrist.

"I am going to make an offering."

"Shall I come?"

"Yes."

Alexander found a priest and offered a ram to Herakles. Standing by the altar stone, in the light of the fire, he offered it for both of them, a gift in return for a gift, that of true friendship. When he turned away he had the look of his mother when she served the gods – his eyes unfocused and fixed on an image that shone in his mind. "We'll sacrifice when we get to Troy," he said, "to honour Achilles and Patroclus. We'll find their grave mounds and run a ceremonial race around them. You'll do it for Patroclus and I'll do it for Achilles." He brought his compelling gaze to his friend's face. "Yes?"

"Yes, Alexander." Hephaistion had his reward.

But the next day Ptolemy raged at him. "You told him! When you knew I was keeping it quiet. You knew better, it seems. Can't you keep guard over your tongue, boy?"

Hephaistion was unshaken. He looked straight into Ptolemy's rather protuberant blue eyes in the scowling face above him and said, "You know he would have heard it from someone – anyone. He goes everywhere, in the barracks, on the drill field, in the hospital. – everywhere among the men. You wouldn't tell him yourself. I had to. It was better from one of us."

Justice prevailed. Ptolemy's stiff shoulders relaxed, he gave a grudging nod of acknowledgement. "Well, see what you can do to keep him from thinking too much about it. I know what he's like in this. There's nothing the king can do. This, mind you, is between you and me. I'm trusting you. Pausanias wanted them punished – Attalus and his clan. But how can Philip put that evidence before the Macedonians? Even if he wanted to. Attalus is one of his best commanders in the field – his friend, too. He's done what he can – promoted Pausanias into his Bodyguard, promised advancement, shown him favour. There it will have to end."

Hephaistion nodded."Can I tell him this – the last bit – if he asks me?"

"He'll see for himself what's been done, as far as it can be, to mend matters. As I say, let it end there."

Olympias was less careful. It pleased her to tell Alexander a tale to discredit the lion-hunting, victorious king of the previous summer. "So the little fool rode in front of him when Philip was hard-pressed and took the spear thrust meant for him."

"Yes, I know. He was brave." He regarded her coolly, a closed look. She had no right to mock any soldier's death.

"Oh yes!" said Olympias. "Brave and foolish. He did it to prove his honour. Who told you? Ptolemy?" She was jealous of Ptolemy's influence with him. He was growing away from her into this world of men.

"No, not Ptolemy. A friend. But everyone knows it."

"That boy who is always with you – Hephaistion?"

He did not answer.

She softened her harsh tone. "It is unwise to have too close a friend,

Alexander, to single any one out. Your father–" she touched the word always with a note of scorn – "your father bestows his favours freely. Other kings have done so before him. It is a dangerous mistake. King Archelaos was killed by a jealous favourite. He was not the only one."

He thought, 'Being a king is dangerous. Living is dangerous.' Aloud he said: "Achilles had Patroclus, Mother."

Her face lightened for a moment at this reminder of these shared stories, but she said, unrelenting, "And his own death followed close upon the death of Patroclus. Do not give too much. Do not trust too much. The gods may be jealous of human friendships."

He went to her and put his arms around her as she bent towards him, knowing that she was jealous, too. "Mother, I love you most, you know that. And I know that the only thing to really fear is fear. It's in all the stories – about Herakles and Achilles and all the heroes, and I hear it when the men tell me about their battles. It is only of fear that we have to be afraid."

Chapter 18

The Singing

Philip used his time of military inactivity to see to home affairs – with plans for road-building, for transferring scattered populations to new towns, to gathering intelligence from his wide network of informers. The great military machine he had created built up its strength. The cavalry squadrons wheeled in formation on the plain; the infantry phalanxes marched and counter marched, executing controlled advances and well-managed retreats, changing from extended lines to deep columns and back again, even reversing their rear ranks to form a defensive square, and swinging their long sarissas into position with deceptive skill. The engineers held competitions to assemble and dismantle siege engines at speed and improve the performance of their giant catapults. New garrisons went out to relieve others at the outposts in Thrace and Illyria, but no new campaign was planned. The boys watched and criticised and admired and imitated whenever they were freed from their own practice, their lessons and duties.

"I used to think Father would leave me nothing to do," said Alexander. "But it seems I may have time to catch up."

"What next then?" wondered Hephaistion.

"The Greek cities of Asia. It's been in his mind from the beginning. I've always known it. To free them from Persian rule and win back the glory of Greece."

"Agammemnon?" asked Hephaistion, raising a wicked eyebrow.

"To my Achilles you mean? Don't tempt the Fates." He made the sign against evil; Achilles' quarrel with his commander King Agammemnon had brought disaster to their army. "But what else is there? Thessaly is his, he is master of most of Thrace, he has the gold and silver mines, Kersobleptes is his vassal. Since last year he has the leadership of the southern states, even kept the alliance with Athens. That means he can use her navy. What's to stop him now crossing the sea to Asia?"

"He must take the cities of Eastern Thrace first," said Philotas, Parmenion's son. "Whoever has them controls the sea crossing, they're a base for the Athenian ships."

"Rebellion," said Ptolemy. "As soon as he lifts his hand from Greece and moves to Asia. Illyria may flare up again, or Kersobleptes break his treaty, or the southerners may renege on him. How do you think Demosthenes relishes being an ally to the King of Macedon?"

"Yes, he'll have to make all certain here. And divide his forces. But we're strong enough. He's ready..."

"So you'll be in time," said Ptolemy, grinning. "Maybe you'll even get to be a general." They laughed. The older of Alexander's friends had rejoined him while their units were stationed at Pella. No-one thought him too young. Hephaistion felt occasional stabs of jealousy.

Suddenly he threw out a challenge to a foot-race. Young men and boys flung off cloaks and tunics, poised on the starting ridges, and hurtled forward on a shout and a signal from Harpolas, who, being lame, could not compete. Those who were now men, Ptolemy and Philotas, pounded powerfully ahead, but first Hephaistion, then Alexander, sped past , the ground spurned lightly by their flying feet. Alexander finished well ahead, flushed but seeming scarcely out of breath.

"Alexander always wins!" said Harpolas, laughing.

"Of course he does!" said Philotas. He plunged his head and shoulders under the fountain and came out shaking off the wet. "It's a waste of time to run against him. The only competition is for second place. It's the Blood Royal, you see." Philotas was laughing too. But there was a slyness behind the laughter and the emphasis he gave to the last remark – a suggestion that Alexander had been given the race.

Alexander paused in the act of flicking his fingers through his wet hair, his brows drawn together suddenly as doubt struck him – he had always assumed he was the fastest – was it possible they let him win, these older men, because of his rank? It made him feel like a spoilt child.

"You ought to have gone to Delphi," said Hephaistion. "You should run in the Olympics. You'd win a crown there. Didn't the first King Alexander run in the foot race and take the prize?"

"He tied for first place."

"Well then, why not you? You would take it outright."

"Well I would," said Alexander, "if all the competitors were the sons of kings." He looked straight at Philotas. "Then the Blood Royal would make no difference. We should see who was truly the fastest."

In Lion Month the court moved to the holy city of Dion. The day before his birth day Alexander received a summons to attend the king. His father was in his book room which had a window looking out towards the mountain; its summit was hidden in storm clouds, trapping the summer heat below. He brushed aside Alexander's formal greeting and began abruptly:

"These boys who share your lessons, they are your friends?"

"Yes, sir."

"Hephaistion son of Amyntas, Nearchos the Cretan, Krateros, Harpolas, Leonnatos..." Philip named the half dozen most often seen in his company.

"Yes, sir." He sounded wary, ready to defend them.

"Oh, I approve. They were all chosen from families of men I wish to honour. You've been with most of them four or five years. You know whether you can trust them. Do you ?"

"Of course, Father!"

"Huh! Why of course? But if you tell me that you can, we will give them their proper title – Companions of the Prince. A Companion is the man beside you in battle who will save you from the spear thrust you didn't see coming. It is not an empty title."

As their eyes met, Alexander thought they both saw the Illyrian spears advancing and heard the wild war-cry of a reckless boy. There was a moment's speaking silence, then Alexander's caution gave way to a grave smile of gratitude and pleasure. "Thank you, Father!" This was promotion from a school boy into a prince with his own guard, the acknowledged heir of Macedon, a young soldier in training. He risked asking for more – "I would like Ptolemy – and Philotas."

Philip shook his head. "No, they are men and have their rank already. But not too old to be your friends. Ptolemy, especially, a steadfast man." He stood up, suddenly more at ease himself, and rested a hand on the boy's shoulder for an instant as he turned to the window. "Tomorrow your Companions will ride with you to the shrine. Wear court dress, your finest – let your Mother have her pleasure too – trappings on your horses, outdo the Persians – make some show for the people. I will make the offerings but this year I won't offer for you. You shall make your own."

He turned, pausing to appreciate the slight shock he had deliberately provoked before continuing blandly: "Oh, you won't have to cut the animal's throat. But you will provide the beast and present it. What can you afford?"

"It must be a bull, Father. It's always been a white bull. How much would it cost?" He mentioned a possible sum.

"That's sufficient. Choose your own animal. Remember he stands for you before the god and must be worthy of you both. Take the advice of the herdsman and the priest."

"Yes, Father, of course." He felt already years older. A king sacrificed every day for his people. He looked at his father, seeing him for a moment, not as Philip with his ruined eye, limping when he rose from his chair, the fighting ruler of Macedon, but as the heir to the Argead Kings, descended from Perdiccas and Herakles, from heroes and gods. It was his inheritance, too.

Philip noted the tilt of his head, his taut, eager stance, like a hawk about to fly, as though the world was his to be conquered, and smiled to himself, satisfied by the effect he had produced. He moved back to his desk. He had one more gift. He opened a silver box embossed with the star of Macedon and tipped out a tumble of gold work. It resolved into several cloak pins, each made from strips of gold engraved and twisted into the lucky knot of Herakles, and set with red stones. "An insignia for your Companions. Give them on your birth day."

"Thank you, Father!" They stood looking at one another. The impulse of each was to move to the other, for Alexander to hug his father, for the king to lay an arm across his son's shoulders and offer a kiss. Neither moved and the moment passed.

The king sat behind his desk and began sifting the correspondence in front of him. "Come in to supper tomorrow," he added as an afterthought. Alexander, feeling himself dismissed, had turned to the door. He turned back.

"Shall I sing, Father? I have a good song about hunting." He had searched for one following the lion hunt. Lysimachus had found one written by Pindar to celebrate the victory of an athlete born on the island of Aegina, home of Achilles' people, the Myrmidons. He had been delighted by it – it told of the hunting exploits of Achilles when only a child. His music teacher had set it for him. It was a difficult piece but he had mastered it. He would offer it as a return gift to his father.

"Mmmm, a song perhaps," said the king, his mind already veering to other matters. "Not a recitation. Don't quote half *The Iliad* at us. It's a Macedonian night – no foreign visitors. A song will do. Something lively and not too long."

"The boy needs a better horse," said Philip.

He and Parmenion were riding back from the stadium where games had followed the early morning sacrifices at the shrines. Alexander had done well in the boys' events, but had been beaten in the horse race.

"Hadn't the staying power," agreed Parmenion. "Good action, fast, but no staying power. He rode it well enough."

"He has the pick of the army stables," said Philip, "but they are re-mounts, after all. Good enough for a gallop with his friends, but it's time for him to train one of his own." The shabraque given to Olympias came to mind. He rationalised – "I thought I'd let him grow a bit first."

"He's put on growth this year."

It was true that he had. And his childish beauty had altered. His face had lengthened and he was developing the high-bridged nose of the Argead family and heavy brow bones above his deep-set eyes. Philip could feel a similar, though less prominent, ridge above his own good eye.

"I'll talk to him," he said. "He'll want the best though. Once I've put the idea in his head."

They laughed together, and Philip, not a man to lose time once he had made a decision, slewed round to see who was in the cavalcade following them. The boys in their white cloaks were not in sight. Given their insignia by Alexander the night before, they had immediately decided to furnish themselves with a uniform and each had found himself a white cloak. Some of their proud mothers had sewn on purple borders which the others would soon copy. Told of their new title, 'Companions of the Prince', they had decided to name themselves 'Alexander's Own.' Now they had ridden off together, still overflowing with high spirits, unwearied by the games in the stadium, looking for more to achieve. Philip sent a Page to find the prince and tell him that his father wished to speak to him, while he rode on with Parmenion.

The boys cantered across the green foothills, and through beech woods, to come out upon rockier slopes. Far above and beyond them the many heights and peaks of the mountain rose beyond forests of oak and pine, a lighter blue against the burning morning sky, streaked white with the everlasting snow fields. The riders drew up at the edge of a slope overlooking a steep ravine, green water rushing far below. They circled about, steadying their mounts, their white cloaks settling about them, half-laughing, breathless, waiting for something – something else to crown their day. Harpolas rode to the edge of the bluff, his dark hair lifted a little in a stirring of the mountain air, he cupped both hands to his mouth and called across the distance –"A-LEX-AND-ER!" He was a musician, the notes of the syllables rose and fell. The last of them came back to him, echoing from the rocks – "*sand – er and –er!*" The horses shook their heads, stamped and swished their tails. Hephaistion, his face alight with laughter, urged forward and threw a ringing cry to another cliff-face, harder than Harpolas, less harmonious – "ALEX-AN-DER!" And the cliff returned it – "*ex-ander – ander !*" It fired them all, like summer lightning igniting resinous pines – they began a paean, sending his name to the mountain for the mountain to return – "A-LEX-AND-ER!" From rock to rock the echoes resounded among the crags that the giants had thrown down here at the beginning of time. There came, from the clear sky somewhere above and beyond the mountain peaks, a low rumble of thunder.

"Enough!" Alexander raised his hand. "Enough. Stop now!" When they began he, too, had laughed with pleasure, accepting their joyous offering. But he was wary of hubris – of presumption in the presence of the gods – they always punished it.

The boys surrendered. They had had their release, their celebration of what seemed to them then to be the most glorious of fortunes – to be young and to be chosen by Alexander to share his. Their horses circled about – they glanced toward the upward path and the way down the slopes to the road back to the city – for a moment undecided. A small group of riders crossed a sunlit patch between trees, mounting towards them. Two men and three women.

Queen Olympias was accompanied by Phoebe, and a young girl whose horse seemed to share her nervousness, shaking its head and flicking its ears. The queen led, riding astride, her skirt kilted up, her veil tossed back over her shoulders. Two senior Pages rode guard behind them.

She said, when Alexander went to meet her, "Let us go up." They moved on, side by side. The boys slipped away through the trees like woodland deer. Hephaistion hesitated – for a moment – then he followed the others. No-one else was welcome in the place Alexander shared with his mother.

They left their guards to wait for them, with Phoebe and her maid, where the rocky path led into a broad pasture. Olympias and Alexander went on, leading their horses up steep, stony tracks; sometimes skirting landfalls of huge, broken boulders; sometimes looking down into ravines where water rushed, loud but unseen, far below. They came to upland meadows, where the air was quite still and the heat was trapped between woods of ash and pine. The trees and their shadows looked black against the bright green turf under the blazing mid-day sun. Here, among the trees, was a small, round temple, very old; ivy and honeysuckle crept across the roof, lifting the tiles, and, as they approached, two tiny, crested birds flew out from a gap in the broken frieze. Inside was an altar of rough hewn stones, the ashes of fires and bones of sacrifice scattered around it. Alexander glanced at his mother; she knew this place. She took a leather flask from her girdle and poured wine over the stones. That morning she had offered more than a hundred beasts at the public ceremonies. This was a secret dedication, a whisper in the listening ear of the god, alone on his mountain.

They scattered red and white *'flowers of Zeus'* over the temple floor, and drank cold water in their cupped hands from a rivulet. While their horses lazily cropped the short turf, they lay with their backs to a rock in a patch of the deepest shade. She made garlands for them both from oak and ivy leaves, tying them with ribbons from her hair, and he ate the honey cakes she had brought him. The peaks of the mountain were hidden from them here but a hammerhead of soft white cloud was climbing slowly into the blue sky above and thin trails of vapour drifted lower among the treetops. The god spoke to them, gently, a low murmur.

Alexander turned his head to look at his mother. "Yes, he speaks to you," she said. "You know you are special to him. I have told you. He knows the day of your birth. He spoke on the night you were born."

"Why?" He was half afraid of it. It seemed stranger to him now that he was older and to impose some kind of burden.

"Who knows why some are chosen? There are enough men in the world, swarming like ants. Only a few who make a difference. You will be one."

The rumble of thunder came again, a little louder, as though confirming her words.

"The heroes?"

"The heroes. All sons of gods."

"Or a goddess."

He saw her smile. It was only a game, he thought, but she loved to play it. "The sea goddess," he murmured.

As they came down from the mountain, the sky darkened, the familiar dark blue cloud spreading across it, trapping the heat, pushing it down on them. Thunder rolled around the peaks above, louder and longer, loosing flickers of white light. Alexander felt trickles of sweat between his shoulders and on his face; there was a tight band across his forehead – he

They went on up the mountain

had not worn a sun hat on the mountain, and his fair skin would burn tomorrow.

King Philip saw them return. He had not been surprised when the Page sent to find Alexander reported that the prince had ridden out to the hills with his friends. It was no great matter – the offer of the horse could be made some other time. But when he saw that the boy had been with his mother a spark of irritation flared. They were laughing together. As Olympias dismounted Alexander leant down to give her a kiss, gathered the reins of her horse and led it off with his own to the stables.

Philip waited on the stairs to the women's rooms. When they saw him, Phoebe and the maid slid smoothly away like lizards.

He glowered down at her. "Where have you been with the boy?"

She let her gaze flicker slowly over him, deliberately provoking. She said coolly, "On the day that I bore him, Philip? To give thanks to the god. Where else?"

"Where have you been taking my son?" He laid emphasis on the words, my son.

So did she – mocking him softly – "*Your* son? Your son – do you think he's yours? There is *nothing* of you in him – nothing!"At that moment she meant just that – there was nothing in him that derived from his father – as she saw him he was all hers.

Philip stared at her, unsure of her meaning, then interpreted it differently. He remembered something the child had shouted at him once. He stepped down towards her, his hand lifted as she backed away. "What lies are you feeding him? He's mine and you know it. What have you told him?"

He pushed his hand below her throat. She said nothing. Her eyes mocked him, bright with the pleasure of rousing him to anger.

"I'd know if you'd betrayed me, but you're not capable of it. No-one's fit to touch you – that's so, isn't it? Not even the king!" He had a fleeting memory of the young initiate on Samothrace with the firelight in her hair – how long ago that was!

"So – who got the boy on you?" Mocking in his turn.

"Look at him, Philip, and you'll see. Look in your mirror and tell me if you see anything of Alexander there. He is mine, mine and the god's. There is *nothing* in him that comes from you!"

"Ha!" His fingers tightened. "I warn you. Go on filling that boy's head with your lies and fancies and I'll take him from you." He would, too, he thought. He would send her back to her people in Epiros, soon he would have her young brother on the throne to be his ally there – as a political surety she would not be needed any more. But that would make the boy his enemy – he must find some less obvious way to separate them that neither could oppose. He was, after all, a diplomat. He pushed her away from him and heard her flicker of laughter as he limped away.

By the evening the storm drew nearer, clouds rolling in low from the mountain. Philip stumbled on the step as he went in to supper. A quick hand at his elbow steadied him – Pausanias on duty as door guard. Philip gave a grunt that might be interpreted as thanks and shrugged off the hand. Pausanias looked at the hand and then wiped it down the side of his tunic.

The king was earlier than usual, causing a flurry among the stewards setting out small tables and the slaves lighting lamps, but enough Companions were already there. Some of his Pages slipped away to warn others that the king was early in hall. Philip flung himself on his couch. He needed easy company – thank the gods there were no foreigners to impress. It would be a Macedonian night. He called for wine before the food came in.

Lysimachus went to fetch Alexander. The boy was flushed from sunburn, or his headache, or both, his eyes overbright and heavy. Lysimachus pushed away a lock of hair on his forehead to see if he felt feverish, but Alexander jerked his head aside. "I'm well, Phoenix. It was hot on the mountain."

"But you're not dressed yet. The king is in hall."

"I'm ready. This is what I'm wearing." He was in his hunting clothes and wearing boots. He held up his lionskin cap. "I'll put this on for the song."

Lysimachus laughed. "A performance then. A pity Thettalos isn't here to enjoy it." The air was oppressive, bearing down on them as they crossed the courtyard.

Philip had forgotten that the boy was to sing until he saw the lyre in the crook of his arm. If he noticed his clothes he said nothing. He gave him a perfunctory kiss and did not offer the empty place on his couch. Alexander went to sit with Lysimachus.

He had looked forward to the supper. Now he could not enjoy it. He felt the tension in the hall, coming from his father. Even in here the air was hot and heavy, and whatever had disturbed the king his mood seemed to be contagious. The drinking was heavy almost from the start.

Alexander 's wine was well watered, but he was also drinking too quickly, having a raging thirst. Lysimachus motioned the Page hovering with the wine jug to move away. "Wait a while, Achilles. Save it until you're ready to sing. It will be some time yet. And there's good water here." "The water's warm. They've cooled the wine." But he drank it and it was better than the wine which did not quench his thirst.

The main dishes had been eaten and cleared away, the fruit and garlands brought in, Kleitos had just told a tale of new recruits mistaking the scuffle of boar in woodland for enemy scouts, which won a brief laugh from the king, and Lysmachus seized his moment to call out: "Philip, your son here has a hunting song."

"Come up here, then, boy. Let's hear it." He beckoned, with an easy, tolerant grin. Get it over with, then the boy could go.

Alexander came up to his couch, smiling. He put on the lionskin cap, sure that his father would remember and share his pleasure. "A song about Achilles, Father. A victory song, by Pindar. About a lion hunt and the Trojan War!"

He tested the strings of the lyre, adjusted them, and with another confiding and confident look ran his fingers over them to sound the opening chords. Then, as he sang, his gaze went beyond his father to some distant forest where Achilles, the bright-haired child, son of a king and a goddess, lived with the centaur Chiron –

'in his house of stone,'

– a brief glance at Lysimachus, who raised a hand slightly and smiled in acknowledgement – then the singer was back in the forest with his other self, the boy –

'who from a child would rather hunt than play,
hurling his short iron javelins to bring down his prey,
and mighty boars and ravenous lions would slay –"

He looked to his father, a half-smile in his eyes. Philip's bloodshot eye did not return the smile. The crease deepened between his swooping brows. The boy still sang like a girl! His high, clear voice, strong and pure, soared upward; his face flushed from heat and wine, his eyes bright with unshed tears as the words moved him. His hair, overlong, curled in loose damp waves on his forehead and down his neck, crowned by the lionskin cap. It struck Philip as childish, this piece of play-acting – like his mother with her snakes – and recalled that other face, flushed with triumph, the grey eyes bright and challenging; the dark gold hair , loosened by the ride and the loss of its ribbons, tumbling over her shoulder.

'*He is not yours! There is nothing of you in him.*'

'*No!* He is not my son! My seed maybe – but not mine. No, my son would be sturdy, dark. If he sang he would belt out a song soldiers could sing on the march – at the camp-fire – a song for a man – but you made an idiot of *my* son, my Arridaios – you cursed my seed, you witch, and this is all I have – this boy who is all of yours and none of mine.'

Who had taught him to sing like this? What had these tutors been doing with him? Philip for the moment forgot that he had instructed Leonidas to 'make a Greek of him.' He thought only of entertainers trained to sing, beardless men, who gave their manhood to it, who sang like women, like his son...... He looked around at his men. They were shifting, uneasy, picking up his mood – he caught a covert smile or two, quickly hidden behind a lifted wine cup, at some of the high flourishes in the music. They were waiting for it to finish, for something with a chorus they could join in. Philotas, grinning, murmured something in his companion's ear.

The song was reaching its climax. Achilles' childish exploits had prepared him as a warrior, ready

"*to withstand the clash of spears and battle cry,*
when strong sea winds should bear his ships to Troy."

Alexander's triumphant gaze came back to his father as he struck the final chords, sure that the message would reach him... ' Isn't this is our destiny, Father ? This is where we, too, will hunt together as we did on the mountain...I am preparing as Achilles did ...'

The king made a sound between a growl and a roar that startled the boy and the company. His wine cup hurtled to the floor, spilling the dregs, the metal clanking on the stone and rattling as it rolled over. Alexander's half-raised hand fell discordantly on the strings and he stood staring at his father with a dazed, uncomprehending look, like a sleeper suddenly awakened.

Philip heaved himself upright. "Is that a song for a man?" He tore off the garland that had slipped across his forehead and flung it after the wine cup to the floor. His voice rose – "Is that a song for a man? They have castrated slaves in Persia trained to sing like that!" He meant like a woman and everyone knew what he meant. "You should be ashamed to make such an exhibition of yourself! I am ashamed – no son of mine – ! I'll not have any son of mine –" He choked again on his anger and flung out his arm, pointing to the door.

Alexander stood with a wide, blank stare, stunned by shock, the words at first incomprehensible. Around him men sprawled on their couches, cups half way to their lips, their silence as loud as their spears beating their shields. The sweaty, glistening face of his father came into focus, his choleric, bloodshot eye, his wine-wet lower lip which had spat out the words still thrust forward.

The gods lifted the shield of shock. Shame and anger scalded the boy. His hands clenched on the lyre, pressing its carved frame into his palms. For one blind moment he was ready to hurl it at that scornful face. Then the goddess took him by the hair, as she had once held back Achilles from Agammemnon, and restrained him. A crimson flush rose, staining his face, neck and breast, then faded, leaving him white-lipped and pale under his tan. He made a slight bow to the king, then turned and walked to the door between the silent couches, his face a cold, stiff mask. He would not hurry. At the door someone briefly touched his arm. It was Pausanias.

As he walked away, he heard the silence break behind him, the king calling thickly for more wine and a song fit for men to sing, and, as he reached the turn of the corridor leading to the stairs, Kleitos' rough voice responding with the first line of a chorus and some uncertain laughter as others joined in.

Lysimachus rose from his inconspicuous couch and made his way out unnoticed. He could have wept for the boy. He was also angry and afraid, but by the time he reached Alexander's room he had composed himself. If he was to help he could not indulge his own feelings.

Alexander stood by the window, looking out into the dark. Now and again the sky fluttered with light.

The lyre had been thrown on the bed, the lionskin cap on the floor. He had wrapped his arms in a cloak as though he felt cold, although the night was still hot.

When he turned and looked at Lysimachus his eyes were clear, lit by a cold flame of anger, blue like the lightning. As the man came towards him with outstretched hand to offer comfort, he drew back and swallowed hard as though to check a tremor before he said in a voice that stopped Lysimachus dead: "Why didn't he kill him – Achilles?"

Lysimachus tried to re-organise his thoughts.

"Don't touch me. Tell me. When the king insulted him, why didn't Achilles kill Agammemnon?"

Wishing not to fan this heat, Lysimachus said calmly, "You know that.

Wise counsel prevented him. The goddess Athene took him by the hair –
  'Cease from strife, take your hand from the hilt of your sword,
  taunt him with words .....'"
Alexander continued:-
"'throw them in his teeth,
I promise you this will come to pass,
glorious gifts three or four times as many shall be given you
in compensation for this insult...'"
He turned back to the window, his fist clenched against the frame, and
broke into the speech of Achilles:
  "'You drunkard with the face of a dog and heart of a deer,
  you shall gnaw your heart out in anger,
  for you did not honour the best of the Achaeans.'"
Lysimachus sat on a stool by the bed. He said, "Well, he was a little
drunk, but you ought to be used to that. Something's wrong-footed him. You
know he didn't mean all he said. He'll regret it tomorrow, if he remembers."
  "I shan't forget."
  "Now that is foolish and not true. You never bear grudges. And you don't
feed your anger as Achilles did. In that you'll never be like him." His voice
dropped into the spell-binding rhythm:
  "'Anger that spreads like smoke through the breast of a man,
  that trickles into his heart, becoming sweeter than drops of honey.'"
Alexander made an impatient movement under the cloak. "Leave me,
Phoenix. I don't need anyone." Lysimachus acknowledged this with a
raised hand and left. He had never had a battle wound himself, but he
remembered that the warriors who fought at Troy found that wounds
hurt less at first, more as the flow of blood dried. He had done as much as
Alexander would allow to assuage this one.

The small room seemed more oppressive when Phoenix had gone.
Alexander felt a swelling in his throat. A sudden clap of thunder so loud it
must be almost overhead decided him. He ran out to the storm, down the
stairs and out into the courtyard. A guard on duty at the door called him:
– "Alexander – where –?" He slid behind a statue as lightning momentarily
blinded the man. The rain came then, streaming down, beating the stones
so hard that it leapt up again in small fountains. It almost drowned the
noise coming from the dining hall.
  There were lights still in the women's rooms. On impulse, because he

seemed to have nowhere else to take his hurt and anger where it could be borne, he ran up the stairs. The guard there, startled, saluted and when he said, "Mother wants me," let him pass.

The heavy door swung and closed again behind him, dimming other sounds. Perfume of roses and lamp oil, the whisper of voices and robes brushing over stone – a woman came to the doorway – "Alexander! The queen – "

"Is my mother asleep?"

He heard her soft laugh as she came. "You know that I never sleep before midnight. And never when the god speaks." She meant during a storm, which she loved. "How wet you are! You should have come sooner, before the storm broke. Come, let me dry you hair." When she touched him he knew that she knew. It showed in her voice, too, and in her eyes – and it pleased her.

How had she heard already? Her informers were everywhere, like mice, like spiders, like flies: serving women, guards and the women who went with them, young Pages under her spell or afraid of her, singers and dancers, scribes, even the chamberlains, telling her or her women, sometimes without knowing they were telling anything, what was happening outside these closed rooms. In a way, he was glad of it – he need not repeat it himself. Glad of it and shamed by it – people were talking of it already – tomorrow his friends would know. He waited to see what she would do – try to heal the wound or make it bleed.

"Achilles!" she said, "What does a man like Philip know of Achilles? He is always Agammemnon. That was a foolish choice." She took a towel from Phoebe to mop the dripping ends of his hair. He moved away impatiently, flicking his fingers through it himself. "It was about hunting and going to war in Asia. I meant it as a gift – and he threw it back in my face. Agammemnon shamed Achilles, but he was not his father."

She stood for a moment looking at him, quite still, as though alerted to something. A movement of her hand dismissed Phoebe and her maid. When they had gone, she walked slowly to the window, the hem of her robe whispering over the stone, and turned, lightning flickering in the dark space behind her, and said softly: "Philip is not your father."

It meant nothing. "What do you mean?"

"Come here."

He came, uncertainly, and met her eyes. She said again, in the voice that had always murmured secrets to him, "Philip is not your father." He heard the little sting of triumph in the softness. This is what she meant; she meant this.

For an instant it seemed that even his breath and his heartbeat stopped.

Not the king's son? Thoughts and images like a swarm of wasps assailed him. If he was not Philip's son, who was he?

Not Philip – then who? His mother ...and a man...not the king. Indistinguishable faces swam before him. *Who?* He could not conceive of it. She had no lovers. No man ever looked at her in that way, despite her beauty. She was the queen. Her pride made her chaste – and men feared her. Even Philip, he thought, would be unwelcome to her now. Philip – this powerful presence dominating his life as surely as the sun passing each day across his sky – if he was loosed from it where would he fall? – where would he be thrown? – falling like Icarus through empty space leaving his father to fly on alone.

Not his father.

Not the king's son. Not heir to Macedon.

A bastard. Half royal.

Like Arridaios, who now had a better claim than he. Arridaios, son of the king. *Alexander, son of a foreign witch – and who?*

A useless sword, unless the men acclaimed him and he fought for the throne. Rivalry, bloodshed and murder. But – not flesh of Philip's flesh.

That man did not get me. He has no part of me. I am not his.

Her words of long ago came back to him. "You are not his." Not Philip's.

But whose? She is smiling. Is it better, then? How can it be?

"Mother, who?"

"Do you not know?"

She came to him. He had grown. They were almost of a height. Her hands slid over his temples, stroking his ears and his cheeks, sliding down his neck onto his shoulders. He was aware of her perfume, the faint clatter of her jewels, her quick, warm breathing. He was rigid, resisting the urge to pull away.

"May it not be forbidden to speak of it, my son. The god...the god came to me."

Child of the god?

The stillness caught him again, a chill in his blood. His skin was hot to touch but she felt him shiver. The thought was too large, too much to dare. He would rather have kept to familiar, painful truth. But what was true?

As though she knew his thought, she lifted a bronze mirror from the sill and held it so that the lamp reflected the pale image of his face. "Where," she said, "Where is Philip in that face? Have you never wondered?"

"Mother, how did he come – the god?" How dare he ask her that? He remembered childhood stories, the god descending in a shower of gold upon his chosen princess, or enveloping her in the white wings of a swan, or carrying her off on his back as he took the form of a bull. He had never doubted the stories, but he had never been called upon to believe them either, except as stories.

In a swift, flowing movement, with a dancer's grace, the queen went to the hearth stone and gathered up from its basket the largest and glossiest of the tame snakes. As she rose and turned towards him, holding the serpent, she was both queen and goddess. The lamplight glittered on her jewels, the witch-fire burned in her eyes, and she looked through him and beyond him.

He could not speak again. What could he ask his mother?

She said in the same soft, low voice, "The gods take many forms, Alexander. They come to us in dreams. I dreamt of fire when you moved in my womb. I dreamt of the thunderbolt that fell from heaven and a flame sprang up out of my body as though the god claimed you then for his own. The snake shared my bed. He coiled against me in the darkness. I caressed him. He was smooth and strong. Look in his eyes, Alexander. He is as old as time. He knows all things. Ask the snake who is your father."

He looked reluctantly into the black and gold eyes. She held the snake out and put its head upon his shoulder; its body glided over him with smooth contractions, across the back of his neck, coiling over his arm. Its head reached his hand and rested there. With his other hand he stroked it. He knew the stories of the birth of Dionysos – of the god entering the cave of the earth mother in the form of a snake. A half-fearful ecstasy crept into him. He looked at his thoughts, not at the room. He ceased to see his mother, and when he awakened and became aware again of the sights and sounds around him she was standing watching him, careful and quiet. The light had gone from her face. The god had left her.

"Give Menelaos to me," she said, as though nothing had happened, as though he had merely passed to bid her goodnight on his way to bed. Dazed, and suddenly tired, he stretched out his arm and the snake slithered back to her.

"Yes," she said, "You feel your destiny. You are greater than he, as Achilles was greater than his mortal father. I was promised that I would know when it was time to speak. Now we will not talk of it again. Go now. Good-night, Alexander." She kissed him, softly and swiftly.

"Goodnight, Mother." There seemed nothing else that words could accomplish. He went out from her room.

He slept heavily. Leonidas had to wake him in the morning. All that had happened in his mother's room seemed unreal, part of a feverish dream. But the shame and his father's betrayal at the supper was like a raw wound and bled.

He burnt the lyre on the altar of Herakles, as he had burnt his last childish toy years ago, and never played or sang in public again.

He would be a soldier – a general – and in the end a king – and he would be the best. He set himself free – from whatever seed he had sprung, whether he was Philip's son or the child of a god – he would achieve his own honour, prove his own worth – and he would excel because he was Alexander. This was the part of every man that came from a god. "I am my self – I am Alexander – that's who I am!"

Chapter 19

The Boar Hunt

Sometime later Alexander went to Ptolemy and said: "Will you do something for me?"

Ptolemy raised an eyebrow and looked at him. "What is it?" His chin was tilted in the way he had when expecting opposition, and Ptolemy was suspicious.

"It's time I killed my boar. Will you help?"

Ptolemy congratulated himself on his caution. "I thought you were up to something. No. Not yet."

Alexander flushed with anger. "Why not? I'm ready. I know what to do. I've read all that Xenophon says about it, and you've taken me along to watch –"

Ptolemy interrupted: "Knowing what to do isn't enough. You need strength. Wait until you're older and bigger."

"Demetrius says I'm strong. I can throw any boy at wrestling – boys much heavier than I am."

"Yes, because you're quick – and quick-thinking. And all right, you're strong too. But for a boar you need weight. You know that as well as I do. As you said, you've carried spears for the men at a score of hunts. You saw how Amyntor had his spear ripped out of his hands by a big tusker, and the wound he got when it charged him. Lucky he wasn't killed. It took two of us to finish that one off. We could set you up a smaller one than that, of course –"

"You will *not!*" Alexander was furious. "You will set up nothing! When we go to the forest we'll take what the god sends us. Do you put me down for a coward?"

"No," said Ptolemy, "nor a fool. So don't talk to me as if you were. Your courage isn't in question. Boys take their boar when they're fifteen or more. Why must you do it now?"

Alexander's mouth set in stubborn lines and he thrust out his chin in the gesture that came from his father. He said, "I'm going into supper as of right with the men, not waiting on his invitation or sitting on *his* couch."

"So that's it. I might have guessed. Alexander, put that behind you. A drunken speech, that's all it was. He was sorry for it after." His look said, 'And you and I both know *why* he was like a bear,' but he did not say so. "Let it be forgotten."

"Yes, I'll forget it – when I've shown him that I'm truly a man." He looked up quickly, tilting his head a little, with the eager look of affection and entreaty which few people could resist. "Ptolemy – ? –"

Ptolemy hardened himself, thereby becoming one of the few. "No. It would be stupid and the king would hold me responsible."

The bright look went and the boy's face closed in hurt and disappointment. He turned to go. Struck by a sudden apprehension, Ptolemy added sharply: "And don't think you can go off and hunt boar with that pack of boys who run with you. You'd be putting their lives in danger as well as your own."

Alexander's back stiffened. "I shouldn't do that."

"No. I hope not." There was a brief pause. Ptolemy sighed and said ruefully, "I'm sorry, Alexander. Come and ask me again in a year or two."

Taking advantage of this lowering of his opponent's guard, Alexander delivered a sharp thrust. He gave Ptolemy a brief, cold glance over his shoulder. "Don't apologise. I won't wait. I'm ready now. If you won't help me someone else will."

He was walking away. Ptolemy lunged after him and grabbed him by the wrist. "Who?"

"What's that to you?" He looked down at Ptolemy's hand. "Let go of me."

Ptolemy let go at once. They stood facing each other. "I want to know who, Alexander. No-one I could trust would do it for you."

"Some men will think it an honour to be asked. If I told you who I have in mind you'd get my father to stop them. Don't concern yourself. They're all grown men and know what they're about." His stiff, cold face softened deliberately as he cast a reproachful look up at Ptolemy. "I would have preferred you, of course; that's why I asked you first."

He turned on his heel and walked away. Ptolemy watched him in exasperation and despair. He would do it if he had resolved on it, and if he was going to hunt boar Ptolemy wanted to be there to look after him. He pictured an impetuous Alexander over-ruling the judgement of an easy going hunt-master; excited young men crowding one another in their eagerness to protect him and share his triumph; ill-trained dogs; a wounded boar breaking out of the nets; Alexander falling and no-one fast enough to keep the boar off him. These swift images were followed by another, almost as unpleasant, of Alexander triumphant, feasting in hall, his arm resting affectionately on the shoulder of the one who had led the successful hunt – Kleitos perhaps, or Philotas – while they recounted their exploit. He called: "Alexander! Come back!" Alexander turned and stood still. "You'll do exactly as I tell you?"

"Of course. Hunting is like war. The hunt master is the general." His eyes began to gleam.

Ptolemy gave a sigh and a shrug of resignation and nodded. Alexander radiated joy and affection. He flung himself at Ptolemy and hugged him. If he had been a young hound he would have barked and wagged his tail. A reluctant grin disappeared quickly from Ptolemy's large, bony face. He held Alexander away from him with hard hands. "Remember it's a serious business. Not a boy's prank. Prepare for it as you would for war."

Eagerly, Alexander rattled off a sensible list of preparations and rules of conduct, culled partly from conversations with Lysimachus, and his observations in the field, but mostly from reading Xenophon's treatise on hunting.

"Yes," said Ptolemy, as soon as he paused for breath. "That's all well and good. And most of it's by the book. Now remember – you said it yourself – hunting's like war, and in both it's the unexpected that often happens. Be ready for it. The boar hasn't read Xenophon and the enemy wasn't trained by your drill instructor. Something will happen that you didn't bargain for, and turn the rules upside down. So think for yourself. There's just one rule that always applies – and don't forget it. What do you do if you lose your weapon and the boar comes for you?"

"Lie down," said Alexander promptly.

"Lie down flat and grab hold of the undergrowth. His tusks are curved, and he gores upwards. He can't get them under you if you lie prone. He'll bite and try to trample you, but before then someone will have drawn him off."

"You!" said Alexander, laughing. "But don't kill him. I must get to my feet and go after him. Xenophon says that safety without victory is not honourable."

"Hmmmph!" Ptolemy grunted. "Don't do anything rash for the sake of glory. If you don't get the first animal there'll be others." He crossed the court, found a guard just about to come off duty by an inner gate, and borrowed his ceremonial spear. He came back and presented it to Alexander. "It's not as heavy as a boar spear, but it will serve. All right.

The dogs have flushed him out of a thicket. We're driving him towards you. He's over there –" Ptolemy pointed – "show me what you do."

Alexander took up a wrestler's stance, feet apart, knees slightly bent. He held the spear inclined downward, his left hand in front to guide it, his right hand further back to drive it.

"Bend your knees more, to take the shock. What are you looking at?"

"His eyes. The movement of his head."

"Yes. He'll be quick. Where will you aim?"

"Just above the collar bone. Into the throat."

A voice in his head said: *'Where life can be taken most swiftly.'*

Ptolemy leapt without warning and grabbed the spear shaft and shoved it back with all his weight upon it. Alexander, in the split second it was given him to realise what was happening, braced back and thighs and clamped his hands to the spear with an iron grip. It took all Ptolemy's weight and impetus to force him back, and he kept his feet and his hold on the spear for several seconds as Ptolemy wrenched it back and forth, trying to pull it from his grasp, finally bringing him down, panting, on one knee.

"Good. You think fast. And if that happens to you, wedge the butt of the spear against the ground. But don't tackle him until we have him in the nets unless you have to – *wait!* That's a hard word for you, Alexander, but remember you promised to obey orders."

"Yes, sir. But don't baby me."

"Baby you! I thought you knew your Xenophon. – *'don't crowd each other... let the hounds bring him out...throw stones and javelins to drive him deep into the nets...'Then let the most experienced and most powerful man in the field approach him in front and thrust a spear into him.'* Isn't that so?"

"Yes."

So they parted company. Alexander went to practise with the heavy boar spear he was borrowing. He knew as well as Ptolemy that he lacked weight; he must strike first and hard at the vital spot above the collar bone. Ptolemy went to confer with the king's hunt master and to call on the friends from his own hunting society that he wanted to take with him. One of these was Philotas.

A few days later, Ptolemy received a summons from the king. "I hear," said Philip, "that you've been asked to set up a boar hunt."

Who had told him? Had the huntsman lost his nerve? Hard to blame him.

"Yes, sir."

"He hasn't the weight for it yet."

"So I told him, sir, but if he doesn't attempt it with me he will go with someone else."

"Not," said Philip, tilting his head and glaring from under his formidable brows, "not if I forbid it."

There was a silence. They both knew that if he was set on it he would do it.

"Who is going with you?"

Ptolemy told him. The men were well chosen, steady, cool-headed and brave.

"Who's training him in this?"

Ptolemy told him the names of the drill instructor, the huntsman – and himself. Philip said, "You know what you're risking?"

Of course he did. The only son of the king. The heir of Macedon. "He's quick, sir, and strong. If he goes straight for the neck vein –"

"And if the boar plays by the rules –"

"I'll have the best men close about him, sir, and I'll be ready –"

"When?"

"When we get favourable omens."

Philip ruminated. 'In two or three years,' he thought, 'I'll be sending him into battle against the Illyrians or the Thracians. Is it time he saw blood on his spear?' It was too late to regret the drunken speech, foolish to suppose that Alexander would forget it. And he knew Ptolemy's worth – he had seen him in action.

"Very well. I give you permission to set up this hunt for my son. I have one condition. You tell me the day before when it is to be and where, and the time you will set out. And you do not tell Alexander that I have spoken to you. Those are orders. You understand?"

"Yes, sir."

"Understand this, too. I shall not hold you responsible. This is his decision and mine."

"Yes. Thank you, sir."

"Your offerings had better be good ones. You may go."

'And,' he thought, 'if the gods do not accept them, Olympias will kill us both.'

Two days later, the hunting party met before daylight in the stable court. The hills in the surrounding country-side had been reconnoitred, local shepherds consulted, and a wood chosen which was known to shelter several young animals, but no breeding sows with families to protect, and no male beast notable for its size, age or ferocity. The hunters prepared their ropes, nets and stakes with exceptional care, and Ptolemy had chosen his men as much for the qualities of their dogs as for their own – he could afford neither who were excitable, slow-witted, or of doubtful courage. He and Alexander sacrificed to Herakles – Macedonian hunting societies were dedicated to him under his various epithets – Ptolemy's was to Herakles Lionslayer.

They consulted the soothsayer, who chose the day, giving them favourable omens. Ptolemy put more faith in his own careful preparations, but he was glad of the god's sanction.

Men, dogs and horses assembled by the flaring light of torches, which glittered on the long blades of the boar spears with their sickle-shaped guard teeth, and multiplied the number of moving arms and legs by their elongated shadows. Muted voices and the chink of weapons gave the stir of preparation in the moonless dark the air of a cattle raid or battle sortie. It chilled and excited Alexander like snow-cooled wine, but his excitement was contained. Alert and cool he presented himself to Ptolemy and placed himself under his orders. Phylax, his big brown and white hound, one of Bia's offspring, was at his heels; although fully grown there was still something of puppy-hood in his large, bouncing feet and grinning, trustfully expectant face.

Neatly and quickly the apparent confusion of shadowy shapes resolved into an ordered pattern. The men mounted and rode off in couples, their dogs running beside them; the net-keepers followed with nets and stakes strapped onto mules; the torch-bearers trotted beside the cavalcade, their dancing flames snatched away into the dark wind, diminishing in brightness as the sky above them lightened. The king's hunt master led the way; Ptolemy and Alexander rode behind him. Alexander was quiet, although exercise and anticipation gave a sparkle to his eyes. Phylax, prancing alongside and glancing eagerly up at him, sensed his master's mood, and settled to a sober, steady trot.

By the time they reached the appointed wood, it was grey daylight and the torches had been extinguished. The horses were tethered under the first trees; the hounds were leashed, and the men went into the whispering green labyrinth where night still lingered. This was the kingdom of Artemis, moon goddess and virgin huntress, armed with deadly silver arrows. The boar, with his white, crescent-shaped tusks, was one of her beasts, and sacred also to Apollo, Lord of the Silver Bow. On the threshold of the wood the hunters dedicated a share of their spoils to Apollo and Artemis.

The hunt master loosed his favourite hound, a wise, grey-muzzled bitch, still agile and strong. "Seek, seek! Good Hebe! Good girl! Go, seek him out." Hebe lowered her head and snaked in and out of the undergrowth, casting about in wide circles. When she picked up a scent, she raised her head, bayed once, and set off nose to the ground, tail wagging slowly, following the trail. One of Ptolemy's dogs was loosed to run with her, and the men followed closely in single file, the huntsman and Ptolemy encouraging their hounds with coaxing cries whenever they seemed to waver. Alexander ran lightly behind them, his face bright and alive now. Phylax was whimpering with excitement, his cold nose bumping into the boy's legs as he ran leashed by his side.

They soon came upon signs that the men could read as well as the dogs: cloven tracks in soft, black mud; droppings near the tracks; an oak tree with bark shredded near the ground where white tusks had slashed it. Hebe bayed once, and Ptolemy's Bryas chimed in, a deep, full sound with a challenging undertone like a battle call. Alexander's blood leapt, and the sensation of being struck by a snowball hit him just below the waist. He caught his breath and it had gone; everything around him seemed very clear and yet at a distance as though he was looking at it through water, and his hands on the shaft of his spear were cool, hard and dry.

Hebe and Bryas stood baying a thicket, a dark tangle of bushes and young trees, into which led a track of trampled and broken undergrowth. Ptolemy took Alexander's arm in a grip like an iron vice. "Stand here, in front of this tree. Keep both your hands on your spear and watch that opening. Let me have your dog. We'll put up the nets, but he may not wait for that. If he comes before we're ready, don't rush him. We'll drive him to you. Keep the tree behind you and butt your spear against it if you can."

Hebe and Bryas were called off and all the dogs tied up at the edge of the clearing, except those sent with their handlers to watch the far side of the bushes. The keepers put up the nets as close about the opening of the thicket as they could, hooking the meshes over tree branches, driving in stakes where the ground was soft, tying the ropes to the trunks of trees. The hunters, in two groups to the right and left, watched the boy and the boar path. Ptolemy stood beside him. The sun, climbing higher behind the trees, sent spears of light through the branches, advancing across the clearing.

Now they loosed all the dogs. The hunt master and Ptolemy cried, "Bravo! Bravo!" and the hounds ran, leaping and yelling, into the boar's lair. After the first outburst there was silence. The men stood like statues, their spears pointing to the tunnel mouth. The dogs appeared to have vanished; not a sound came from the thicket. A butterfly floated down a shaft of sunlight and rested on Alexander's boot, opening and closing its wings.

Darkness moved at the mouth of the tunnel, and the boar was there, like some ancient wood spirit roused from slumber. He stood feet apart, head down ready to charge. His bristling mane stood up like the crest on a warrior's helmet, his tusks were two small white crescents either side of his long snout, and his small eyes sparked red fires of anger as his glance darted about the ring of his enemies. Ptolemy had a moment to see that it was a young animal of moderate size and to let his held breath escape in a hiss of relief, before the stillness snapped like a catapult and the boar hurtled across the small clearing, a bolt of destruction to gore the invaders of his kingdom. Around him came the dogs like skirmishers, snapping and growling. He ran to one side, in spite of a flurry of hurled stones and the working of the dogs, but was still caught in the nets. He stopped in his tracks; here, apparently, was a boar who *had* read Xenophon. The hunt master urged on the dogs. The men shouted and hurled stones to drive him further in. Ptolemy and Alexander ran to get in front of him.

Then several things happened so rapidly that to Alexander they seemed caught in the same moment of suspended time. Instead of plunging further into the nets, the boar drew back, and, slashing his head from side to side, freed himself. A dog tried to fasten itself to his shoulder and others snarled about his legs. He rounded on them, and one was flung squealing into the air as he charged at the group of men on the left of the clearing. Seeing all the dogs round him clawing at his sides, they hesitated to discharge their weapons; Lysander, quickly side-stepping to better his position, caught his foot, stumbled before he could throw, and went down under an avalanche of snarling bodies.

As the boar charged, and Alexander's feet began to move of their own accord, although he was too far away to get there in time, at the edge of the rush of movement before his eyes he was aware of something dark and still and menacing. Another boar had come out of the thicket. This one was bigger, its hunched shoulders like black rock, its tusks yellow with age, the bristles round its jaws white-tufted. Alexander turned, running, and whatever Ptolemy shouted to him he did not hear. The men on the right of the field ran with him, but he was quicker, running to claim the boar the god had sent him.

The old boar gave a squeal like a battle cry, and came for the moving figure. A brown and white hound leapt between them. The boar's head jerked upward, the hound screamed, twisting over with legs sprawling, and fell like a bundle of thrown rags. Its speed unchecked, the boar came upon Alexander like a boulder thundering down a hillside.

One part of his mind heard its feet like a rainstorm on the dried leaves. Then earth's fire and darkness, death hot and stinking, leapt out of the Underworld to overwhelm him. He saw two things: the blade of his spear glinting before him in the sun, and the destined place of that spear's entry into the boar's dark throat.

'He drove it in with the weight of his strong hand.'

But it was not he who drove it in, it was the boar, with the charging force of its own weight. Blood spurted and splattered his legs and hands. A detached part of his mind wondered that the bones in his arms and the shaft of his spear had not splintered on impact. He held on with a strength he did not know he had because it was death to let go, his feet inside their soft leather boots gripping the earth, the muscles of his back and thighs straining to bear the weight. With a length of metal inside him, but the vital artery not touched, the boar fought to get at him along the shaft of the spear, squealing and trampling the bloody ground, held back only by the curved guard teeth at the base of the blade. Out of the corner of his eye, Alexander saw Ptolemy, as large as a Cyclops, whirling in; the sun glittered on his raised weapon.

"No!" Alexander spat out the word with his sobbing breath. "No! I can hold him. Keep back!" His feet slid on the blood-slimed leaf mast; his hands, slippery now with sweat, were welded to the spear shaft by a will that operated apart from his thinking mind. His shoulder struck something. A loud voice in his head, but it must have been Ptolemy's, shouted, "Use the tree behind you!" He wanted to butt the spear against it, but the boar's weight fixed him. He was fastened to the darkness of earth, to the grim power of Hades, as though the giant dog Cerberus had been sent up from the Underworld to pull him down, Cerberus, whom only Herakles could hold –

"Herakles! *Herakles* – hear me!"

The boar gave back with a sudden-ness that nearly wrenched his arms from their sockets and the spear from his wet hands; it twisted in his sliding grasp, and he would have lost it if the beast, instead of wrenching it aside, had not flung itself at him again. His back smashed against the bark of the tree, the butt of the spear rammed against it, the boar stood suddenly still; blood ran from its mouth, it gave a sighing grunt, the great weight sagged on the end of the spear, and, as it died, Alexander went down with it, stumbling to his knees beside the body. One red eye, from which the pain and fury were fading as the last embers of life from a fire, looked sidelong up at him. Then the fire was cold, the eye sightless, and as he looked a film came over it. He felt for a moment that a comrade had died, a fellow-warrior with whom he had shared life.

There was a noise about him of cheering and shouting. It seemed to have nothing to do with him, or with his vanquished enemy. He looked up and Ptolemy was looking down at him, standing feet astride, arms akimbo, grinning. Tears of exhaustion were running down Alexander's face and his body felt light and shaken with the sudden relief from effort. He became aware of the tears and brushed them away with the back of his red hand, giving Ptolemy a shaky smile. His kinsman reached down and hauled him to his feet. He was praising him, and other voices joined in.

"Lysander – ?"

"He was gored along the thigh. Nothing very serious. Demetrius is binding the wound. Laertes killed the first boar. Are you fit? Pull out your spear."

Alexander nodded. Demanding a last effort from his aching body, he put his foot on the carcass and dragged out the weapon. He put it in Ptolemy's hand, then gently pushed him aside, and stepped over the body of the boar. Three paces away the brown and white hound lay on his side, panting in long, slow gasps of painful breath. Flies whined about dark, sticky patches on the crushed leaves beneath him. Alexander knelt down and gently slid one hand under the dog's head, with the other softly ruffled the fur on his neck and behind his ears, and murmured an endearment. The dog's eyes, misted with pain, greeted him; he was the god who would bring relief. "Ptolemy," said Alexander quietly, "can you bring me some water?"

"Don't," said Ptolemy. "Let him go quickly. Shall I do it?"

"No," said Alexander. "He's my dog. But give me some water first. I won't try to move him."

One of the men had a leather flask. Carefully, Alexander trickled a few drops over the dog's tongue, wetted his fingers and moistened his gums and lips. Then, as Phylax tried to lick his fingers, he loosed his hunting knife with his other hand, and, bending low, holding the dog's gaze with his own, and murmuring to him, he felt for the place and then struck, quickly and hard. He wiped the knife on the undergrowth, and stood up. Ptolemy's large hand grasped his shoulder and turned him round. He was dry-eyed. The king's huntsman was waiting to offer his congratulations. The men began joking and laughing in the sudden relief from tension. In the midst of it, Alexander felt remote, serene. Even his hurts – his grazed back, his bruises, his swollen wrist wrenched by the boar – seemed to belong to someone else's body. Outside the walls of Troy, Diomedes had ignored his minor wounds. The god had sent his boar to him, Herakles had leaned on his spear and he had taken his battle prize.

At the edge of the wood, where they had left their horses and mules, they lit fires. The boars were broken, offerings made to the gods, and the hounds given their reward. Phylax and Laertes' dog were buried there. The heads of the boars were mounted on spears, the butchered carcasses slung from poles, and they rode homeward as the sun climbed towards its zenith.

At the cross-roads outside Pella, King Philip waited for them with a small troop of the Companion Cavalry. If the boy had been injured, or worse, he intended to send Ptolemy and the huntsman under escort into safety before the news reached Olympias. What anxieties he had endured he kept hidden.

"Father!" Alexander drew rein so sharply that his horse reared. He cast a furious, hurt, accusing look at Ptolemy. While he quietened his horse, Philip rode forward. He regarded his son, bloodied, dirty, triumphant, and angry. "Before you accuse them, none of your companions betrayed you, although perhaps I think they should have done. Is the kill yours?" He did not need to ask. Ptolemy, grinning, answered for him, "The largest one, Sir."

"A clean kill?"

"Of course!" Alexander spoke for himself.

"Who helped you?"

"No-one!" He thought, 'So, if I sing like a woman, I hunt like a man.' Perhaps Philip saw that in the defiant face. "It was well done, then."

The urge to boast a little was overwhelming. "I aimed straight for the neck vein. Herakles leant on my spear. I invoked his help." A fleeting reluctant grin as tension relaxed. "I was nearly overborne. Ptolemy wanted to interfere but he let me do it."

They eyed each other, still warily, on the edge of reconciliation.

Philip about to laugh, to say, "Well, boy, what next? Another lion hunt?" Alexander demanding admiration, some warm praise. He had earned his reward.

Achilles and Agamemnon. Philip decided he had gone as far as he would. The boy had gone out, in a way, to defy him, to get the better of him. Now the anxiety was over it began to be replaced by annoyance. No reason to make him too cocksure – he was full enough of himself as it was. Philip knew where over-confidence could lead. However, he was prepared to make one more generous gesture. "Give me the tusks later," he said. "I'll have them mounted for you in silver."

"Thank you, sir," replied his disappointed son, coldly, "but they are for my mother."

He had first to make his peace with Hephaistion. The other boys, now officially Companions of the Prince, basked in his glory, boasted of it as though it was their achievement, too.

Hephaistion sulked. Expecting a shared triumph, admiration and laughter, Alexander encountered a closed face, a stone silence.

"What is it? What have I done?"

Hephaistion turned his shoulder. "You didn't tell me. You didn't trust me." He spoke to the ground.

Alexander put a hand on the rigid shoulder. "You would have wanted to come."

"So?"

"I couldn't risk your life as well as my own."

"I can risk my own life if I wish."

"No. I would be responsible. And Ptolemy would never have taken us both."

"I thought we were to do everything together."

"Listen!" Alexander put both hands on his friend's shoulders and turned him. Their eyes met, Hephaistion's troubled and stormy, Alexander's compelling. "Listen, when I'm a general, when I'm a king, I'll have charge of the lives of my men. I'll have to judge where they will do best, for themselves, for the army, for me. I'll have my friends, friendship is sacred, no man can live without his friends, especially a king. But friendship is a thing apart. It has nothing to do with battle plans and this hunt was a battle."

Hephaistion was stubborn still. "You mean you didn't think me capable."

"No, you fool! I don't know whether you're capable or not. I *had* to do it. But you can do it when you and your father know you're ready. Don't you see? I'm responsible, even now. Don't you remember – even Achilles forbade his friend Patroclus to outrun his luck and his strength in battle."

He dropped his voice to the magic rhythm of Homer, invoking that powerful spell. His look was one of love.

"When you have driven the enemy from the ships, come back.
You must not in the pride and fury of fighting go on slaughtering Trojans
for fear some one of the everlasting gods might crush you."

He did not say, or even remember, that Achilles also feared that Patroclus' success might limit his own glory.

He said: "We are part of each other, like Patroclus and Achilles. I've always known it, since we rescued Bia together. So may the gods be kind to us, and we to each other."

Hephaistion's face cleared, and Alexander knew that, once won, he was won completely. His grudge vanished. In a sudden rush of remorse he said, "I know you had enough to think of without being concerned for me. And if I had been there, I'd have been thinking about you. We'd both have been chopped, I daresay."

Alexander felt that he should concede something, too. "I expect I should have trusted you and told you. I'm sorry. I was eaten up with myself."

Embarrassed, Hephaistion said: "You don't have to tell me everything. Why should you? I ought not to expect it... you are the prince ... and I don't ... but it's your fault you –"

"That's enough!" said Alexander, laughing and slipping a hand through his arm. "After this we do everything together. We must. We're going to war together and we'll get used to sharing danger. In battle you won't be looking out for what's happening to me when half a dozen Illyrians are coming at you."

'Well,' thought Hephaistion, 'I won't be far away from you if I can help it.' But aloud he said: "I'll ask my father how soon he'll let me try. I'll be joining you at supper before long."

From Olympias, too, Alexander had a cool reception. He had gone to make his peace with Hephaistion first. By the time he came to her it was after noon, she had heard from others of his triumph, and she knew also to whom he had gone first with the news.

"So you come at last, Alexander. Who is this boy who must know before your Mother?"

There was no protest, no quick step to fling his arm around her as there might have been a year ago. He stood still, looking, a warning in his eyes. For a dangerous moment it held them both, then he lowered the sword.

"Mother, I brought you the tusks."

She swept away from him, her gown making a soft hiss of sound on the stone floor as she turned. She went to the window and leant against it, looking out.

His arms, warm and strong, slid round her, he kissed the side of her neck under the fold of her hair.... his hands, held out before her, slightly cupped, with a boar tusk on each palm. She had them set in gold and wore them, constantly, in a necklace.

Chapter 20

Bukephalus

The first day of the autumn horse fair dawned clear with a strong wind blowing. Alexander, up at daybreak, was aware from the moment of waking that this was a day blessed by the gods, a day of good omen.

For the horse fair dealers came from Thessaly, Thrace, even – sometimes – across the sea from Asia. Along the roads from north and south a tide of horses flowed into the markets that grew around Pella. The best stock, brought by well-known dealers, found its way into the royal paddocks. From these the cavalry men would be choosing new mounts, horse-masters looking for draught animals to haul transport, landowners for breeds to improve their stock, and the wealthiest, maybe, for horses with racing blood. Philip himself needed a war horse. He had never replaced the brave charger killed under him on the Illyrian frontier, making do with a succession of army mounts. But now, having spent over a year on home affairs and on consolidating his position in the south, he was preparing for a new campaign to capture the cities of Eastern Thrace. It was some years since he had led his spearmen on foot, even before his injury left one leg shorter than the other.

Alexander, too, wanted a horse. "A young one I can train myself," he said to Hephaistion. "Xenophon says send the colt to a professional groom to train him, but that's because he reckoned a man of affairs had too many other things to do."

"Well, Leonidas may see to it that you have other things to do," said Hephaistion, grinning.

"He may see this is important, too. I don't want a horse someone else has trained. It takes time to build understanding and trust and your horse bears your life in battle. I've saved enough from my allowance for a good colt; Mother offered to help me, to sell some ear-rings, but I want it to be all my own."

Philip had not followed up his intention of offering him a horse – other events had crowded it from his mind, they had had little time together, and they were guarded in each other's company since Alexander had been humiliated at supper and then triumphed in the boar hunt. If they both regretted their loss, the king was too impatient and Alexander too proud to attempt to repair it. And always Olympias was between them.

Not my father! The thought seldom recurred to him. It was too strange. What did she mean? He quietened it by thinking that seed and spirit were separate; he could be Philip's son and carry Divinity within him too. But even that was disturbing. And how was it then that the heroes of Troy could be called the sons of gods? He put it away from him. And Leonidas and his instructors did indeed see that he had many things other things to do.

But today was a holiday. Everyone went to the horse fair. Alexander stood at the window of his room, stretching up naked in the new morning light, drawing a deep breath of cool air and freedom. The sun rose higher and the vigorous wind sent tree shadows dancing across the courtyard below. It had the feel of a day when the gods smiled and were kind, a day on which they granted victory.

Alexander grasped his happiness. He took the white cloak from the clothes chest and, flinging it round him, ran down to the inner court. Xenophon said, '*Before any enterprise gain the good will of the gods.*' His father had been before him. His offerings lay on the smoking embers before the shrine. Had the omens been good? This was the altar where he had offered Balios when Leonidas came, and last year had burnt his lyre. He rinsed the libation bowls carefully with water and poured in the wine. Then he made his petitions to Herakles and to the Warrior Twins, Pollux the Boxer and Castor the great Tamer of Horses, whose stars were in the night sky below the Great Bear.

He went to find a good breakfast in the officer's mess room at the barracks. The talk was all of horses and of one in particular, whose reputation had preceded it. "A horse fit for a god!" declared Kleitos, imitating the speech of the Thessalian dealer and drooping an eyelid over one eye.

"Where was it bred?"

"Oh, in Thessaly, there's a Nisean strain in the blood – so he says." Nisean horses from the plains of Persia were stronger and swifter than any native to Greece – even to Thessaly – breeders there imported them to improve their stock.

"Who says?"

"Philonicus, he's the dealer." The others laughed.

"Well I heard about it from the Arcanian," said Philotas. "He saw it being paraded yesterday."

"Lysimachus?" Alexander sat up straight. "He knows horses. What did he say?"

"That it has every quality Xenophon admires," said Philotas. "Strong legs well-spaced, broad chest, double back, deep flanks and broad haunches. He didn't get to look at the hooves, but if he had no doubt he'd report them *'high and hollow!'*"

The men grinned but Alexander disliked the slightly mockng tone, whether it was aimed at Lysimachus or Xenophon, both his instructors in horsemanship, and said, "But he'd have heard them – the sound they made on the road."

"A perfect horse then," said Ptolemy.

"Well, no, not quite. He also said it looked mad. Rolling its eye and foaming at the mouth. Two grooms could scarcely control it."

"What use bringing it then? A killer. Who would want one like that to carry him into battle!"

"They say it's for the king. One of his guest friends from Corinth picked it out for him. Philonicus brought it here for that reason."

The men made dismissive sounds of scorn and disbelief, pushing back from the tables, slinging on their cloaks. Ptolemy said to Alexander, "Will your father let you buy?"

"Why not? I've saved enough for a colt. I need not ask him."

"I'll help you look for one. Lysimachus will be with the king."

"How much do you think is true about that horse?"

"We'll see for ourselves later on. Someone thinks he's worth something – I've heard the price is thirteen talents! So not for us!"

On the riding field, the Companions gathered round them. Hephaistion had brought apples. They went about the field, watching horses being run to and fro, being mounted, trotted and galloped, buyers haggling over prices, bargains struck. Alexander and Ptolemy, looking at colts, pointed out the good and bad points of the animals, Alexander quoting Xenophon, "*'The shanks don't increase much in size, the rest of the body grows to them.'* That one will make a big horse, he has long shanks." Ptolemy speaking from experience, "He doesn't respond well to the bit – mouth may be uneven. Keep looking."

A bustle of noise and consequence, laughter and loud voices marked the arrival of the king on the field. He had come from making public sacrifices in the temples but was wearing his riding clothes. The crowd fell back, leaving a space around the royal pavilion, where the bodyguard were taking up their positions. The king dismounted, limping swiftly up the steps of the dais, talking and gesticulating in considerable animation with a group of close friends. It had been a political year for him, re-organising the administration in Thessaly, overcoming Demosthenes' continuous attempts to undermine his treaty with Athens, conciliating the southern states – where he had succeeded so well that some had erected statues of him in gratitude for his protection. But now he was with his soldiers and Companions, his Macedonians, and free to enjoy the pursuits he loved best – the pleasures of riding and the chase. He was with Antipater and his eldest son, Kassander, Parmenion with his youngest boy Hector riding on his shoulders, and Lysimachus, and beckoned and called to others nearby, including Ptolemy, to join them. Alexander and his friends kept back. When Lysimachus saw them and lifted his hand Alexander shook his head at him, meaning, "Don't show him I'm here."

Horses singled out for presentation to the king were in a separate paddock. Their owners had drawn lots for precedence, with some cheating and quarrelling, but the order was settled now and they had to make the best of it. A handsome bay with a light mane and tail, superbly groomed, was led up before the dais, trotted and cantered to and fro on a leading rein. "Moves well," nodded Philip. "Let's see him ridden." A groom mounted him, and, riding up to face the king, brought the horse up on his hind legs to prance in the manner used to show off horse and rider at public parades. Philip growled. "I need a war horse, a charger, not a dancer showing his belly to the enemy." The generals laughed.

Alexander said to Hephaistion, "Father says that's a stupid practice. Even on parade it interrupts the procession and holds everyone else up."

"How do they teach it?"

"Strike the horse under the hocks with a stick. I'd do the same to them."

Harpolas, on the edge of the group, murmured provocatively, "But *Xenophon* says it displays horse and rider at their best – very impressive!"

"Oh well – the Athenians! They like show."

The next three horses were unremarkable. The generals asked to see one or two galloped about the field. Antipater picked out a strong, sensible-looking brown horse, went down and examined its mouth and hooves, rode it and bought it. None took the king's fancy.

A balding, bow-legged man holding a whip came up to the pavilion, smirking and bowing to the king. "Philonicus!" murmured Alexander, who had had him pointed out by Ptolemy earlier on. "Now we'll see!" He felt hairs prickle on the back of his neck.

The horse came. Two grooms were holding the reins close to his head, one each side. Their combined shadows were thrown ahead of them by the morning sun, like a lumpy monster with several heads and legs, advancing across the grass. The horse was stepping as though about to put his feet on red-hot coals and fighting to free his head. His black skin glistened with sweat and Alexander glimpsed a rolling, glittering, bloodshot eye and flaring nostrils. There was something barbaric about the spectacle, degrading and cruel, like seeing a noble royal captive dragged before you in chains. Alexander involuntarily put out his hand and moved forward. His soul was satisfied. The horse was the most splendid, noble creature – broad-backed, broad chested, with strong legs, an arched neck and small bony head – every virtue that Xenophon extolled was there – except docility.

The horse looked mad. There was foam and blood on its lips. Its eyes and nostrils were red. It snorted and stamped in fury. The men trying to hold it were obviously afraid – of the horse and probably, thought Alexander, of Philonicus. The stallion wrenched its head up, scattering drops of blood, and aimed a bite at one, who let go of it and darted aside. The horse whipped its tail, then lashed out with powerful hind hooves and cavorted, pulling the remaining groom round with him.

Philip looked from the horse to Philonicus in astonishment. "Tell me how I've harmed you, Philonicus. I've never had an assassin brought to me openly before."

Philonicus had been standing, tight-lipped and rigid, watching the disgraceful display. He said, biting his lip, "Your pardon, King Philip. The animal is high spirited – " there was a guffaw from Parmenion and Antipater together – "it was alarmed just after we arrived at the field. Allow it time to calm down and get used to the crowd and we'll show you its paces. You can see what a superb animal it is – and such a horseman as yourself – "

"My friend," said the king with deceptively gentle irony, "I am in need of a war- horse! War is apt to be frightening. There is generally a crowd on a battlefield. As for my horsemanship, I am satisfied with my existing reputation and have no wish to prove it further." He flicked out his hand in a dismissive gesture. "Take the horse away."

Something like a moan came unconciously from Alexander's mouth. He said in a fierce undertone, "He's *not* frightened! He's *angry!*" He had moved nearer to the dais and the king heard him. His brows went up but he took no further notice. Until that moment he had not been aware of his son.

The horse had quietened, standing sideways to the king. His strength and beauty were evident and marked by his proud carriage. Lysimachus stooped and said something close to Philip's ear. The king said to his chief groom. "Have a look at him then, Simonides." The man walked about him from a safe distance, while the horse stamped and sidled, and then approached him from the side, making coaxing noises and speaking in a quiet, soothing voice. The animal let him come. Slowly, Simonides put up a hand and took the bridle rein from the groom and with the other stroked the animal's neck, while squinting at his mouth. He kept his voice low, "Not a youngster, Philip. I'd guess ten – maybe even twelve." His tone implied that the horse was spoilt – it was too late for change.

"Who's going to ride him?" asked the king, rising to his feet. Antipater and Parmenion chuckled and shook their heads, but followed him down the steps. Pausanias put down his spear and stepped out of line; he gave the king a challenging look: "I'll mount him for you, Philip." He was a bold horseman. The king gave a curt nod. The guard strode up to Simonides to take the rein. Parmenion said in his deep voice, "I'd have put a smooth bit on him with larger discs." As Antipater began to contradict him, the king raised his hand to his friend's shoulder and also began to speak and the fury of Ares was unleashed again. Snorting, biting, kicking, the powerful stallion dragged at its handlers. Its long black tail lashed like a whip. The king made a gesture of throwing something away and said: "Waste of time! Stand aside, Pausanias. He'll break your neck. You're a fool, Philonicus. Herakles himself couldn't tame that one! Take it away."

Alexander received the word *Herakles* like a jab between the shoulder blades. It couldn't be *this*, for him, the gift of the god? And then he believed it could be, if he had the courage to take it. He said in his penetrating high voice: "That's the best horse I've ever seen! How could they turn away a horse like that!" It was too loud to be ignored. Philip had his foot on the lowest step to mount the dais. He stood down again and turned, head tilted back, to confront his son. Alexander came a step towards him. "Father, the best horse I've ever seen. A superb horse! And you're sending him away because no-one knows how to manage him."

"Oh?" Philip's swooping brows drew into a formidable frown. "And you do I suppose?" Alexander said coolly, "Yes, I do. I could do better than they have." He nodded towards the grooms, striving to quieten the horse again, while Philonicus hovered, uncertain what turn events were taking now.

"How old are you?"

"Thirteen in Lion Month, Sir."

"Ah! Accustomed to riding a war-horse?"

Alexander flushed and thrust out his lower lip, which made him resemble his father. "I do know about horses. About this one. And Xenophon says –"

"Ah, Xenophon! you do well to quote him, boy. That man knew what he was talking about. And what does he say about an un-manageable horse? You'd be safer with a traitor in your ranks. He'll be a greater danger to you than the enemy."

"Father, he wouldn't be un-manageable if –" Philip said with heavy good humour, "You'd like me to risk my neck on him, would you? Or are you offering to take him in hand and break him in for me first?"

Parmenion grinned and Alexander saw Kassander nudge Philotas and both of them laughed. It made him control his anger. Lysimachus and Ptolemy were both signing to him to let go but he ignored them too.

He said in a level voice, "Well, I think I could ride him for you, Sir, if you'd let me try."

Philip's brows went up. He had allowed himself to goad the boy and was pleased by the cool reaction. He said quite pleasantly, "Simonides hasn't cared to try it, and he's been training horses these twenty years. I won't risk it. Parmenion won't." He turned his head to catch Parmenion's affirmative grin. "But you will."

"Yes, Father."

"Hah! Why?"

Alexander took another step forward. He said, a little breathlessly, "Don't you see, Father? He's *angry*. They've brought him here like a king in chains. I think they've beaten him. I'd behave like that if they'd whipped me. It's his courage that makes him fight them, not his fear. They're not fit to be his slaves, those men. I can see what excites him. Let me go to him. I'll show you!"

The intensity of his son's eager, burning look in his enthusiasms was not often turned upon Philip. Now he received the full force of it and it made him uncomfortable. This reminded him unpleasantly of the night of the singing and the passions of Olympias.

He said roughly, "That'll do now, boy. That's enough. I'll have no boasting where your word can't be put to the proof."

Alexander flamed with anger. "I'm not boasting. I'm telling you. I can ride him."

Philip signed to the grooms. "Take the horse away."

Alexander spun half round, held up a hand to stop them, and turned back to his father in desperation. "No! Don't let him go! I'll wager you, Father. I'll wager! I can ride him!"

It was Philip's turn to feel goaded. He was angry. What had got into the boy, openly defying him, making fools of them both in public? He had hardly seen him during the last few months. What had Leonidas been about? Where was the celebrated Spartan discipline? That precocious boar hunt had gone to his head. Time his father taught him a lesson or, rather, let him teach himself. He accepted the challenge.

"So you'll wager, will you? I'll take you on. If you can ride the horse I'll buy him for you. Now, what are you staking?"

Alexander's face glowed with joy. He grinned broadly. "If I can't ride him, Father, I'll pay for him myself." There was a rumble of laughter from some of the onlookers – those not concerned with the outcome. Reckoning Alexander's allowance in his mind, the king said scathingly, "*Could* you?"

"Yes, if you give me time to pay."

More grins passed between the men. Philip was less amused. His glance flickered to the dangerous animal, still pulling against restraining hands, the sun high-lighting the powerful muscles under the gleaming coat. He would have liked to pull Alexander back from the contest, but it was too late now that the bargain had been struck and witnessed. And, he told himself, the boy needed to be taught a lesson. He nodded. "Go ahead, then. Show us what you can do." He limped to his chair and sat down, unconsciously settling his hands over the end of the arms, where the carvings afforded a good grip. No-one ventured to interfere.

Alexander drew in and let out a deep breath. He ran his hands down his sides as he turned away from his father and stood facing the horse. It was, for the moment, quiet, only nervously flicking its ears.

He walked a little distance to one side before he approached it. He had seen that it disliked shadows passing over the ground in front of it, and that its own shadow, when it moved, made it start. When he had the sun shining almost full in his face he made a low, smooth gesture with one hand, and said to the grooms : "Move away from him – all except the red

"Go — like kings"

haired one – over there, that way, quietly." And to Philonicus: "You too!"
They glanced at the king and, receiving no counter command, obeyed.
Alexander unfastened the pin of his cloak and let the garment slide gently
to the ground. The horse's head jerked as he followed the slight movement
with an apprehensive eye.

The onlookers had been quiet before, listening to the exchange between
the king and his son. Now the silence felt as if the crowd held not only its
tongue but its breath.

Philonicus felt cold sweat running down his spine. He would be known
as the man whose horse had killed the king's son. Lysimachus, who had
signalled ' *no*' to Alexander and been ignored, folded his arms and prayed to
Castor the Tamer of Horses. Alexander's Companions fiercely and silently
willed his success; he was theirs and they were his, whatever happened to
him, they shared. Hephaistion's mouth was set in a firm line. As Alexander
stepped past he made the sign for good luck, and slid one of his apples into
his hand.

The horse had experienced a moment of stillness, when the clamouring
of men, the harsh breathing and muttered cursing of his tormentors and
the pulling of their hard hands at his mouth were withdrawn, leaving him
uncertain. In the stillness, he heard clearly the assured note of command in
Alexander's quiet voice. He looked towards him, snorting , and pawed the
ground. His tail flicked a cautionary warning.

Alexander moved smoothly and quietly, but his approach was swift. He
reached the horse as it lifted a foot to back away, put one firm hand on
its neck and with the other stroked down its muzzle. The bony nose of the
horse pushed up hard against his hand, its eye rolled uneasily, showing
some white, and it snorted again.

The pressure of the boy's hand was firm but not forceful. He stroked
down and, as the horse lowered its head, blew into its nostrils in the way he
had seen horses greet one another in the field. The head tossed up again,
but less violently and the wild eye quietened a little. Alexander spoke
gently. He offered the apple and the stallion accepted it. Then, with a tiny
shake of its ears, arched its neck and nuzzled the top of the boy's head.

The black horse, before it was sold to a dealer, had only one master, the
son of the man on whose land it had been foaled, and the boy had trained
it himself. When the young man was killed by a fall on the hunting field,
his grieving father sold his horse. Its life underwent rapid and bewildering
changes at the hands of hard men to whom horses were passing trade.

Philip's friend saw it, admired its strength and beauty, and suggested a royal buyer.

One morning, in an unfamiliar stable yard on the way to Macedon, the horse, led out of semi-darkness into sudden brilliant light, met the shadows of tree branches, writhing across the ground in front of it like black snakes. It screamed and reared up to strike at them and hit a groom with its fore-hoof. Another man, frightened, raised his arm and fetched it a heavy blow across the face. In the seconds before it was struck, the horse saw the man's shadow also leap threateningly across its path. Philonicus, hearing the row, came out and added his own voice and weight to the job of controlling the horse. He was furious at the mistreatment of this animal intended for a royal buyer, and after the horse was mastered he beat the grooms. The horse hated them all. He fretted at the changes each day brought to confuse him. He wanted only to kill his tormentors and escape from them, although at times exhaustion quietened him and revived Philonicus' hopes, but then he seemed likely to pine into sickness. They drove on hard to Macedon.

When the horse was brought to the riding ground it was just such a day of wind and sunshine as that on which he had first met the black snakes and he met them there, too. Then into the bewilderment of noise, uncertainty and fear, the hated presence of men with their harsh voices and rank sweaty smell, their accoutrements that clanked and rattled, their hard hands that forced him this way and that, held down his head and jabbed the bit against his tender jaws, came this other presence. It was like one he had known before. It was small and made no noise. It brought no black demons with it. It smelt of grass and apples. It touched caressingly and its voice was light. It seemed to put itself under his protection rather than to threaten him, yet there was a certainty about it, a reassurance in its presence, an authority it was safe to trust. He wanted to stay near this presence.

Alexander took the leading rein in his left hand and motioned away the remaining groom. He was talking in a low, cheerful voice, as if telling a confidential tale to a friend, while he still stroked the horse. He was saying: "You have a mark on your forehead like a white ox-head with horns. Did you know that? That's what I shall call you...Oxhead...Bukephalus. I am Alexander. We'll ride together, Alexander and Bukephalus, like Achilles and Chiron..."

He was leaning and stroking, coaxing the horse round to face the sun. Their shadows lay behind them. "Did you know that a god sent you? Be still now. Remember you're a king. Don't show them your anger. Obey because you choose to do it, like the Spartans at Thermopylae. That's how I treat Leonidas and the schoolmen. They can't master you then."

His left hand gathered up the reins and he took a firm hold of the long black mane just above the withers. A quiver ran down the horse's shoulders. It struck the ground a ringing blow with its hoof.

"Yes, we'll go now. The god is waiting. We'll go with him, but like warriors, like kings. Go gently now."

He gave a little push against the animal. As Bukephalus moved forward, he ran a few steps at his side, then took an agile leap which carried his leg over the horse's back and brought him neatly to his seat. Bukephalus pranced sideways. Alexander took the reins in a firm hold, spoke to him clearly, and within a few steps brought him to a standstill. He settled himself comfortably on the broad back, feeling the strong heart beating against his legs, the contained power quivering through the tensed muscles under him, a sweet steam of sweat rising to his nostrils above the tossing, impatient head. The horse's ears pricked towards him. He laughed softly. "Yes, now we'll go. But not like flying Scythians. Remember – like kings!"

He tapped his heels against the horse's sides. Bukephalus broke into a gentle canter, lengthened his stride to a gallop, a contained gallop. They began to circle the field. The crowd, wanting to cheer but having the good sense not to, expecting still to see him thrown, or the horse run away with him, muttered in excitement. The king stood up. Hephaistion uttered a breathy whistle of triumph.

Alexander, feeling that he had control, kicked his heels and shouted, "Charge!" Bukephalus threw up his head, rattling the harness. His flying legs, his flowing mane and flaunting tail became part of the wind. The light weight on his back was no burden. It became part of himself, a part that was courage, certainty and joy. The sun flamed around them. Alexander sang the battle song of the Companions. The sound of it drifted back to his father on the wind.

The horse and its rider neared the end of the long field. The king watched anxiously for the turn. They were going too fast and the horse would be too strong for the boy. But they steadied, slowed, and the black horse swung round easily in a graceful arc. Then the crowd did cheer. It roared with delight. Hephaistion yelled the war cry – *alalalala!* – and the other boys joined in, punching the air. Alexander's victory was theirs, too. Bukephalus understood applause as well as Alexander. He tossed his head and neighed. They both feasted on the adulation, drinking the wine of the gods.

As they came nearer to the pavilion, Alexander brought the horse to a trot and then to an easy walk. Their shadows, which had been alongside them, crept to the front. He felt Bukephalus quiver, the horse sidled and shook his head. Alexander soothed him with hands and voice, and brought him up to where the king was standing.

The boy on the horse's back sat upright, easy, looking the prince he was, his hands low in front of him, his legs straight, gripping with the thighs, hanging loosely from the knees, as Xenophon and Lysimachus taught. The horse, too, bore himself with a princely air, his head up, neck arched, stepping proudly – not mastered, but won. The two of them belonged together. With the sun behind them, lighting a crown in Alexander's hair and outlining their shadowed bodies in radiance, Lysimachus saw for a moment an apparition of a young centaur riding out of the legends of the golden past – or a boy and a horse about to make new legends of their own?

They halted in front of the king and Alexander sat still, looking at his father. There was a glow in his eyes, his breath came quickly, but his face was remote, peaceful. The king stood without moving, unsmiling, looking back at his son. He had not made a sound since he sent the boy to the horse. With a shock of mild surprise, Alexander saw that he did not speak because he was weeping. His good eye was wet, tear marks glistened on his cheeks and he swallowed convulsively.

The most unexpected love for him flowed into Alexander like wine. It mingled with his love for this magnificent horse, proud, angry and untameable who had given him love in return; love for this beautiful morning of sun and cool, clean air, on which the gods had smiled for him; and love for himself, who had known his time and taken it, without fear, with knowledge and self mastery. His glance swept round, taking in the approving, smiling faces of the generals, the glowing, laughing faces of his friends, and his love flowed out to them all, and came back to his father. It burned in him like fire.

The king came forward and held out his arms. Alexander spoke quietly to Bukephalus, swung his leg across, managing the reins carefully to avoid jerking his mouth, and slid down into his father's embrace. He was folded to the king's broad chest in hard arms that held him with the strength of a bear. Philip hugged him, kissed him, then ran his fingers through the boy's thick locks to pull back his head and look into his flushed and laughing face, those brilliant eyes that generously shared with him the triumph and the victory.

"Boy! Boy!" said Philip, laughing a little now, and scraping his cheek with another damp and hairy kiss, "What are we going to give you for a kingdom? Macedon won't be big enough for you!"

Alexander laughed back at him. "Is the horse mine, Father?"

"Yes, he's yours. You've won him. A prize of honour."

"Thank you, Father. I call him Oxhead."

Philip gave a snort of amused surprise. "Oxhead? Not Balios or Xanthos?" These were the immortal horses of Achilles. Alexander stirred uncomfortably under the hands resting on his shoulders, reminded of his song. He was being mocked again. He flushed resentfully, drawing back. But Philip, the diplomat, leader of men, charmer of women, yet so often maladroit where his son was concerned, knew his mistake the moment the words left his mouth and he felt Alexander stiffen. He thumped his shoulder in comradely fashion. "Present Oxhead to me," he said.

Alexander relaxed and grinned. Hephaistion was standing nearby, shining with love and admiration, waiting until he should be noticed or needed. Alexander gave him the look that shared everything and said, laughing, "Have you any more apples?"

Hephaistion's hand delved into his tunic. "Two."

"Keep one."

Alexander gave the apple to his father and took him up to the horse. Bukephalus had been standing quietly enough, flicking his ears and once or twice tossing or shaking his head and stretching out his neck towards Alexander. The grooms were poised ready to grab him, but had not come too close. Philonicus stood grinning from ear to ear.

Alexander held his father's hand and stroked Bukephalus. The king offered the apple and was acknowledged and allowed to pat the horse.

"Father," said Alexander, "I want to make an offering to the gods."

"You shall, boy."

"A good one. Since you've bought me the horse, I have some money saved. It ought to be my own gift. May I buy incense – a talent's worth?"

"You shall have what you want. The gods have been generous. We won't be stingy in return."

"I ought to ride him again before I take him to the stable. I'll look after him myself at first. I don't suppose he'll let the men near him yet. I'd like to take him away from everyone, across the marshes and by the lake. May I?"

"Take Simonides and Ptolemy with you."

"Yes and Hephaistion and Lysimachus."

The king grinned and nodded. Lysimachus, meeting Alexander's enquiring look, nodded too. When they had gone, followed by the applause of the crowd like athletes leaving the arena, Philip said to Antipater, "The boy's outgrown those schoolmasters. I've thought so some time. He knows all he needs to know of poetry and hero-tales and playing with weapons. It's high time we thought of giving him a proper education and a grown warrior's training." He was not looking at either of his generals. His gaze was inward, seeing the future commander, the King of Macedon, and the leader of all the Greeks.

Alexander, followed by his companions, rode away from the noise and tensions of the court about his father into the wind-swept, sunlit spaces of grassland, water and sky, sharing it only with startled birds and hares. The men and boys were a little in awe of him and his charger, cooled after their earlier excitement, and rode almost without speaking. They let him draw ahead of them.

Alexander had been looking out for something. He guided Bukephalus towards an oak tree, standing on a clean little knoll. The shadows of the branches and foliage danced over the green slope. Alexander drew rein. Bukephalus pranced and sidled, eyeing the black shapes that advanced and retreated so unpredictably.

"It's nothing to be alarmed about," said the cheerful, quiet voice he trusted and had already begun to love. "Look, I'll show you. Stand still." A re-assuring hand patted him. The boy slid down from his back and, holding the reins at full length, advanced upon the threatening black snakes wriggling over the grass. In front of the horse he knelt down. The black snakes played over his back and arms. He spoke with the voice of love and courage.

"We know fear, you and I, Bukephalus. The brave ones do. Those who are not afraid are stupid. Father says so. But we know how to beat him, this enemy. Come and walk on him. Come on! Put him under your feet!"

He held out his free hand, gave a gentle pull on the reins, and made a little chirruping sound. "Come on, king of horses, Bukephalus. Walk with the god. It is a lovely thing, I promise you."

One step at a time, raising his feet as though about to put them on hot coals, the horse advanced. As he came, Alexander stood up, and when he reached him under the tree embraced him, stroking his nose and patting his sides. Bukephalus put down his head to sniff at a black patch, and jerked back with a whiffle of alarm when the leaves overhead shivered and the patch moved. Alexander put his foot on the shadow and lifted it again. Bukephalus trod on it hesitantly, lowered his head and sniffed at it, blew at it softly and then straightened up, stepping away and casting a nonchalant glance over his shoulder at Alexander as though he said, "Well, what are we hanging about here for? There's nothing more to see."

Alexander laughed delightedly, calling him a fraud. As the others rode up he said to Hephaistion, "Come and reward him. He has just vanquished an enemy. Give him your other apple."

Hephaistion came, and Alexander put an arm round him as he patted and fed the docile horse. "You must love him if you love me, Oxhead," said the prince. "He is Alexander, too."

Ptolemy wound sprays of oak leaves into garlands and they put them on. Then they rode in a victory procession to the marshes, where the horses kicked up sprays of glittering water, and the boys lost their crowns to the wind in a mad gallop along the lake shore, and where Bukephalus so far out-distanced the others that the older men suffered agonies of cheated responsibility and anxiety until the ride ended safely in breathless laughter.

Alexander offered his special thanks that evening to Herakles and the Divine Twins at the garden shrine, but the next day there were public ceremonies at the temples in the city. The king sacrificed bulls, Olympias gave sheep and goats in extravagant numbers. The meat would feast the people after the gods' share was burnt on the altars.

Alexander bought frankincense from the Treasury. The dusty golden granules were heaped on three silver dishes; he poured one onto each of the altar fires of Zeus, Herakles and the Warrior Twins. Clouds of fragrant smoke rose from the glowing charcoal with its little leaping flames. Alexander watched the columns rise, white in the morning sun, taking his grateful thanks with them, confirming the gods' blessing on him. He felt skin-tight with a deep and flawless happiness.

Leonidas, present because it was a court occasion, watched the extravagant offerings with austere disapproval. Like the king, he had felt the time of change coming, The boy who had killed his boar and tamed Bukephalus, though he still obeyed him, did so in a detached way as though this were a temporary courtesy now. It made him angry because there was nothing to condemn, no obvious opposition, yet the independence was there. He had come to shape and train a future king, but he knew that somehow the real Alexander had eluded him and shaped himself.

As the prince turned away from the altars with a deep sigh of satisfaction, the man aimed a shaft at the serene self-assurance that radiated from his face. Moderation in all things! "Your offerings are too extravagant," he said sharply. "Be less wasteful of precious things, Alexander, until you are master of the lands they grow in!"

The sarcasm was lost in the meaning Alexander took from his words. He stood for a moment startled by the discordant note. Then he looked up into his father's face. Philip's expressive brows flared above his prescient eye; the king and his son regarded each other, pricked like horses who had heard the war trumpet. Then they both smiled. Alexander said gravely to Leonidas: "I will remember your words."

Ten years later the man received a gift from the Great King of Persia. It was a fabulous quantity of incense, worth a fortune. With it came a letter. *'Alexander to Leonidas, greetings. We send you frankincense and myrrh in abundance so that you need no longer be stingy in your offerings to the gods.'*

Epilogue

General

"In all his early battles he led the cavalry charge riding Bukephalus. They thought as one, man and horse. He was eighteen when his father fought the Athenians and their allies at Chaironeia. He led the Companion Cavalry against the Thebans and broke their battle line.

At Gaugemela, six years later, he rode other horses early in the day, but saved Bukephalus for the final charge – against the Great King and his Immortals... they broke through!... yes, the Great King fled..."

The Pharaoh's deep voice, slightly husky from the long morning's dictation, thinned and was lost in reverie, his eyes focused on distant memories. The scribe paused, stylus half-raised, uncertain whether their work was finished for the day.

A deep chuckle surprised him. Ptolemy said, "I swear the old horse expected the honour, took it as his due – no, don't put that in. He knew he carried the king. Now continue...

"Bukephalus let no-one else ride him. He came with us all the way to India. He was stolen once, when tribesmen ambushed the Pages leading horses through a forest. Alexander threatened to fire the forest and burn the villages if he were not returned unharmed. They brought him back next day, wondering perhaps why one old horse meant so much to a king who had all the finest horses in the empire at his command. He died in India. He must have been thirty years old, though no-one knew his true age when he came to Alexander. We gave him a soldier's honours and the king named a city after him – Bukephala. I've heard that the people there claim to have horses sired by him. Well, maybe... but there could only ever be one Bukephalus."

A long silence followed. 'And,' thought Ptolemy, 'only ever one Alexander. None of us could succeed him.'

The scribe, watching him, put down his stylus. The slight sound recalled Ptolemy to the present. "Yes... yes... enough for today. A good place to stop. The end of his childhood. Have a fair copy made and add to the others in the library. We'll have a public reading on his birthday."

A hound nosed its way round the open door, followed by Ptolemy's eldest grandson.

"I saw the scribe going away. Are you finished for today?"

"For today. I've told the story of Bukephalus. The end of childhood. Next, his schooling by Aristotle, his early battles, his quarrel with his father and his exile – and – the death of Philip."

"Killed by Pausanias."

"Pausanias used the dagger. But there were powerful men behind him. His escape was planned...horses waiting...a ship. Parmenion's advance force had crossed into Asia. The Persians knew that Philip planned to follow soon. Alexander found evidence of their involvement later. And how did Demosthenes know that he was dead before any messenger had time to reach Athens?"

"How then?"

"My guess – bonfires on the hills. A chain of fires carrying a message. But you must know what message it is that they confirm. Antipater's spies said that Demosthenes put on a festal wreath and went out into the streets of Athens to spread the news of Philip's death before anyone else knew."

"Will you write that?"

"I write what I know and saw. Not what I surmise. But Demosthenes was receiving silver from Persia. We know that."

"Why didn't Alexander kill him?"

"He was plunged into war straight away. Rebellion flared up on every border once the news spread that Philip was dead. Alexander was twenty. How could they know that the cub already had the jaws of a lion?" Ptolemy laughed and slapped his hand down over the golden lion head on his chair arm.

His grandson looked at him curiously. The man he spoke of had been dead for more than thirty years, but seemed still a living presence to his grandfather. "What was it like," he said, "when you were with him. When you were young?"

"A large question! Don't expect me to be able to answer it." Ptolemy stood up and paced about the room, his hands clasped behind him as, the boy imagined, he might have walked beside Alexander, his large frame and long stride still more suited to battle armour than the robes of the Pharaoh.

"Philip was king of Macedon but Alexander's kingdom was the army when we crossed into Asia. We had our engineers, surveyors, craftsmen, our doctors, architects and armourers, our grooms and stewards and servants. We gathered women and children. We lived in camps outside the cities.Traders followed us and set up their markets. Alexander had his seers and priests, his chamberlains, his secretariat, historians and tutors for the royal Pages. The business of empire came to him wherever he was. He had records kept of the plants and animals in the lands we crossed, of the people, their customs – what they produced. He was always hungry –"

"Hungry!"

"Hungry for knowledge – eager for new discoveries, new experiences, greater challenges. It was what led him on as much as the necessities of war."

"What was the best time?"

"The best time! The first years were the best. When we were young."

"Tell me about the battles."

"What! All of them?"

"When you fought the Great King."

"The first was at Issus. Between mountains and the sea. In a rainstorm. After a night march. The Persians had a great army without the space to deploy it. The Great King fled. We chased after him but he escaped in the dark through mountain passes choked with fugitives.

At midnight we get back to the battlefield, to Darius's base camp. The stewards have a meal for us – in the Great King's tent. We stand in the entrance – and stare. Like hillmen come down to Pella for the first time. But there was nothing at Pella like this. Hanging lamps of silver. Censers breathing perfume. Silk carpets and curtains, cushioned couches. Tables inlaid with lapis and ivory, dishes of silver and gold. Even a throne! Alexander says, 'So *this* is what it means to be a king!' There was a bath, too! That pleased him!"

Ptolemy's deep rumble of laughter disturbed the dog, who sat up and barked. He bent to soothe it.

"While we were eating, we heard people wailing, women's voices. Alexander sent Leonnatus to find the cause. Darius had left more behind than his furniture – he'd abandoned his family – his wife, his three children and his mother. Told that his empty chariot had been found, they assumed he'd been killed and expected slavery – or worse. Alexander sent Leonnatus back to re-assure them. Darius had escaped alive, they would be treated with honour.

Next day, after he'd seen the wounded, he went to them himself. He took Hephaistion I'm told the Queen Mother prostrated herself before him, thinking he was the king. He was taller – they seldom thought of precedence, those two – I expect they walked in side by side. The attendants hissed a warning to her, he stepped back, but Alexander laughed: 'Never mind, Mother, he is Alexander, too!' She knew *some* Greek, but I don't know what she made of that! I'm told the six year old boy came up and hugged him. Alexander said it was a pity Darius hadn't the courage of his son.

After that the family were kept with us for their protection, given their servants and their royal status. The queen lived secluded – she was young – said to be the most beautiful woman in Asia – but the Queen Mother had no need for strict privacy and Alexander visited her often. If Darius had surrendered would Alexander have given him a satrapy and re-united him with his family? Hephaistion thought so. He'd been told a story like that about Kyros, who captured the beautiful wife of an enemy and through his kindness to her won her husband's allegiance. He always believed he could make his hero- tales come true. Sometimes he did. But not this time. The queen died in childbirth."

Returning to his chair, Ptolemy reached for a cup on a nearby table. His grandson poured water for him and waited until he put down the cup.

"Was that the greatest battle?"

"The decisive one? No, that was Gaugemela. But the Persian forces were broken for a while. We came here to Egypt. The Egyptians welcomed us. Under Persian rule their temples had been desecrated, their gods mocked – the Great King – it was Xerxes then – had their sacred bull slaughtered. Alexander restored their temples and founded this city. They made him Pharaoh and we held a great festival – famous actors and athletes came from everywhere – the army held games and contests. Then he left men to govern and we went back to Persia.

The Great King had had time to gather an army from his farthest provinces – Medes, Bactrians, Armenians, Scythian archers, Indian cavalry, Syrians, Hyrcanians, Cappodchians – and a tough core of Greek mercenaries. An army five times the size of ours. He had chosen his ground this time. Not a narrow coastal plain cut by rocks and rivers between mountains and the sea, as at Issus, but a wide, flat plain – he'd had thousands of slaves smooth and flatten it still more – where his scythed chariots could run free and he could deploy his cavalry on their powerful horses and use his elephants."

"Elephants! He had elephants!"

"This time – yes. Our horses were afraid of them. Now, having chosen his ground he could not move from it, but stayed there – waiting for Alexander. What does that suggest to you?"

"The men might get frightened, waiting."

"So we thought. Alexander didn't hurry. An eclipse of the moon made the men uneasy, but Aristander said it foretold the Persians' fate.

When we were ready to be engaged, Alexander ordered the men to eat a good dinner and get some rest. He rode out to reconnoitre with Parmenion and his scouts. Parmenion suggested an attack before dawn to take the Persians by surprise. The Great King expected that and kept his entire army standing to battle stations all night. Alexander sat up late, too, planning. The lamp in his tent went out not long before dawn. So he overslept. But we had the men ready. And, as I told you, his plan was not to hurry.

He formed us up on low hills in sight of the Persians. And he sacrificed to Fear – the god of Fear. He reminded us how Darius fled at Issus. 'It's only of Fear,' he said, 'that we have to be afraid.' He said we didn't need any speeches from him to encourage us. Our own pride and courage would do that. Aristander pointed to an eagle soaring over us. – he could always find us a good omen.

We advanced. In silence. According to his orders. Across the plain. In perfect order. And in silence."

The boy watched his face. His grandfather was advancing again in his mind. His eyes were not looking at the room. They were seeing that battlefield. The dust rising under the relentless marching feet, the trampling hooves.

"The dust – ?"

"Oh yes, the dust. A dry plain at the end of summer! The Persians watched the smoke of it rolling towards them, concealing numbers... It half-blinded us, too, but we knew our drill. Darius hoped to break our front with his elephants and chariots, then sweep his wings round to outflank us. That was the danger. But in that event our infantry were trained to form a defensive square – spears bristling on all sides. So we advanced towards his trap. Then Alexander swung us into an oblique line of attack – . Darius began to move his crack troops to the centre. And we raised the war cry!"

For a moment it seemed that the elderly Pharaoh of Egypt hovered on the brink of lifting his head and bringing guards and frightened servants running and setting the dog barking with the Macedonian howl

– ALALALALALAI! But the moment passed with a relinquishing gesture of his hand. "The infantry had been well drilled. Their ranks parted to let the scythed chariots through without much harm. The Agrianians leapt on them to cut the traces and cut down the riders.

A gap opened up in the Persian ranks and Alexander led the Royal Squadron straight for Darius. He'd mounted Bukephalus. The last battle for the old horse. The king's charioteer fell wounded. Darius seized the reins and once again the Great King fled. He'd sent a picked band of troops to rescue his family from the base camp but the Queen Mother refused to go with them.

The Persians saw one of the riders in the chariot fall – many of them thought it was the king. They fell into dis-array. Only Parmenion on the left still had hard fighting. So did Alexander when he rode to help him – thirty Companions fell. That's why they didn't capture the Great King. He escaped again but he was finished. Later his own people killed him before Alexander could rescue him.

After that, the cities surrendered to us. The great cities of the fertile plain where grain and fruit grew, where the treasures of the empire were laid up in palaces of a splendour beyond imagining – palaces the gods might envy. The first was Babylon. The satrap fought against us at Gaugemela, when the king fled he retreated. Afterwards he came with his wife and children to surrender his city.

Alexander was doubtful. We approached in battle order. But the gates were open – and the walls un-manned. The citizens came out to welcome us. They brought a golden chariot for Alexander. An escort of cavalry – un-armed – on their beautiful horses. Priests with censers. Dancing girls. Musicians. They showered our way with flowers We rode and marched in along the Processional Way between the blue tiled walls – there were golden lions pictured on the walls and lions in the procession! It was as Alexander had half-dreamed as a boy when he listened to the stories of the Persian exiles.

They came to him after the death of Darius. Old Artabazus and his sons. They'd been recalled when Darius came to the throne and served this new king faithfully until his murder, when they came to Alexander, who loved and honoured them. Darius's brother came, too, seeking revenge for his death, and joined the Companion Cavalry, with Artabazus' grandsons.

Alexander knew then that he could be Great King himself. They took us to find Kyros' tomb, a small chamber of rock in the mountains. Inside was the stone coffin, his robe and jewellery, his bow and scimitar and an inscription:

'Know traveller it was I Kyros who founded the empire of the Persians
Do not grudge me this small piece of earth which covers my body'

We wondered if Alexander meant to use the regalia himself in a ceremony to confirm him as Great King. But like the nomad shepherds who leave offerings of milk and honey on the steps when they pass by, he paid his own homage and went away."

Ptolemy did not tell the boy that later the tomb had been found robbed and the bones scattered by Macedonian soldiers – no need to smirch the dreams of the young too soon. He reached for his cup, drank, and picked up his tale again – vigorously, to dispel the unwelcome recollection.

"Babylon was the beginning of our wealth. The treasures of the empire had been stored in the strongholds of the king. Alexander set it free. He loved to give. After Gaugemela every man was given two months extra pay. He gave gold to the Babylonian priests to rebuild temples Darius had destroyed. He gave prizes for valour on campaign – to men of all ranks, chosen by acclamation. Once he came alongside a treasure train. A mule had gone lame and the man in charge had shouldered the load himself. 'Just get it as far as your tent, Coinus,' he said, 'it's yours.' For the first time he gave eight common soldiers command over a thousand men – a reward for their valour. We were beginning a new world, Alexander's world."

For a moment or two the boy watched him. He wanted to know more, to keep him talking. Was he getting tired? There was something he wanted – needed – to know, amid the glitter and the glory. The question sprang from him before he had decided to ask it, surprising him almost as much as Ptolemy. "What was the worst time?"

"The worst time!" Ptolemy's bark surprised the dog, which leapt instantly out of sleep and began barking, too. By the time they had quietened it, he was ready.

"Why ask that?"

"I want to know. There were bad times. There must have been."

A glint of approval lifted his grandfather's frown. "There were." He pondered which to choose. The boy needed a true answer.

"Was it crossing the desert?"

It would be easy to say yes, that was the worst, the terrible desert march when so many died – or – the death of Hephaistion, from fever – when grief had brought Alexander to the verge of madness, hastening his own death.

Any of these would do, would satisfy his grandson. But Ptolemy decided to speak the truth. Otherwise, why speak at all? He said, "When he killed Kleitos."

"He killed Kleitos! How? In battle, hunting, an accident?"

"It was murder. He named it so himself."

"Murder! Why? When?"

"It was a feast day of Dionysos, but Alexander held a great supper in honour of Castor and Pollux the Warrior Twins. There were Persian guests whom Alexander honoured. He was trying to build a kingdom that included all his people. But it angered some of the older Macedonians who wanted him all theirs. These men had fought with Philip and resented seeing younger friends of Alexander rise to power in a new empire with ways that were foreign to them. Kleitus was one of the most outspoken, having known the king from childhood.

He had just been appointed governor of a province – an honour in its way, but it would take him out of the high command. That night he brought two sheep to sacrifice to Dionysos, and dedicated them, but then the trumpet sounded and he went in to the feast. The sheep followed him in through the door. Everyone laughed. It made him angry, but Alexander said it was a bad omen and sent to tell the priests to pray for his safety.

We were drinking heavily – neat wine – the water was bad thereabouts. Hephaistion and Philotas and others – well most of us to tell the truth – began talking up our exploits – Alexander, too – soldiers' talk, friendly boasting. The young men began a raucous song – mocking the veterans who'd failed to relieve the siege of Samarkand – Alexander had to go himself. Others were soon saying how far Alexander had surpassed his father. Kleitos let out a roar like an angry bull and shouted: "Ah! Philip's not good enough for you now, you son of Ammon! Where would you be without the men Philip trained? These soft Persians won't hold your kingdom for you, for all their bowing and crawling on the floor." Alexander shouted back and so did Kleitos, telling him again he was no match for his father – it was the Macedonians who had done it all for him . There was a bowl of apples on the table – Alexander grabbed one and threw it – he always aimed straight – it hit Kleitos in the teeth. We laughed but Kleitos made for him. Alexander shouted for a weapon, but no-one goes armed to a feast. I grabbed Kleitos and pushed him outside. I walked him away, still struggling and mouthing insults. But then, in the night air, he quietened down and I left him stumbling off towards his quarters."

There was a moment's silence. Ptolemy's chest heaved – a deep soundless sigh. Then – "He came back. He burst in through a side door, shouting 'I'm here, Alexander!' and some insult he'd just thought of. Something about the men doing the fighting and the boy getting the glory. There was uproar. Alexander was scarlet with rage. It was his pride never to ask his men to do anything he did not, he always led from the front. He grabbed the only weapon in the place – a spear from the door guard – and ran it into Kleitos."

There was a silence. Just as there had been in that supper room.

Ptolemy said, "He knew at once what he'd done. Killed an unarmed man and a friend. He pulled out the spear and stared at it – as if it were a thing that had moved of its own volition. We leapt forward to hold him before he could turn the spear on himself. Someone wrenched it away."

Again he was silent. His grandson looked into his deeply furrowed face. "Perhaps he thought Kleitos meant to kill him – like his father?.... he was the king...?"

"A Macedonian king. Who cannot take life without trial. Who must accuse a man before an assembly of Macedonians. And our men always had freedom of speech.

We led him to his room. We tried to tell him it was Kleitos' fault. But he knew it was his own temper. He'd killed a friend, the brother of his childhood nurse, and not as a king but like any common soldier in a drunken brawl. We thought he'd kill himself. We dare not leave him alone. He refused to eat or drink – and a man can die in three days without water in that heat. By the third day he was barely with us.

The men were afraid. Without him we were nothing – a headless dragon. They held an assembly and condemned Kleitos for treasonable speech – so that his death would be lawful. It wasn't enough. I daresay Alexander loved them for their loyalty but he knew it was a deceit.

Aristander brought the priests with better comfort. They said the god had been angered – the god Dionysos who drives men mad. It was his feast day, but Alexander had sacrificed to the Warrior Twins and Kleitos had not made his offering – his sheep, still alive, had followed him. Alexander had known the power of Dionysos from childhood, he could believe that the god had sent his madness upon Kleitos and himself as punishment."

Ptolemy paused. "And", he said, "if you had been there that night you might have believed it too. It was hot. The torches flared. The wine burned in your throat, and in your head. There was something – something dangerous there."

"So he believed the priests?"

"He had to. The lives of hundreds, thousands depended on him. He couldn't abandon them for one man. He took food and drink again. We held sacrifices as they did at Troy when the gods were angry with the Achaiens." Ptolemy brooded, frowning a little. "His mother's temper. It didn't betray him often. Not even when the rain and the heat and the snakes in India defeated his men as no army had done and they refused to march on. He couldn't move them. They wanted to go home – he could bring out younger men, their spokesman said, to carry his conquests further. Alexander made offerings to the gods and took omens from the sacrifices and it seemed the omens agreed with the men. Well, he did everything with style. He held games and ceremonies, turning defeat into a kind of victory. He led some of us back a different way, still exploring , to reach the shore of the Encircling Ocean and launch his fleet – and nearly killed us all crossing the unknown desert!"

"Wasn't that the worst time then?"

"No. Men are strange creatures. And kings are men, too. It bound us together – the survivors. We took him water in a helmet once when we found a little in a pool. There wasn't enough for us, so he poured it out as an offering to the gods. We suffered, and we conquered the desert, too."

In a brief silence, the elderly Pharaoh looked back at the endless hills of sand they had climbed night after night – when it was cooler. "He marched with us, refusing to ride, although breathing still caused him pain after a chest wound that had nearly killed him. He made the officers walk, too. It's why the men loved him. We shared his rewards – his commanders lived like kings, he paid all the debts his men incurred, no questions asked – looked after their campaign wives and foreign children – and he shared our dangers. Never a battle but he was in the forefront, as his wounds showed.

Only once did the men turn against him. Because they were jealous –" He broke off abruptly. He'd spoken before he thought, not meaning to tell this story. But he'd aroused curiosity.

"Why? When was it? What happened?"

Ptolemy gave in with a slight shrug and shake of his head. "It was in the last year of his life. He was working to make a united people, appointing Persian satraps with Macedonian military governors in his provinces, training Persian boys for his army. He proposed to send his veterans home, those whose age or disablement made them unfit for active service, and held a parade to dismiss them. He promised them enough to make them rich men in Macedon, and to send Kraterus, his second-in-command, to take charge of their journey And they rebelled. For the first and only time. They shouted him down. They yelled back at him to discharge them all, send them all home. "And you can go fighting on your own with the god if he's your father!" They knew that story.

He jumped down from the platform. We followed him fast – the mood was ugly. I never thought we'd fear for Alexander, but we knew that Philip's half-brother had been cut down by his own men. He went for the ring leaders, had them dragged off."

Ptolemy pushed himself from his chair and crossed to the window. Looking out, his gaze was not on the busy wharves and harbour below, but on the angry upturned faces of the Macedonian soldiery. He knew Alexander's words by heart. They had burned into him that dangerous morning.

"He was back on the platform. No-one had touched him. He shouted at them: 'Go! Go then! I won't stop you. But first understand what I've done for you.' Then he talked, striding up and down.

"'Philip found you dressed in skins, feeding a few sheep in the hills, fighting to keep them from your neighbours. He gave you cloaks instead of skins, brought you down from the hills to the plains, taught you to fight. He brought you law. He civilised you. He rescued you from subjection and slavery and made you masters of those who had harried and plundered you. He opened your coasts to trade and brought you the gold and silver mines. When he was made commander of the Greeks for the war against Persia, he claimed the glory not for himself alone but for the Macedonian people.

Now the wealth of Egypt, Syria, Babylon and Lydia, the treasures of Persia are yours. You are my captains, my generals, my governors of provinces.

I've kept nothing for my own – no treasure apart from what you yourselves possess or have in safe keeping for your future. I eat the same food. I wake earlier than you and watch that you may sleep.

Perhaps you will say that I had none of the labours and distress which you endured to win for me what I have won. Come now, if you are wounded, strip and show your wounds and I will show mine. There is no part of my body but my back which has not a scar, no weapon that men may grasp or fling that has not left its mark on me.

Over every land and sea, across rivers, mountains and plains I've

256

led you to the world's end, a victorious army. I married as you married. Some of you will have children related by blood to mine.

Some of you owed money. I paid your debts, never asking how they were incurred, in spite of the fact that you earned good pay and grew rich from the sack of cities. Those who have died in battle have been commemorated with statues of bronze and pensions granted to their parents and their children. But under my leadership not a man of you has fallen with his back to the enemy.

It was in my mind to dismiss any no longer fit for service, to return home to be honoured and admired. But you all wish to leave me. Go then! and tell them that Alexander your king, who vanquished the Persians, Medes and Bactrians, who crossed the Caucasus beyond the Caspian Gates, the Oxus and the Indus, which none but Dionysos had crossed before him, who crossed the desert of Gedrosia and was brought back by you to Susa when his ships had sailed the ocean from India to Persia – tell them that you deserted him and left him to barbarian men whom you yourselves had conquered. Such news will assure you praise on earth and reward in heaven. Go! Out of my sight!'"

Ptolemy's ageing voice had taken on the ring of youth, of the long-dead, loved commander. His grandson saw a muscle move in his throat.

Ptolemy said, "He flung himself from the platform and back to the palace. No-one tried to stop him. He remained out of sight of the men all that day. Ate nothing. They hung about, returned to camp, came back to the parade ground, not knowing what to do. The next day too. The day after that they saw Persian officers going in and out. Heard rumours. We made sure the rumours spread. Alexander was taking them at their word. They were leaving him. So he was dividing the army commands among Persian officers, replacing Macedonian troopers with Medes and Persians."

Ptolemy's face creased into a grin.

"What did they do?"

His grandfather's smile broadened. "Ran to the doors of the palace. Flung down their weapons, their shields and armour, the sign of surrender in the field. They stood there shouting and calling to him, begging him to hear them. They would condemn the men who led them to rebel against him. They wouldn't go, they would stay there day and night until he pitied them and gave them a hearing.

When he came out he was in tears and so were they – well, they'd been to the world's end together. While he struggled to master his voice so that he could speak to them, one of the older Companions called out to him, 'What hurts us, Alexander, is that you've made Persians your kinsmen, and Persians are allowed to kiss you' – that was a Persian custom, not ours – 'but no Macedonian has had that honour.'

And he said to them, 'But I regard everyone of you as my kinsman.' Then the man came up and kissed him and after that anyone kissed him who wished. Then they all went cheering and singing back to camp. Alexander held a public thanksgiving, with ceremonies conducted by Aristander and Greek seers, and Persian magi, at an enormous open air feast for his Macedonians *and* Persians. After that, Kraterus led ten thousand retired soldiers on their return and Alexander gave a talent to each of them"

"Do you think he truly was the son of a god?"

"His mother told him so. Herakles was a son of Zeus. Achilles the son of a goddess. So – who can know? Believing it helped him to do more than most men would attempt. It was here that he tried to find out the truth of it."

The boy nodded. He had heard of this. "He went to Siwa. You went too?"

"I did," said Ptolemy. "He took his closest friends. We went along the coast from here and across the desert to the oasis. They say it's the oldest sanctuary of Zeus in the world. A sandstorm blew up and we lost the way. We followed a flock of crows. They led us through the mountains. Then across desert again. When we saw the trees we doubted the evidence of our eyes. Thousands of green trees – thousands! – and when we came nearer – fountains, streams, rivers, wells – all manner of fruits, grapes, pomegranates – and people with healthy flocks of sheep and goats. That was Siwa, a miracle in the desert, a place the god had touched, like Delphi, although it was very different.

Out of the trees rose a citadel of rocks, a kind of mountain, a natural tower. On that was built the sanctuary of Zeus Ammon.

We went up. Alexander wouldn't stop to eat or drink or wash – he'd waited too long for this. The priests greeted him as Pharaoh and Son of Ammon – but the Pharaoh to them is a god-king. He went alone into the sanctuary just as he was . We had to change our clothes and then wait outside. They have strange rituals – singing and music and they carry a boat hung with symbols that sways and dips to answer petitions and questions. But what Alexander said or did or what he was told we weren't to know.

When he came out he smiled at Hephaistion. He said later that he heard what he wanted to hear. Someone overheard him ask if all his father's murderers had been caught and punished, so it seems he accepted Philip as his mortal father still – and I was told he asked to which gods he should sacrifice when he reached the world's end." He shook his head, smiling. "That sounds as if it might be true – true to him, what he was."

"So was he the son of a god? People worship in his temple."

Ptolemy was silent sometime. Then he said: "He cast his spell. He could inspire men to believe – in themselves, in him, in his ideas. And his ideas were larger than most men's. If he'd lived he might have made us one people – we can't do that – we each took what we could. But who knows the truth? For myself, it doesn't matter. I loved him. I'd have followed him – we nearly did – to the end of the world and back again. And I serve him still." He got up again and moved to the window. "I brought him here. They would have taken his golden sarcophagus to Macedon. Would Kassander have buried him with honour? He killed his wife and his son."

His grandson said, "People come here from all over the world to honour him."

"They do. Well, he still casts his spell..."

A cooling breeze blew in from the sea. Ptolemy said, "His city, his first Alexandria – well, apart from a hill fortress in the wilds of Thrace that he named Alexandria during his first campaign." He chuckled. "He was sixteen then! Now there's Alexandria in Babylonia, Alexandria Margiana, Alexandria in Areia, Alexandria in Arachosia, Alexandria at the Confluence and Alexandria the Furthermost!" He laughed again. "Well, this was the first. He had a good eye for a site, he saw the advantages here – between the lake and the sea, two sheltered harbours, access to the Nile. He strode about, followed by his engineer and his architect, marking the roads, the outer walls – someone gave him a bag of barley meal when the chalk ran out. Crows came down and ate the meal – Aristander was quick to say it was a good sign – the city would prosper – well, so it has."

"Our Alexandria must be the best. We have the harbours – and the library!"

"Yes, that would please him. Wherever he was he sent for books to read."

"Will you get every book there is in the world?"

"I'll try!" said Ptolemy, smiling. "If we use his name we must match the largeness of his mind." In this campaign the boy knew the elderly general was ruthless – borrowing books from Greece and returning the copies – having ships searched for trophies – persuading scholars to come and work in Alexandria...

"And there'll be your book about him. That would please him, wouldn't it?"

259

"Oh yes, he loved his fame."

The dog fidgeted and whined. Ptolemy looked down. "Take him out. It's cooler now. Let him run by the shore."

When the boy had gone he stood by the window looking across at the temple, the winged Victories on the pediments, the golden garland reflecting the sun's rays. Ships would catch the flash of light as they drew into harbour.

After a moment he was looking at the sun in a courtyard casting shadows through a colonnade, lighting the tangled hair of a small boy in a torn tunic: "Take me with you, Ptolemy. I can come! Father wants me to cheer him!"

At a barefoot boy running into a soldier's messroom, scanning the almost empty table: "Do you have anything to eat? I'm starving!"

And at the stiff back of a boy who said coldly, "I won't wait. If you won't help me, I know someone else who will!"

Ptolemy half-smiled and shook his head. "So I helped you. I never refused. Few people did – or could. We made you Great King. Well enough. But for me you can just be Alexander."

Appendices

Sources

Polyaenus, Stratagems of War (wrestling story and soldier's pay)
Public Orations of Demosthenes Vols 1 & 2 (embassy to Philip and its aftermath)
Demosthenes and Aeschines Orations, Penguin
The Speeches of Aeschines, trans. Charles Adams, Heinemann
Oxford Book of Greek Verse in translation, O.U.P. (Odes of Pindar)
Odes of Pindar, trans. C.M. Bowra, Penguin 1969
Athenaeus (feast for Companions)
Diodorus Siculus, History Bks XVI & XVII, Loeb Classical Library
Aelian, Varia Historia (for the singing)
Justin, Philippica
Xenophon, Scripta Minorca. On the Cavalry Commander, On the Art of Horsemanship, On
           Hunting, trans. E.C. Marchant, Loeb Classical Library, Heinemann
Arrian, The Campaigns of Alexander, trans. Aubrey de Selincourt, Penguin Classics
Quintus Curtius, History of Alexander, trans. J.C. Rolfe, Loeb Classical Library
Plutarch Lives: Life of Alexander, Life of Demosthenes
           Moralia: On the Fortune or Virtue of Alexander
           Sayings of Kings and Commanders, Penguin Classics
The Iliad, Homer, trans. A. V. Rieu, Penguin 1950 (for reference)
The Iliad, Homer, trans. R Lattimore, University of Chicago Press & London O.U.P.
The Iliad of Homer, William Morris, O.U.P. 1934
Euripedes, The Bacchae and Other Plays, trans. Philip Vellacott, Penguin.
Aristophanes, The Complete Plays (The Frogs trans. R.H. Webb), Bantam

Chapter 8 and Chapter 16 are entirely ficticious. It isn't known how Alexander and Hephaistion
first met, but it was probably in childhood if Lord Amyntas was one of King Philip's Companions

Reference books

Philip of Macedon. George Cawkwell, Faber & Faber 1978
A History of Macedonia Vol 2, Hammond / Griffith
The Gods of the Greeks, Professor Kerenyi, Thames and Hudson
The Heroes of the Greeks. Professor Kerenyi, Thames and Hudson

Philip of Macedon, edited Miltiades Hatzopoulos and Louisa Loukopoulos. Contributors: Andronicus, Cawkwell, Ellis, Griffith, Hammond, Rider, Leveque and Sakellarion, Ekdotike Athenon. S.A. 1980

Vergina, the Royal Tombs, Manolis Andronicus, Akdotike Athenon 1988

Alexander the Great, Robin Lane Fox, London 1973

Alexander the Great, N.G.L Hammond, Chatto and Windus 1981, Bristol Classical Paperbacks

The Nature of Alexander, Mary Renault, Penguin 1975

Hippocratic Writings edited Betty Radice, Penguin Classics

The Wars of Alexander the Great, Waldemar Heckel, Osprey Publishing 1984

Roumeli: Travels in Northern Greece, Patrick Leigh Fermor, Penguin.

Facing the Lion, Growing up Masai in the African Savannah, Joseph Lemasolai Lekut and Herman J Viola, National Geographic & Amazon U.K. 2005

The Army of Alexander the Great, N. Sekunda, Osprey Publishing 1984

ASSISTANCE IN TRANSLATING AND INTERPRETING GREEK TEXTS
F. A. Lepper M.A., F.S.A.

MEDICAL INFORMATION, particularly concerning Philip's eye injury
Dr. A.J. N. W. Prag, Keeper of Archaeology Manchester Museum
Mr. Richard Neeve, Dept. of Medical Illustration, Univ. of Manchester Medical School
Mrs Beryl Yates, Nursing sister in the Eye Unit, The Herts and Essex Hospital

My thanks to the above for their generous help,
and to George Mann for his care in preparing this publication.

Illustrations

Front cover – Alexander – youthful version of head from Sparta
Back cover – Lion from hunting scene – floor mosaic at Pella.

Colour, full page

"Are you a goddess, Mother?"

Chiron on Mount Pelion

They went on up the mountain

"Go – like kings!"

Portraits in colour

Alexander – from the Pergamon head in Museum of Archaeology, Istanbul

Philip as a young king – based on a head in N. Y. Carlsberg Glyptothek, Copenhagen

Hephaistion – from Greek commemorative monument in Paul Getty Museum and 3rd century B.C. bronze head in Prado, Madrid (some believe this to be Alexander – they were supposed to be alike)

Ptolemy – a youthful version adapted from a marble head of an older Ptolemy I in N.Y. Carlsberg Glyptotek, Copenhagen

Philip II – based on a head in N. Y. Carlsberg Glyptothek, Copenhagen and ivory head from tomb at Vergina.

Alexander – based on a head in Acropolis Museum, Athens.

Pencil drawings

Frontispiece: Alexander in the lionskin cap – youthful version of a head from Sparta in Boston Museum of Fine Arts and a similar head from Kerameikos, National Museum of Athens.

p56: Dionysos – from Greek amphora by Phinias, Minical Museum, Cometo

Dionysos – part of a procession with Pan and Bacchante, bas–relief National Museum, Naples

Dionysos riding a panther – 4th century B.C. mosaic from Pella, Athens Archaeological Museum

The voyage of Dionysos – adapted from the inside of a drinking cup by Exechias, 6th century B.C.

p66: The duel – two handled cup 5th century B.C. from Museum für Antika Kleinkunst, Munich

p75: The tomb of Kyros the Great at Pasargadai

The Persian king Xerxes – relief carving from Persepolis c. 480 B.C.

Elamite bowman – mosaic from guard of Immortals on wall tiles at Susa.

Coins

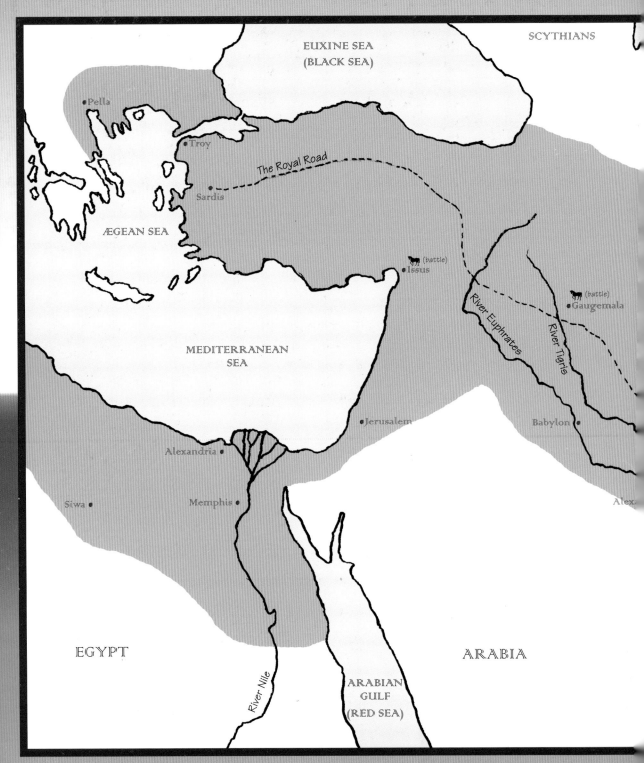

SCYTHIANS

EUXINE SEA
(BLACK SEA)

• Pella

• Troy

The Royal Road

• Sardis

ÆGEAN SEA

(battle)
• Issus

• Gaugemala (battle)

River Euphrates

River Tigris

MEDITERRANEAN
SEA

• Jerusalem

Babylon •

Alexandria •

Siwa •

Memphis •

Alex.

EGYPT

ARABIA

River Nile

ARABIAN
GULF
(RED SEA)